WAITING FOR THE MAN

WAITING
FOR THE MAN

The Story of Drugs and Popular Music

HARRY SHAPIRO

William Morrow and Company, Inc.
New York

Library of Congress Cataloging-in-Publication Data

Shapiro, Harry.
    Waiting for the man : the story of drugs and popular music / Harry
Shapiro.
        p.   cm.
    Bibliography: p.
    Includes index.
    ISBN 0-688-08961-5
    1. Drug abuse—United States—History.   2. Popular music—United
States—History.   I. Title.
HV5825.S4495   1989
362.2'9—dc 19   89-3028
                                                                          CIP

Printed in the United States of America

First U.S. Edition

1 2 3 4 5 6 7 8 9 10

For Kay and Hannah, from a man twice blessed

CONTENTS

Author's Note and Acknowledgements

Except for purposes of comparison, this book excludes any detailed consideration of alcohol. This is not to suggest that alcohol is not a drug; whatever other drugs have been in fashion among musicians, alcohol has never been out of favour. In health terms, it has caused more problems than all the other drugs put together and claimed lives across the spectrum of popular music from Bix Beiderbecke to John Bonham. However, alcohol is an accepted legal drug in Western society. Its use is not surrounded by the excitement, fear and ignorance which attends the use of other drugs like heroin, cocaine and marijuana – a phenomenon central to the narrative which follows.

For this very reason, there are some people whose valuable assistance I have promised not to acknowledge publicly. Instead I nod gratefully but silently in their direction. I can, however, say 'thank you' to: Roy Carr, Andy Cornwell, Paul Du Noyer, Pete Frame, John Gribbens, John Glover, Lee Harris, Dick Heckstall-Smith, Graham Langley, Ken Leech, Tony Levene, Dennis Muirhead, Paul Oliver, John Platt, John Tobler and Andrew Tyler. Thanks are also due to the staff of *Billboard* and *Variety* magazines for allowing me access to back copies and to take up office space looking through them all; the National Sound Archive; officers of the District Court of Macon, Georgia; the Middle Georgia Regional Library; and the library of the University of Pennsylvania. Special thanks to Julian Bourne, my editor at Quartet, for his belief in the project and his patience and understanding during tough times. Closer to home, a hug and a cheque to Claudie Mernick for the index and gasps of admiration to my mother for her staggering keyboard skills.

The members of the author's family suffer most when an enterprise of this nature is undertaken. Like the author, they are isolated, but without the satisfaction of creating something out of the chaos and turmoil. So undying gratitude to Kay for her guidance, inspiration and support, all the more remarkable when I say that our daughter Hannah was born when the book was only half finished.

Extract from *On the Road* (André Deutsch, US edition, 1980) reproduced by kind permission of the publisher; extract from *High Times* interview with Peter Tosh (November 1981) reproduced by kind permission of the Trans High Corporation, 211 East 43rd St, NY 10017. Lyrics of 'Tea for Two' (Caesar/Youmans) reproduced by kind permission of Chappell Music Ltd, 129 Park St, London W1Y 3FA; of 'Wacky Dust' (Adams/Levant © 1938) reproduced by kind permission of SBK United Partnership, 3-5 Rathbone Place, London W1P 1DA; of 'Reefer Man' (© 1932) and 'Light Up' (© 1938) reproduced by kind permission of J.R. Lafleur and Son Ltd, 295 Regent St, London W1A 1BR; of 'Cocaine Habit Blues' (© 1930) and 'Pipe Dream Blues' (© 1924) reproduced by kind permission of Southern Music, 8 Denmark St, London WC2 8LT; and of 'Minnie the Moocher' (Calloway/Mills) reproduced by kind permission of EMI Publishing Ltd, 138-40 Charing Cross Rd, London WC2H 0LD. Attempts to contact copyright holders of some other lyrics reproduced have not proved successful at the time of going to press; the author apologizes for any resultant inadvertent breach of copyright.

WAITING FOR THE MAN

Introduction

Society has undergone the most remarkable changes since the turn of the century. Projected into the future, an inhabitant of the 1920s would find the eighties a strange, fantasy world straight from the science-fiction pulps. He would feel more at home, however, if he read the current media coverage of the drugs scene. Here he would find the same words and images with which William Randolph Hearst, role model for Murdoch and Maxwell, filled his dailies: dark enticing tales of dope pedlars, playground pushers, opium dens and teeny addicts.

Serious discussion has been allowed on most social and political issues of today – gay rights, censorship, abortion, racial discrimination and the position of women in society. But the drugs issue remains at the level of base propaganda. Any attempt at raising the level of debate is swamped by allegations of being 'soft on drugs' or condoning their use. The press retains an invidious grip on providing drug 'information' for public consumption.

Since the enactment of the Harrison Narcotics Act in 1914, America has led the way in the global war against drugs. Under American instigation, international treaties have obliged nations to combat drug use in their own countries and American-influenced international agencies have been at work in third-world producer countries, attempting to channel agricultural activities away from the production of opium, marijuana and cocaine. America has also used its economic and political influence abroad to coerce producer nations and often accuses those hostile to American influence of being centres or transit points for illegal drugs, Cuba and Nicaragua being two recent examples.

The most recent tactic in the war has been to seize the money and property of convicted drug smugglers. Given the extent to which drug money passes through the world's legitimate banking systems, much will depend on the extent to which the time-honoured secrecy of these systems can be overcome. However, taken together with the breaking of

1

insider-dealing rackets, enforcement agencies are making previously unheard-of in-roads, into the heartlands of international finance.

These global efforts have been stepped up dramatically since the early sixties when drugs 'came out of the ghetto', and frightened WASP America to its foundations. In practice, these 'wars' have amounted to just yet another reorganization of the drug enforcement agencies and further millions being thrown at the problem.

The statistics of today's drug scene are both mind-boggling and meaningless. Nobody knows how many people use any particular drug, what the illicit drug market is worth or how much of it is seized by police and customs. Millions of dollars of government money chase a business worth billions, which supplies the drug demands of yet more unquantified millions. In magic there is an ancient saying that 'to know a devil's real name is to be its master'. So too with drug statistics: a belief exists that quantification – however inaccurate – puts you on the road to taming the beast.

One small story will illustrate the scale of the illicit drug market. In 1985, a trafficker was sentenced to fifty years' imprisonment in Florida. In six years of dealing, he had sold 1.5 million pounds of Colombian marijuana, amassing in the process a personal fortune of $750 million. The problem was that he could not find a bank that could 'launder' such a huge amount – so he bought one.[1] His was one case among thousands going through the American courts every day.

Widespread public concern about drugs in Britain was also born in the sixties. Then as now, heroin, the staple drug of all drug scares, was the focus of attention. In fact, in contrast to marijuana and amphetamine users, this sector of the illegal drug-using population numbered only a few hundred in the London area. There was virtually no black market in imported heroin; most of the heroin sold on the streets came from a handful of doctors, some greedy, some misguided, who over-prescribed. Policies devised to head off the development of a black market in imported heroin failed and in the eighties, with addict figures at record highs, media and government attention reached unprecedented levels. In 1985, a drugs advisory service in Liverpool reported that during the first few months of its operation, for every call received from a drug user three came from journalists. Earlier in the year, a delegation of British politicians from the Home Affairs Committee was shown around New York as part of a fact-finding mission on drug problems. Haunted by the spectre of Christmas to Come, they returned home to recommend using the army and navy in Britain's own war against drugs.

When 'sending in the gunboats' was an integral part of British foreign policy in Victorian times, the drug scene here and in the States was very

2

different; large sectors of the population consumed opiate drugs, cocaine and marijuana provided by a patent-medicine industry run by a handful of men who became exceedingly rich. And it was all legitimate. Drugs now feared and reviled were then standard entries in the medical pharmacopoeias, and far from using military might to keep drugs out of Britain, the Navy protected British exports of opium to China. We were the first international drug traffickers, fighting not only against the Chinese to protect our market, but against increasing pressure from the international community to end the trade.

Cliché it may be, but in the light of current government strategies towards 'stamping out drug abuse', its attitude to alcohol and tobacco is both contradictory and ironic. It must be said that no previous government has acted any differently, nor can one imagine future governments breaking the mould. Huge revenues accrue from the tax on products that unequivocally cause thousands of premature deaths in Britain every year. Willing to attribute devastating side-effects to some drugs on the flimsiest of evidence (e.g. the chromosome damage attributed to LSD), the government fudges the effects of cigarettes with its 'warning' labels, while no warning at all appears on a bottle of whisky. Such is the power of the alcohol and tobacco lobbies. Replicated the world over, these contradictions demonstrate that the formulation of drug policies has very little to do with the pharmacological reality of the substances under review.

In their book *Drug Control in a Free Society*, James Bakalar and Lester Grinspoon state:

> Looked at as a series of incidents, the history of the social and legal responses to drug use, especially in the last century and in the United States, sometimes seems melancholy and haphazard. It is easy to find inadequate pharmacology, inconsistent *ad hoc* responses based on poor information, indulgence of passions and prejudices, including racism, in response to drug scares, institutional self-aggrandizement by narcotics police and a fair amount of hypocrisy and corruption.[2]

The social history of drugs is replete with examples of the importance of symbolism. In other words the effects of any drug have always been overshadowed by who is using it and for what purposes. Some users and purposes are socially and morally acceptable, others are not, and laws are enacted to set the parameters, to determine social deviancy, to establish what is 'beyond the pale'. This is important for the history of drugs and music, because by very dint of their occupation musicians have often been regarded as 'beyond the pale', associating with other fringe elements such as prostitutes and criminals, in areas of predominantly immigrant or ethnic minority population. With little political status or influence, groups within this sector have tended to suffer most from the implementation of laws against drugs that were previously in legitimate use.

As each new drug has been introduced, it has passed through various status positions dictated by political, moral and economic expediency. Celebration is the first stage. From England to China, tobacco was heralded as a cure for everything from headache to malaria, cholera, venereal disease and worms. Approbation followed as the upper classes and the clergy began to use it recreationally although the problems of dependence became apparent. Inevitably, use of tobacco began to percolate through society and the authorities became anxious that it was diverting the working man away from his labours and damaging his capacities as a unit of production. In addition, it was considered that relaxing with a pipe or a cup of coffee or even a drink was tantamount to plotting against the State. Pubs and coffee houses were branded as 'dens of iniquity'. The banning of youngsters from pubs was originally to protect them against the corrupting influence of political intrigue, not against the evils of drinking. James I's counterblast to tobacco (1604) was a blueprint for future attitudes regarding recreational drug use by the working class whereby certain drugs became vilified and/or legislated against:

> Whereas tobacco...was used and taken by the better sort, both then and now only as physic to preserve health, it is now at this day through evil custom and the toleration thereof, excessively taken by a number of riotous and disordered persons of mean and base condition who contrary to the use which persons of good calling and quality make thereof, do spend most of their time in that idle vanity to the evil example and corrupting of others...by which great and immoderate taking of tobacco, the health of a great number of people is impaired and their bodies weakened and made unfit for labour.

The oldest documented drug is alcohol, so that by the sixteenth and seventeenth centuries, when the first attempts were made around Europe and the Middle East to curb smoking and coffee drinking, alcohol was firmly established as an acceptable recreational diversion. What laws existed were against drunkenness rather than drinking itself. Would-be smokers and coffee drinkers, however, were subject to the most vicious punishments. In Turkey, a sly puff was likely to result in your having a pipe shoved through your nose and a free ride backwards

4

round town on a donkey. Amurath the Cruel, the aptly named Sultan of Turkey from 1623-40, later decided that the pipe through the nose was being 'soft on drugs'. He had a neat line in entrapment: tracking down a tobacco dealer, the Sultan, in disguise, offered him a huge sum of money and total secrecy if he sold him a pound of tobacco. The hapless dealer produced the goods, whereupon Amurath produced a scimitar and sliced his head off. Elsewhere, limb crushing, beheading and quartering were decreed. Selling tobacco in seventeenth-century Russia earned you the right to be flogged to death. Smoking in China was deemed to be 'against the national interest', and heads rolled. Even as late as 1832, smoking in public in the streets of Prussia was regarded as a demonstration against the government.

Despite such horrific retribution, successive rulers discovered that they could not stop people enjoying themselves, so they decided that instead of making people pay with their lives, they should pay with their money. So drugs such as tobacco and coffee moved into the assimilation phase, as the revenues derived from each became vital to royal coffers everywhere. Attempts at prohibiting alcohol, especially in America, continued into this century, but the era of Prohibition demonstrated the impossibility of a nationwide ban on a drug that had earned such universal acceptability.

The period 1820-1920 saw opium, its derivatives morphine and heroin, and cocaine and marijuana pass through the integration pattern to vilification and legislation, where they remain over sixty years later. Those with a libertarian view on drugs can draw little comfort from the response of governments since the days of 'flower power'. The political and economic interdependence of nations, modern communications systems and sophisticated intelligence networks bind Marshall McLuhan's 'Global Village' tighter than ever. The political and social tensions of many Western nations, caused by urban decay and unemployment, are kept in check by right-wing law-and-order administrations steeped in the rhetoric of 'traditional values'. Thus it seems most unlikely that the 'flowers of evil' will ever turn their faces to the sun again.

PART ONE

1

Step Right Up For God's Own Medicine

Nowadays, the public perception of heroin and cocaine is that they are dangerous, enslaving drugs which destroy young lives while making vast sums for the evil men who supply them; such men are often regarded as worse than murderers. The image of marijuana is not so destructive as it once was, but the belief is still strong that an inexorable path leads from marijuana use to heroin addiction.

It is hard to imagine that the situation has ever been any different but up to the First World War, opium, morphine, heroin and cocaine were freely available to anyone who could afford them from respectable doctors, pharmacists and even street-corner grocery stores and business-men selling patent medicines. The famous herbalist Nicholas Culpeper remarked in his *Complete Herbal* that cannabis was so well-known to English housewives that he would not bother to list all its uses round the home.

For most of the nineteenth century, medical science was still wedded to the theories of the ancient Greeks, modified by the barbaric practices of so-called 'heroic therapy'. Driving out unpleasant maladies with even more unpleasant remedies was the guiding principle. Patients 'could expect to be leeched, cupped, blistered, amputated, sweated, trepanned, scourged and flayed to a fare-the-well'.[1] Small wonder that doctors in the eighteenth and early nineteenth century lost many well-to-do patients to fashionable herbalism, until the virtues of opiate drugs became apparent.

With so little knowledge of how the body worked, doctors could treat only the symptoms, not the causes of illness. Pain was the most distressing symptom and, as the world's greatest painkillers, opium and its derivatives were a godsend to beleaguered doctors traditionally regarded as little better than butchers and charlatans. The noted English physician Thomas Sydenham spoke for all his colleagues when he said 'among the remedies which it has pleased almighty God to give to man

9

to relieve his sufferings, none is so universal and so efficacious as opium'. Doctors prescribed it for ailments great and small and 'it would be almost easier to list those areas where it was never employed than to attempt to deal with every therapeutic possibility'.[2]

Today, a 'typical' heroin addict might be a young unemployed male (black or white) living in a deprived inner-city wasteland. The nineteenth-century addict was more likely to be a middle-aged, middle-class white female who had become dependent on her prescriptions of laudanum (opium with alcohol) or injectable morphine. The problems associated with long-term use of opium were well known but for the most part were regarded as the inconvenient side effects of an otherwise miracle drug. In an era when self-control was a social necessity, some of those who became addicts felt a degree of personal shame and were regarded as self-indulgent or weak, but certainly not as criminals or social pariahs. Injectable morphine was really available only to those who could afford doctors, a rare and expensive service in the nineteenth century.

The patent medicine industry in Britain and America supplied the drug needs of the majority of the population. Thomas Sydenham's own laudanum concoction was the first patent medicine to make an impact in the late seventeenth century, and it remained a clear market leader for the next 150 years. Later it faced extensive competition from Godfrey's Cordial, Battley's Sedative Solution, Squire's Elixir, Mrs Winslow's Soothing Syrup, Daffy's Elixir and many others, all containing opium and on unrestricted sale.

Patent-medicine selling was big business. The manufacturers were the first to realize the potential benefits of advertising and, once the railways opened up distribution networks for the mass circulation of newspapers, the medicine men poured thousands of pounds into advertising. For many newspapers, the medicine business was their major source of advertising revenue.

The story was repeated in America, but on a much larger scale. The first American patent medicine was registered in 1796 – Samuel Lee's Bilious Pills, good for everything from worms to 'female complaints'. Three years later somebody else called Dr Samuel Lee began marketing *his* bilious pills and, through newspaper advertising, a commercial war ensued. Each attacked the other as a fraud and both made a handsome profit, setting the tone for the rest of the industry in succeeding decades: no lie too big, no claim too outrageous, no deception too dishonest. By 1900 some 50,000 preparations were on the market generating an income for the manufacturers of nearly $80 million. As with medicines in Britain, opium was a common ingredient.

In 1898 a German scientist working in the pharmaceutical laboratories of Friedrich Bayer produced a new derivative of morphine, diacetyl morphine. The new drug was tried with sensational effects on a number of intractable respiratory conditions. Bayer marketed this wonder drug as 'heroin', its name in German indicating a lot of power from a small amount. What pleased the research team was that those given heroin seemed free of the usual morphine side effects like nausea and constipation. They assumed that dependence would also be absent, but once adverse medical reports started coming in heroin's career as a widely distributed legal drug was cut short. At about the same time a new drug, derived from a South American bush, burst on to the market as 'the real thing'.

Sigmund Freud was an early champion of cocaine. In his paper 'On Coca', he listed its uses as a stimulant, a cure for digestive complaints, asthma and even alcohol and morphine addiction. But the news wasn't all good: Freud warned that immoderate use could cause 'physical and intellectual decadence', together with 'weakness, emaciation and moral depravity'.

Cocaine found long-term medical favour as a local anaesthetic, but in the 1890s it was its stimulant qualities that encouraged the patent medicine industry to flood the market with tonics and 'pick-me-ups'. Some, like Dr Tucker's Specific or Agnew's Powder, were virtually pure cocaine. Bernay's Catarrh Cure came with its own drug paraphernalia kit – not a mirror, razor blade and spoon, but a small glass tube and short length of rubber tubing. One end of the tube went into the powder, the other up one nostril, relieving catarrh, sinus trouble, and doubtless a lot more besides.

Far more innocuous, containing very small amounts of cocaine, were the cola drinks (including Coca-Cola) and the coca wines. Vin Mariani's (named after its Corsican producer) was among the most popular and became a great favourite in royal circles. Mariani received enthusiastic testimonies from the Prince of Wales, the Tsar of Russia and the Kings of Norway and Sweden. Pope Leo XIII presented Mariani with a gold medal for being a 'benefactor of humanity'.

Like its British counterpart, the American newspaper industry flourished under the patronage of the patent-medicine advertisers. From twenty dailies in 1800, by 1860 America had four hundred and numerous rural and provincial papers, with some manufacturers spending up to $100,000 a year on advertising. But convinced though they were of the value of newspaper advertising, the medicine men were also showmen – they wanted to get out on the road and sell direct to the people. So was born the medicine show.

11

The 'show' might be no more than one man standing on a box on a street corner pitching his wares. At the other extreme was John Healy and Charles Bigelow's Kickapoo Indian Medical Company Show. This consisted of re-enactments of Indian battles, magicians, comedians, musicians – dozens of entertainers putting on a whole evening's extravaganza for crowds anything up to 8,000 strong.

But whatever the size of the show, the guiding principle was the same: the pitchman had to keep his audience interested but not critical, to convince them that it was only a matter of time before they would be ill and in dire need of his latest wonder cure:

> STEP RIGHT UP – HERE YOU ARE! No matter what it is, this little box will save your life. One dose alone irrevocably guaranteed to instantaneously eliminate, permanently prevent and otherwise completely cure toothache, sleeplessness, club feet, mumps, stuttering, varicose veins, youthful errors, tonsilitis, rheumatism, lockjaw, stomach ache, hernia, tuberculosis, nervous disability, impotence, halitosis and falling downstairs or your money back.[3]

To bolster the credibility of the medicine, the pitchmen would either pose as doctors or take a doctor on the road. These were often sad cases who had lost their own practices through drink or drugs. Some of the performers were in an equally bad state: with opium and cocaine so close at hand, overusing them to relieve the boredom of travelling on the road was always a risk. And for the 'has-beens' or 'never-weres' that made up any troupe, these medicines would have provided an escape from the reality of being doomed to tread the boards in one grim hick town after another.

For a young nation with little history of its own, the imagery of ancient and mysterious races held a powerful sway. The Kickapoo Indian Company traded on belief in the healing powers of the American Indian. Many pitchmen donned oriental garb to weave tall tales about the exotic East. Exploiting the trust that the clergy engendered, the Quaker pitchmen spouted thees and thous and wore wide-brimmed hats. But at the most basic level, with so much ignorance about the fundamentals of health care, the pitchmen relied on fear.

> Do you ever feel like it is almost impossible to get up in the morning? You eat well and sleep well, but you hate to get up? Well, folks, you might not know it, but that's the first sign of gallopin' consumption!
>
> You laughing happy audience, you mother, you father, you

12

young man, woman and child – within every one of you are the seeds of death. Is it cancer? Is it consumption? Is it perhaps some horrible unknown màlady?

The medicine shows were full of larger-than-life characters: Big Foot Bill Wallace, Phenomenal Klaus and Wonderful Walton. Ray Black's Tour of the World pitch went on for five hours without a break. He said, 'If they stay with me till the end, they're sure to buy. When I get through with them, their heels are round ... their backs are aching and they're certain they have kidney trouble or lumbago.'[4]

A handful of medicine men became very wealthy; the Rockefeller family fortune has its origins in patent medicine. Nelson's great-grandfather William Avery Rockefeller was as sharp and sophisticated a supplier of drugs as any latterday New York cocaine dealer. Like his criminal counterpart today, he dressed stylishly, travelled under assumed names and never had less than a thousand dollars in his wallet. Big Bill Avery, 'the cancer specialist', made enough money to back his son J. D. Rockefeller for a stake in the Cleveland oil business – and the rest, as they say, is history.[5] One of the very few women pitchers, Madame Dubois, left an estate worth over a million dollars. Another, Violet McNeal, told of life on the road in her autobiography *Four White Horses and a Brass Band*. Violet travelled as 'Princess Lotus Blossom' with her husband Will, who was one of the first pitchmen to develop the 'oriental' sales show. During their most lucrative period from 1906–14, Violet and Will and other successful pitchers could be regarded as the first media stars. Their shows were seen by thousands all over the States; they wore the best clothes, ate at the best restaurants, and sat at the best tables. 'I had twenty-seven diamond rings. I had diamond bracelets and lockets and one of them Hope Diamonds [sic] – a six-carat stone set in a brooch. We called them Sunbursts.'[6] And everybody called *her* Diamond Vi.

Diamond Vi mixed with the fringes of urban and small-town society – prostitutes, gamblers, bookmakers, hustlers – all making a living from the greed and gullibility of straight society, together with other travellers in the twilight zone – actors, prizefighters, gangsters and musicians. She learned of the pitchman hierarchy: the low pitchman who played from a box in the street and the high pitchman who played from a stage and paid large licence fees for the privilege. The high pitchman would mix socially with circus owners (never the performers), saloon-bar and gambling-house owners, madams, politicians, racehorse owners and the better class of thief.

The shows did best in the Middle West and Southern States. The unsophisticated rural crowds were more gullible than city dwellers and more grateful for the entertainment. Aside from the occasional touring minstrel troupe or tent show, the medicine show was one of life's few diversions. Generally modest affairs, they would be staged on a simple wooden platform backed with canvas and flanked by the company's transport vehicles. The show would feature the lecturer/manager, a sketch team who also did solo turns, a song-and-dance man, a pianist and other musicians, and a black-face comedian doubling as MC and producer. The bill often changed nightly, so the performers had to be very versatile. A show lasting two hours would run something like this: the black-face act or a song routine with the whole cast starts the ball rolling and settles the audience down. A comedy routine follows featuring a standard caricature of the negro – 'Jake' or 'Sambo' with big pants in loud colours and outsize shoes, with a straight man acting as 'feed'. More music, or perhaps a speciality act like ventriloquism comes next. Then the first pitch of the evening, selling to begin with some cheap soap, the more expensive stuff coming later. Then music and comedy, followed by the second pitch. There might be a Prize Candy Sale: buy some candy and you get the chance to win a bigger prize, ranging from cheap novelties to bedspreads. The Sambo act closes the spectacle.

Music played an important part in the medicine show, which enabled those struggling to earn a living as musicians to find regular work and gave them a chance to travel. Travelling was a part of the mythology of being a musician: it invoked the wayward spirit, the freethinker, the outlaw untrammelled by social conventions. Once illegal, drugs developed their own mystique which was embraced by the outlaw myth of the itinerant musician.

Before the mass migration to the North early this century, becoming a wandering minstrel or musician was one of the few options for blacks in the South who did not want to work the land as sharecroppers. For those who couldn't break free, the 'travelling coon', as immortalized in songs from around the Southern states, became a figure imbued with almost superhuman powers, fast-talking, free-spending and a hit with the girls. After emancipation in 1865, freedom was equated with mobility and thousands of questing Negroes took to the roads, establishing a pattern which was to become part of the black self-image in America. The travelling musician, who had taken on the role of truth-teller from the Black Preacher, and the role of trickster or 'bad nigger' from the Devil, became the ultimate symbol of freedom. Escape from the monotony and hopelessness of black employment, combined with the potential for earning a living without having to rely on the white

14

man – beating the white man at his own game, in other words – kept the musician's status high.

'At one time or another, most of the top Memphis bluesmen and street singers worked the medicine shows,'[7] states blues writer Bruce Cook. The medicine show was regarded by the blues singers as 'a kind of paid vacation from the rigours of town life', something they did for fun. However, life for the black musician on the road at the turn of the century could be quite dangerous. With the Black Codes, anti-black legislation in force throughout the South, the rednecks had a field day. Black musicians got the worst lodgings if they got any at all, were refused service at restaurants, could expect to be ripped off by managers and agents, were generally subjected to routine harassment and intimidation, and occasionally lost their lives. W. C. Handy was almost lynched after he had saved one of his troupe from being killed, escaping only by hiding in a railway car's secret compartment. Louis Wright, a fiercely proud black minstrel, was not so lucky. Snowballed by whites in Missouri while out walking with his girlfriend, Wright retaliated with a few well-chosen insults. An angry mob quickly formed, but Wright dispersed them with shots from his gun. The sheriff arrived, arrested the whole company but 'released' Wright to the crowd during the night. His mutilated body was shipped home to Chicago for burial.[8] Despite these difficulties, musicians travelling with the medicine shows helped to spread knowledge of the blues throughout the South.

One of the very earliest blues singers was Ophelia Simpson, known as 'Black Alfalfa'. She worked for Dr Parker's Medicine Show, helping to mix a concoction which was supposed to eradicate tapeworms. This was a favourite pitch: the medicine man would suspend a huge tapeworm full length in a glass jar; by the end of the lecture most of the audience were convinced they had tapeworms. Black Alfalfa would sing ragtime songs as a crowd pleaser, but she was better as a blues singer. Her husband Henry worked in a fertilizer factory on the Ohio River near Louisville, Kentucky, which earned him the nickname Dead Dog. Early in 1898, Ophelia Simpson stood trial for the manslaughter of Dead Dog Simpson. She was committed to what the blacks called the Stoney Lonesome (jail) for a while and then released on the grounds that her husband was a 'no-count' and probably deserved to die anyway.

Plenty of no-hopers played in the medicine shows, but some famous names began their careers there up until the forties, when the medicine show effectively died out. (By then of course, patent medicines contained only water, herb and alcohol mixtures.) Buster Keaton's parents ran a medicine show. Harry Houdini and country stars Roy Acuff, Hank Williams and Jimmy Rodgers all paid some dues there. Even the King of

Rock'n'Roll, Little Richard, did his time supporting the 'grinder' (medicine man).

> When I started getting into all this trouble at home, I left and joined up with Dr Hudson's Medicine Show. I didn't tell anybody I was going, I just went. Doc Hudson was out of Macon and he used to sell snake oil. He would go into towns, have all the black people come round and tell them that the snake oil was good for everything. Well, they would believe him. But he was lying. Snake oil! I was helping to lie ... He had a stage out in the open and a feller by the name of James would play piano. I would sing 'Cal'donia, Cal'donia, what makes your big head so hard?'[9]

But long before Little Richard hit the boards, the writing was on the wall for the patent medicine industry as a significant force in American commercial life. The medical profession was growing fast and becoming increasingly well organized and self-assertive as new discoveries in clinical medicine stimulated the development of specialization. Meanwhile the patent medicine business had reached the point where only large companies could launch new products because of the massive capital investments required. Battle was joined for control of the market in medical services.

S.H. Adams, a journalist, fired the first broadside on behalf of the medical profession, with a series of articles written for *Colliers Magazine* entitled 'The Great American Fraud'. The first article appeared in 1905 and began:

> Gullible Americans will spend this year some seventy-five millions of dollars ... in the purchase of patent medicines. In consideration of this sum it will swallow huge quantities of alcohol, an appalling amount of opiates and narcotics, a wide assortment of varied drugs, ranging from powerful and dangerous heart depressants to insidious liver stimulants; and, far in excess of all other ingredients, undiluted fraud. For fraud, exploited by the skilfulest of advertising bunco men, is the basis of the trade. Should the newspapers, the magazines, and the medical journals refuse their pages to this class of advertisment, the patent-medicine business in five years would be as scandalously historic as the South Sea Bubble.

A medical crusader, Dr Hamilton Wright, who figured largely in the eventual prohibition of narcotic drugs in America, seized on this opportunity and had 500,000 copies of 'The Great American Fraud' distributed round the country.

Of itself, the Pure Food and Drug Act of 1906 did little to help the doctor's campaign. The Act's architect, Dr Harvey Wiley, was much more concerned with food adulteration; the measures relating to patent medicines were an afterthought. All the manufacturers were required to do was to list and quantify the ingredients of any medicine that contained opium and its derivatives morphine and heroin, or cocaine. However, the Act did raise public awareness of the amount of opium and cocaine in circulation at a time when general fears about the consequences of addiction were being taken up by the more sensation-seeking newspapers. The real crunch came on 1 March 1915, the day the 1914 Harrison Narcotics Act came into force. From that day on, as far as the Treasury agents enforcing the Act were concerned, anyone who had anything to do with narcotic drugs – suppliers, doctors or patients – was a criminal.

2

From Sambo To Satan

Most writers on the passing of the Harrison Narcotics Act focus on two key elements running in parallel. First, the medical profession's continuing fight to control prescribing, and second, the need for domestic anti-narcotics legislation to give America's international campaign against narcotics trafficking some credibility. But as John Helmer has noted in his book on drugs and minority oppression, the available history of drug use in those years and of narcotics policy appears almost completely divorced from the affairs of the rest of America, and as a result, the forces which shaped that history are not easy to see.

It is well beyond the scope of this book to examine all these forces, but because the story of popular music is essentially the story of black music in America, the changing attitude of the white community towards blacks after the abolition of slavery is of importance both for the history of drug legislation and in the creation of a high-profile bugaboo – the drug-using black jazz musician.

As the nineteenth century drew to a close, America underwent something of a spiritual and moral crisis. A national mythology existed, founded on the belief that 'cultural renewal depended upon movement in space'.[1] The progress of a nation founded on evangelical Protestantism and wedded to the work ethic drew much of its impetus from mobility. Open space and the battles fought against the Indians to win it, had provided a challenge which was supposed to have kept the nation young and vital. But after the last Indian wars of the 1880s, Americans reached the end of the trail. A people born to run and infused with the pioneering spirit had nowhere to go.

Reaching the edge of the frontier also had serious implications for American business. Still recovering from the shock of economic slump in the 1870s, domestic markets were reaching saturation point. For American politicians in the 1890s the search for new frontiers became a priority. Senator Orville Platt said in 1893, 'A policy of isolation did well enough when we were an embryo nation, but today things are different. We are the most advanced and powerful people on earth and regard to our future welfare demands an abandonment of the doctrine of isolation ... it is to the ocean that our children must look, as they once looked to the boundless West.'[2]

America's Holy War against international narcotics trafficking was part of a 'publicity campaign' designed to show the rest of the world that America was a world leader and therefore entitled to a share of the foreign markets carved up at that time by established colonial powers like Britain, Germany and Holland.

The problem on the home front was more intractable. While taking an expansive view abroad, the WASP culture at home closed ranks. America had no unified culture and the Civil War had shown how frail the Union was. The male-dominated WASP ethos, with its innate sense of superiority over the Indians, blacks, immigrants and its own women, was nevertheless insecure. From the earliest days of white settlement, deep fears had existed about contamination from undesirables. These fears were heightened as the crumbling of Victorian social and moral values coincided with a stagnant frontier, throwing up visions of slow decline into Old World decadence. From these anxieties came the idea of 'the enemy within', a useful device for uniting the nation, excusing failures or preparing the people for unpopular legislation. Twentieth-century enemies have included Jewish and Italian gangsters, communists, student activists, sexually and politically independent women and jazz and rock musicians.

Government propaganda often attempted to forge links in the public mind between those labelled 'beyond the pale' and illegal drug users. Thus there were drug-pushing communists and acid-crazed student activists. In the nineteenth century the press, police and politicians combined to generate public fear of two groups: Chinese opium-smoking white slavers and violent black cocaine users.

Chinese labourers were brought over in their thousands to the West Coast of America in the 1840s and 1850s, to work in the gold mines and build the railways in conditions and for wages that no white man would tolerate. As the mines were exhausted and the railways finished, America was shocked by an economic depression in the 1870s which compelled whites to compete with Chinese labour. Until then, the Chinese had at best been tolerated by the white community. Now a wave of anti-Chinese feeling swept the country and the Chinese, who had built up large, thriving communities in many American cities, found themselves the victims of legal restrictions and systematic harassment.

San Francisco had the largest Chinese community. When William

Randolph Hearst took over the *San Francisco Examiner* in 1887, he embarked on an anti-Chinese crusade and singlehandedly evolved the crude mythology of the 'Yellow Peril' through sensational journalism. The Chinese had brought with them their opium-smoking habit and the social institution of the opium den. As early as 1875 the City banned opium smoking as a direct attack on the community. Hearst chose opium as a natural hook on which to hang his crusade. Everything there was to fear about the Chinese became embodied in the opium den.

Polite society steered clear of the Chinese community, but the white underworld and the artistic demi-monde had no scruples about fostering community relations. Unlike the solitary activity of morphine injecting, opium smoking was a social habit and the attractions of the amenable opium den enticed Chinese and whites alike. The paraphernalia and ritual of opium smoking, the sense of belonging and exclusivity felt by smokers, the use of esoteric jargon – 'hop joint', 'long draw', 'yen', etc – set the pattern that all drug subcultures would follow in the next century. The same fascination that drew people to buy patent medicines with an 'oriental' history drew them to buy Hearst's newspaper, to read about 'Ten Slaves of the Poppy's Spell', 'Sunday Vice in Chinatown' and 'Body of Opium Fiend Burned'. Well before the first Sax Rohmer stories about Fu Manchu were published in 1913, the public had a fixed image of devious, inscrutable Chinamen leading young virgins into white slavery and prostitution through addiction to opium.

Chinese immigration was stopped in 1882 and in 1909 the importation and use of opium for smoking were banned. Unlike tobacco and coffee in Europe, the fear was not of *downward* percolation through the social strata, but upward. The architect of all America's early drugs legislation, Dr Hamilton Wright, wrote in 1910, 'Smoking opium has spread steadily to a large part of our outlaw population and even into the higher ranks of society.' But a district court in Oregon discerned the true genesis of the ban. The court, ruling on the conviction of a Chinese for selling opium, acknowledged that the target of the prohibition was not opium, but those most associated with its use: 'Smoking opium is not our vice, and therefore it may be that this legislation proceeds more from a desire to vex and annoy the "Heathen Chinese" in this respect, than to protect the people from the evil habit.' The conviction stood however on the grounds that the court could not take the possible motives behind the law into account.

For Hamilton Wright the devil's fork had two prongs: one was opium and the other cocaine, 'the most threatening of the drug habits that has ever appeared in this country', spread by those whom he imagined were the most threatening social group 'the cocaine-crazed niggers'.

When they were first brought to America as slaves, blacks were regarded as little more than savages. The first American slave owners had viewed slavery as a necessary expedient. The slaves' labour was essential and they themselves would benefit from enforced assimilation into Christian society. But from the turn of the nineteenth century, attitudes began to change: slavery became a necessary evil which must eventually be abolished.

As the notion of 'natural slavery' became increasingly disturbing to many Americans, apologists for slavery sought to change the image of the Negro from brute savage to innocent child. This child was Sambo, lazy, shiftless, ignorant, good-natured, docile and, above all, contented. Sambo became a stock character in tent and medicine shows, but it was the minstrel show that did most to perpetuate this crude caricature. Sambo, the white man with a black face, was presented to Northern urban audiences as the acceptable face of slavery, a safe and comfortable image of the blacks and their lives on the plantations.

The minstrel show presented the Negro as inferior, subordinate and stupid. Black-face comedians played out ludicrous caricatures: exaggerated facial make-up to accentuate eyes and mouth, ill-fitting patchwork clothes, rolling eyes, jerky bodily contortions and heavy 'nigger' dialect. The visual stereotyping was complemented by idealized views of the plantation. In the songs of Stephen Foster, for example, everyone was happy, safe and free from worries – either content to be where they were or looking forward to returning 'home' to Africa:

> It was no accident that the incredible popularity of minstrelsy coincided with public concern about slavery and the proper position of Negroes in America. Precisely because people could always just laugh off the performance ... minstrelsy served as a 'safe' vehicle through which its primarily Northern, urban audiences could work out their feelings about even the most sensitive and volatile issues ... Like every aspect of the show, minstrelsy's racial content grew out of the intimate interaction between the performers and their vocal patrons. When public opinion shifted, the content of minstrelsy shifted.[3]

This meant that during heightened public debate about slavery an element of anti-slavery sentiment crept into the shows, but as soon as the slavery question threatened to tear the Union apart, such sentiments were expunged.

In 1852, Harriet Beecher Stowe's *Uncle Tom's Cabin* was published. The first American novel with blacks as central characters, *Uncle Tom's*

Cabin showed blacks to be human beings, able to feel suffering, misery and humiliation. But the producers of minstrel shows managed to sanitize this when the novel was adapted for the stage. Their message was that:

> there was no need to fight a war over slavery, no need to accept Negroes as equals in the North and no need to feel guilty for contradictions between slavery and the American Creed. Fulfilment for blacks ... came only within the subordinate roles of the plantation; blacks needed supervision and they got it in a benevolent atmosphere of a loving extended family.[4]

Emancipation changed everything. Although most blacks stayed in the South, they gained mobility and a new social and spiritual life through the rapid growth of the American black church. Even as sharecroppers they were not under the direct economic control of whites. Blacks became political leaders and were a presence in many white-collar and professional occupations. In response the whites, particularly Southern politicians, created a new popular image of the Negro – he changed from innocent child to malevolent rapist.

Spurred on by a fear that black voters would ally themselves with low-income whites and threaten the Democratic powerbase, politicians like Thomas Dixon of North Carolina engineered a virulent anti-black crusade in the 1890s, not dissimilar to Hitler's campaign against the Jews. This evolved into formal legislation, the 'Jim Crow' laws which institutionalized segregation in the South and separated black from white in every conceivable area of public life. Fear, harassment and intimidation were part of the daily routine for the black community. It has been recorded that between 1890–1917 a black man or woman was lynched every second day.

The Prohibition movement was particularly strong in the South, on the principle that booze turned Sambo into Satan. But it was his involvement with cocaine which gave the instigators of racial hatred their most potent symbol of black savagery.

Given the popularity of the medicine show among poor Southern blacks they were enthusiastic consumers of tonics, remedies and cola drinks containing cocaine. Moreover plantation owners often kept a supply on hand and passed cheap cocaine to their workers: a happy worker was more industrious, and as cocaine suppressed the appetite, he didn't get hungry so quickly either. A shrewd boss doling out a quarter of a gram per man could keep sixteen workers happy and more productive for a full seven days on a single ounce. With cocaine selling at $2.50 an ounce, he could hardly go wrong. The difficulty of buying alcohol may also have diverted some blacks to cocaine.

The 'cocaine-crazed black' mythology served the purposes of both anti-drugs campaigners and racists (where the two were not the same). Blacks used cocaine, blacks were a menace, therefore cocaine was dangerous; alternatively cocaine was dangerous and when taken by blacks it made them revert to their savage state. Newspaper reports began linking cocaine with black violence. In 1903 a Colonel Watson wrote to the *New York Tribune* warning that 'many of the horrible crimes committed in the Southern states by coloured people can be traced directly to the cocaine habit'. Report followed report: Atlanta's Chief of Police maintained that seventy per cent of all crime was cocaine-related, while Dr Christopher Koch, an anti-drugs campaigner, asserted that 'Most of the attacks upon white women of the South are the direct result of a cocaine-crazed Negro brain.' Under the influence of cocaine, blacks allegedly became unstoppable and superhuman. Writing in the *New York Times* of 8 February 1914, Dr E. H. Williams maintained that a 'cocaine nigger' near Asheville, North Carolina, stopped five men dead in their tracks using one cartridge per man. A policeman from the same town swore that a direct shot in the heart at point-blank range of a 'Negro in a cocaine frenzy' did not even jolt him. Police all over the Southern states used this incident as an excuse to issue themselves heavier-calibre revolvers.

In the 1890s, the Indian Hemp Commission set up by the British found no evidence for any of the claims made that marijuana drove men mad. The commissioners followed up anecdotal reports to check their validity. Hamilton Wright made no such checks; it suited his purposes not to. He assimilated all the unsubstantiated gossip about cocaine and translated it into part of the official and 'authoritative'*rationale for curbing non-medical drug use.

'The corruption of youth' has always been an attention-grabbing rallying cry for campaigns in support of traditional values. For America, this was part of the country's moral 'crisis'. In the era of America's youngest President, Theodore Roosevelt, the youth of the country were revered as standard-bearers of future economic and military strength. The middle-class-based Progressive Reform Movement was active in securing legislation to protect young people against prostitution, abortion and drinking. With supporters in influential government posts, it now put pressure on Congress to move against drugs.

Much was made of the use of heroin among adolescents (a term first coined in 1904 by G. Stanley Hall, a psychologist, to denote those in the fourteen–eighteen age group). Most studies of the period, while acknowledging that heroin use did occur among adolescents, showed that it was far more prevalent among older age groups. Similarly, an outcry was raised about alleged drug use, especially cocaine, among servicemen. But again, from studies carried out it was found that there was no significant drug use in the armed forces, and the fact that so few young recruits had drug problems was further evidence that young people in general were not heavily involved in drugs.

In effect, whatever the parts played by medical self-aggrandizement, international diplomacy and genuine concern about public health, *social disapproval* was central to the banning of recreational drug use in America. Laws were enacted as demonstrations against particular user groups, their lifestyles and the threat they allegedly posed to white society.

Sambo became Satan when he became 'out of control' – on cocaine so they said, but actually out of the economic thrall of the white man. In consequence drugs went underground, an appropriate place for satanic pleasures. Equally appropriate was their association with the new voice of the black community – blues ('the devil's music') and jazz. Blacks, jungle rhythms and drugs: an unholy trinity to make the stiff-necked WASP quail, the gutter journalist rub his hands with glee and the thrill-seeker hit the streets.

3

Light Up And Be Somebody
– Mezz And Marijuana

I's gwina save all my nickels and dimes/To buy me a Mary Jane
                                                    'High Sheriff Blues'

For the cats and kittens of the Jazz Age, marijuana was kicks,
climbs, jollies and high times jumpin' to the beat of a hot horn or a
mean licorice stick.

                                                    Albert Goldman

My ... memories will always be lots of beauty and warmth from
gage. Well, that was my life and I don't feel ashamed at all. Mary
Warner, honey, you sure was good ...

                                                    Louis Armstrong

Once the war in Europe was over and the boys were home, America
experienced a period of spiritual emptiness. The new religion was
materialism, accumulation, the worship of everything new and big. And
as in the 1960s, the affluence and conspicuous consumption of the 1920s
brought a reaction among a section of the younger generation who could
afford the luxury of being unorthodox. They sought escape in anti-
establishment music, sexual pleasure, alternative lifestyles and 'other
worldliness'.

For the flappers 'other worldliness' meant a craze for ouija boards,·
rather than Eastern mysticism. And instead of 'back-to-nature' com-
munes, the adolescents of sixty years ago turned to the 'loose passion'
and 'vitality' of black culture. The idealism of an earlier age gave way to
realism: all the straight world had to offer was disillusionment and
stagnation; the past had been blown up in the trenches and the future
held nothing but the dubious promise of 'progress'. Black culture
seemed to offer honesty, spontaneity and even a new spiritual meaning
to two groups in particular: affluent people looking for excitement

where the rules and pretensions of polite society did not apply; and Jewish immigrant groups sympathetic to the problems of minority status.

Contrary to the expectations of the temperance movement, Prohibition encouraged the well-to-do to 'take a walk on the wild side'. Cafés, cabarets and restaurants had been a feature of urban nightlife for decades, but the speakeasies and basement dives selling illicit booze to the strains of jazz added a new dimension to the thrill of 'steppin' out down market'. Milton Mezzrow, jazz clarinet player and focal point of this chapter, summed up this situation in his autobiography *Really the Blues,* published in 1946:

> It struck me as funny how the top and bottom crusts in society were always getting together during the Prohibition era. In this swanky club which was run by members of the notorious Purple Gang, Detroit's bluebloods used to congregate – the Grosse Point mob on the slumming kick, rubbing elbows with Louis the Wop's mob. That Purple Gang was a hard lot of guys ... and Detroit's snooty set used to feel it was really living to talk to them hoodlums.[1]

Among the young whites (often Jewish or Italian) in revolt against traditional values, the most rebellious were jazz musicians. Jazz had emerged as the urban voice of black culture, essentially a protest music in which blacks played out their daily experiences. This found favour with white kids seeking a vehicle for their own thrash against society, a music guaranteed to shock the squares, as rock 'n' roll did in the mid-fifties. One musician in particular epitomized the religious zeal that alienated whites felt for black lifestyles. He was white, he was Jewish, and he became the archetypal hip musician of the Jazz Age, the first White Negro.

Milton 'Mezz' Mezzrow was born 'on a wintery night' in 1899 to a respectable middle-class Jewish family on Chicago's Northwest Side. As a kid, he spent much of his time on the streets, getting into trouble, fighting, petty thieving and hanging around poolrooms. Throughout his early life he had an unfortunate knack of being in the wrong place at the wrong time. At sixteen, he was caught riding in a stolen car and sent to Pontiac Reformatory. 'During those months I got me a good solid dose of the coloured man's gift for keeping the life and spirit in him while he tells his troubles in music.'[2]

Inside Pontiac, Mezzrow met his first black musicians: Yellow, a cornet player, and an alto saxophonist called King. Race riots inside the prison (and later Chicago's four-day city-wide race riot in 1919), gave

26

him a taste of Jim Crow, although on the streets of Chicago he'd
bloodied himself often enough against shouts of 'Kike'. By the time he
was released, Mezzrow had his life plan sorted out: 'I knew that I was to
spend all my time from then on sticking close to Negroes. They were my
kind of people. And I was going to learn their music and play it for the
rest of my days.'[3]

The Great Migration of blacks from the South to the North saw
Chicago's black population increase by 150% in the years 1910 to 1920,
the largest influx coming after 1916, with the promise of high wages
after the war. Blacks settled on the South Side of Chicago in such
numbers that it became a city within a city, independent of the
mainstream of Chicago life.

Along with tens of thousands of blacks looking for routine day jobs
came musicians from New Orleans. 'Cook's Tour' histories of jazz set
out an over-simplified itinerary for the spread of jazz through America.
The linear journey from New Orleans to Kansas City, Chicago and New
York, prompted by the closing down in 1917 of black Storyville, New
Orleans' red light district, ignores in Kenneth Allsop's words all the
'jazz, semi-jazz, near jazz and tributary jazz' heard throughout the
South and Middle West. Brass-band music, ragtime, tent-show music,
vaudeville, church music and a host of related localized musical idioms
fed into the genre. Nevertheless, New Orleans represented the best the
new music had to offer and gave to jazz its sleazy reputation.

The New Orleans spirit was one of permissiveness and non-
interference, very much a musician's creed. From its earliest days a city
of low life, thieving, gambling and above all prostitution, New Orleans
'tolerated with impartiality small-time hustlers and high crimes, self-
serving royal governors and fifty-cent whores'.[4] In a town of corruption
and easy money, the establishments that thrived were bordellos,
gambling joints, saloons, cabarets and dance halls. The customers
needed entertaining, so music was a growth industry, although there
were few professional musicians. In fact music was a subsidiary of the
gambling business: 'The hustlers, gamblers and racetrack followers were
often hard-working musicians in their off-season or when their luck
turned down and they needed a little ready cash.'[5] They also used drugs
in a big way and naturally, before 1914, everything was there for the
asking. But by the time war came, drugs were illegal and the Navy,
worried about the moral well-being of young sailors, had Storyville
closed down.

In fact the exodus of jazz musicians from New Orleans began much
earlier. Mezz Mezzrow's ears were first turned by the Original Creole
Jazz Band, who had been drawing in the crowds at Chicago's Big Grand

Theatre and the North American Restaurant since 1913. Their star players included Sidney Bechet, Freddie Keppard, drummer Tubby Hall and pianist Lil Hardin, who later married Louis Armstrong. Initially, the Chicago Musicians' Union had made it hard for Southern jazzmen like Jelly Roll Morton, Keppard, Bechet, Jimmy Moore and Nick La Rocca to find regular work, but resistance crumbled in the face of an avalanche of public demand. Chicago jazz really started cooking when Joe 'King' Oliver, a superstar cornettist from New Orleans, arrived in 1918. He formed his own band in 1920, sent for Louis Armstrong, and drew a crowd of open-mouthed white kids like Mezzrow, Eddie Condon, Bix Beiderbecke, Dave Tough, Pee Wee Russell, Jimmy McPartland and Frank Teschemacher, who together pioneered the Chicago style.

Mezzrow was hooked by Bechet's soprano-sax sound, rushed out and bought one, together with some sheet music, and declared himself to be a musician, spending every spare minute learning or listening to jazz.[6] On his twenty-second birthday, 11 December 1923, he became a fully paid-up member of the Local Tenth of the Chicago Federation of Musicians.

> I got to be part of the fixtures at the Pekin and a lot of other South Side spots. Making friends with Jimmie Noone, Sidney Bechet, Joe Oliver and Clarence Williams, I began to feel like I owned the South Side .... Anytime I breezed down the street, cats would flash me friendly grins and hands would wave at me from all sides ... I was really living then.[7]

One of the earliest white bands to copy Joe Oliver's style was the New Orleans Rhythm Kings. The clarinet player was 'a little hyped-up Italian guy with pop eyes' named Leon Rappolo:

> One night during intermission at the Friars Inn, Rapp took me into his dressing room, where he felt around on the moulding and came up with a cigarette made out of brown wheatstraw paper ... He sounded more like he was sighing than smoking ... After a lungful he closed his lips tight and held it until he was about choked and had to cough ... 'Ever smoke any muggles?' he asked me. 'Man, this is some golden leaf I brought up New Orleans. It'll make you feel good. Take a puff.' The minute he said that, dope hit my mind and I got scared – working in my uncle's drugstore had made me know that messing with dope was a one-way ticket to the graveyard. I told him I didn't smoke and let it go at that, because I

looked up to him so much as a musician.[8]

In the early twenties, marijuana, muggles, muta, gage, tea, reefer, grifa, Mary Warner, Mary Jane or rosa maria was known almost exclusively to musicians. Hemp had been grown in the States since the earliest days of white settlement, as a valuable cash crop for clothes and rope making – so valuable, that the state of Virginia fined farmers for not growing it. The plant grew wild in many regions, including along the banks of the Mississippi, but apart from the odd literary figure who picked up on the hashish experiences of French artists like Baudelaire, Gautier and Rimbaud, nobody knew of marijuana's other properties until the Mexican Revolution of 1910.

Marijuana smoking was commonplace in Mexico. The revolution sent thousands of Mexicans streaming over the border with the weed stashed in their packs. Smoking among Americans was initially confined to black soldiers living in garrison border towns like El Paso. Almost inevitably, marijuana found its way along the coast to New Orleans, a bustling sea port where sailors coming from the West Indies and Africa were the other major importers of the drug into America.

The story of marijuana in America was a rerun of Chinese opium smoking and the alleged over-use of cocaine by blacks. Marijuana was branded as an 'alien' drug (nobody made the connection with hemp) taken by a naturally excitable, volatile minority group (Mexicans), who turned nasty under its influence. Wherever Mexicans lived in any number, there were local ordinances against marijuana smoking. By 1933, seventeen states had banned the drug, but it was not regarded as a sufficient national problem to warrant its inclusion in the legislation of 1914 nor had the press latched on to it yet.

Organized crime was not a product of the Prohibition years between 1919 and 1933, nor was it always synonymous with the Mafia. Irish and American gangs had been operating in New York, Chicago and San Francisco for most of the nineteenth century. Southern Italian immigrants came to America after the civil war, but only in the 1890s did Sicilian gangsters begin to make their presence known on the New York waterfront. Jewish gangsters were also well represented in the underworld, and the likes of Arnold Rothstein and Meyer Lansky ranked in notoriety with the top Mafia personalities.

Nevertheless Prohibition did secure the ascendancy of the Mafia in the underground hierarchy and allowed the organization of an enormously profitable service industry, providing the nation with limitless quantities of illegal booze. The mob raked in millions of dollars during Prohibition and used the proceeds to fund every conceivable type of 'personal service': prostitution, gambling, loan-sharking, protection rackets and the supply of illegal drugs on a scale never before known, aided and abetted by corrupt politicians and policemen. It was Arnold Rothstein who during these years developed a new angle to mob operations: the 'laundering' and investment of money earned from the proceeds of crime into legitimate business. The Mafia made a major incursion into the entertainment business and, ironically much to the benefit of jazz, gangsters dominated the clubs, cabarets, dives and bars in many American cities. Indeed, if black musicians had needed to rely on legitimate ballrooms, theatres and restaurants for work, the story of jazz would have been very different.

The gangsters provided endless opportunities for musicians to play. John Hammond of CBS reckoned that three quarters of all the jazz clubs and cabarets were mob-controlled. In New York there were 1,300 licensed clubs and speakeasies, while Chicago boasted 24,000 night spots in 1926. Trumpeter Rex Stewart said musicians never had it so good in the twenties: 'You could get fired at 11 p.m. and by midnight be sitting on another bandstand blowing.'[9]

As most of the gangsters were immigrants, they felt an affinity both with the struggling white musicians from their own cultural groups and with the black musicians from the South. They were largely intolerant of racism and more than one offensive patron found his tyres slashed when he got back to his car. There was also an age affiliation; in 1925 Legs Diamond, Lucky Luciano, Louis Lepke, Vito Genovese, Al Capone, Carlo Gambino and Meyer Lansky were all under thirty. To musicians they liked they were generous. Earl Hines recalled 'Scarface [Capone] got along well with musicians. He liked to come into a club with his henchmen and have the band play his requests. He was very free with his $100 tips.'[10] When the mob moved in, no expense was spared. Louis Armstrong had a long residency in Chicago's Sunset Café; long residencies enabled bands to develop a style and make progress. When the Fletcher Henderson Orchestra from New York were booked to appear in 1927, the Sunset Café was redesigned to accommodate them. The mob owned the Lincoln Gardens, home of King Oliver, and Charlie's, whose main attraction was the Bud Freeman/Dave Tough Quintet. Like many establishments during Prohibition, Charlie's looked like a bomb ruin from the outside, so as not to attract roving Federal agents looking for booze, but inside was a sumptuously furnished, highly exclusive restaurant. The biggest nightspot owner in New York was Owney 'The Killer' Madden and the jewel in his crown was the Cotton Club. Sonny

Greer, the house drummer, was given $3,000 worth of drums. Rival club owners fared less well. The owners of the Plantation Club, set up in Harlem in competition with the Cotton Club, were found dead and the club smashed to bits, two days after it opened – retribution for enticing away Cab Calloway and his Orchestra.

Musicians were allowed loans without crippling interest rates, given investment advice, access to drugs and a free rein for their own sidelines. Jelly Roll Morton sold drugs and ran prostitutes, while Duke Ellington was offered a piece of major bootlegging action in New York.

So what were the rules of the game? Basically, you kept quiet, kept playing, kept straight, did what you were told and didn't ask questions. The environment was tough, nerves were stretched to breaking point, physical injury was not uncommon. Muggsy Spanier saw two men shot dead in front of him, but had to carry on playing. Comedian Joe Lewis survived having his throat cut when he transferred from one gang-controlled North Side club to another. Pianist Pinetop Smith was shot dead on the stand and Bix Beiderbecke, the first of many music superstars to live fast and die young, died from pneumonia brought on by an excess of bootleg gin.

Even the famous had to watch their backs: when Louis Armstrong changed managers, he had day-and-night bodyguards for months. It has been suggested that the careers of Fletcher Henderson and Joe Oliver went into steep decline after they fell out of favour with the mob. Oliver finished up as a janitor in a Savannah poolroom. Mezz Mezzrow once took his life in his hands with Al Capone. Told by Capone to sack his singer at the Capone-owned Arrowhead, Mezz screamed back, 'Can't sing? ... Why, you couldn't even tell good whisky if you smelled it and that's your racket, so how do you figure to tell me about music?' Luckily Capone just burst out laughing. 'Listen to the Pro-fes-sor! The kid's got plenty of guts.'[11]

Mezzrow established himself running his own band, first at Capone's Arrowhead, then the Roadhouse and then the Martinique Inn, Indiana Harbour, all in the Chicago area. The Martinique was run by Monkey Pollack, a Jewish Club owner who spoke Yiddish with a Texan drawl and fancied himself as a gunslinger. It was here that Mezz, albeit reluctantly, first smoked some New Orleans sweet leaf:

> After I finished the weed, I went back to the bandstand. Everything seemed normal and I began to play as usual. I passed a stick of gage around for the other boys to smoke and we started a set. The first thing I noticed was that I began to hear my saxophone as though it was inside my head, but I couldn't hear much of the band in back of

me, although I knew they were there. All the other instruments sounded like they were way off in the distance; I got the same sensation you'd get if you stuffed your ears with cotton and talked out loud. Then I began to feel the vibrations of the reed much more pronounced against my lips and my head buzzed like a loudspeaker. I found I was slurring much better and putting just the right feeling into my phrases. I was really coming on. All the notes came easing out of my horn like they'd already been made up, greased and stuffed into the bell, so all I had to do was blow a little and send them on their way, one right after the other, never missing, never behind time, all without an ounce of effort. The phrases seemed to have more continuity to them and I was sticking to the theme without ever going tangent. I felt I could go on playing for years without running out of ideas and energy. There wasn't any struggle; it was all made to order and suddenly there wasn't a sour note or a discord in the world that could bother me.[12]

Given Mezz's initial reluctance to smoke marijuana, it would have been no surprise if his first experience had been a bad one: expectations of a drug experience play a large part in how the experience actually evolves. But even allowing for Mezzrow's tendency to exaggerate (a further two pages of purple prose follow), his first taste of marijuana was obviously intensely pleasurable and convinced him that he played better for it.

Mezzrow's experience wasn't unique; it was widely felt among the jazz community that marijuana helped the creation of jazz by removing inhibitions and providing stimulation and confidence. Hoagy Carmichael described the influence of marijuana and gin while listening to another *aficionado* of the Holy Smoke, Louis Armstrong: 'Then the muggles took effect and my body got light. Every note Louis hit was perfection. I ran to the piano and took the place of Louis' wife. They swung into "Royal Garden Blues". I had never heard the tune before, but somehow I couldn't miss. I was floating in a strange deep blue whirlpool of jazz.'[13]

Mezz was an instant convert and quickly established a reputation for having the best weed around. In 1925, now based in Detroit, he found the local stuff decidedly second-class. 'A couple to times I had to make a trip back to Chi [cago] to pick up a fresh supply from my connection, a little Mexican named Pasquale. Chicago was home for high-class dope because thousands of Mexicans arrived in the twenties looking for work and traded it to supplement their meagre incomes. In those days, we used to get a Prince Albert tobacco can full of marijuana ... for two dollars. The grefa they pushed around Detroit was like the scrapings off old wooden bridges compared with the golden leaf being peddled in Chicago.'[14]

The marijuana musicians soon formed a clique, sharing the experiences of the drug, writing songs about it, looking down on musicians who drank and the music they made (excepting Bix Beiderbecke, whom they worshipped): 'Their tones became hard and evil, not natural, soft and soulful, and anything that messed up the music instead of sending it on its way, was out with us.'[15]

Not everyone agreed with Mezzrow's perception of the role of marijuana in producing good music. John Hammond maintained that dope 'played hell with time' and Artie Shaw's view was that during the twenties and thirties, a lot of good jazz went down in spite of marijuana rather than because of it. The validity of either viewpoint is questionable; certainly nobody has proved that anyone actually plays better when stoned – the relaxation of inhibitions might push musicians to go for things they might not otherwise try, but if they are too stoned they won't make it and everything will collapse. On the other hand many musicians resent being linked with drugs and like Artie Shaw might play down or deny any possible advantages that might accrue from them.

While the musicians in Detroit used marijuana, the gangsters and (according to Mezzrow) most of the rest of the city had a yen for something more oriental. Despite the general legality of marijuana, as opposed to the total prohibition of opiate drugs, jazzmen got drawn into the illegal camp primarily because they relied on the largesse of the gangsters for continued employment. When a psychotic throwback who is paying your wages laughs at your joint and suggests you try something stronger, how can you 'just say no?' Mezz said 'yes' and from that first time, he liked it.

Moving back to Chicago in 1926 Mezzrow met a bunch of talented white musicians who first played together as a high-school jazz outfit called the Austin Blue Friars, eventually becoming Chicago's star white musicians – Jimmy McPartland (cornet and alto sax), Bud Freeman (tenor sax), Charlie Watts' hero Dave Tough (drums) and Frank Teschemacher (alto sax and clarinet), whom Mezz saved from alcoholism by turning him on to marijuana.

Playing up a storm and getting high with the renamed Austin High School Gang, the years 1926 to 1929 were good for Mezzrow. Then Depression signalled the end of an era on which the curtain finally dropped when Prohibition collapsed in 1933. The love affair with New Orleans jazz and the heyday of Chicago jazz were over. New York was the new jazz town and many musicians, including the Austin High Gang, headed for it. Mezz stayed in Chicago vainly trying to keep the purist jazz flame alight, scuffling around the town to make a living for himself, his wife Bonnie (whom he married in 1925) and his stepson. Eventually the pull of New York was too strong. One night, on impulse and wired up on cocaine to stay awake, he drove there with a friend. On arrival he phoned the hotel where he knew the gang were staying. The first voice on the line was Eddie Condon. '"Hey, Roll, where are you?" The next voice was Frank Teschemacher, "Hey Milton, did you bring any mula?" Then I knew I was home again, back among my own people. Solid . . . '[16]

All accounts of Milton Mezzrow give the impression of a life centred around joyful jazz and marijuana highs. But although he was never specific about them, he had a number of psychological and emotional problems. New York let him down (he couldn't find regular work) and in 1929 he fled to Paris to stay with Dave Tough, who found French audiences more appreciative and enthusiastic. He was trying to buy time, recovering from what appears to have been a nervous breakdown. But things were no better when he got back: the only work he could get was in dismal strip joints, watching leering white businessmen ogle at bored women. Depression got to him again and he resolved to move as close as he could persuade his wife to Harlem, for him the Promised Land. 'My education was completed on The Stroll [a famous Harlem street] and I became a Negro.'[17]

Mezzrow did not actually introduce marijuana into Harlem, but the local stuff was poor quality and he still had access to the best Mexican grass. This was to be Mezz's calling card, his way into a community where he desperately wanted to be accepted. As a musician he was limited and could not hope to compete with black musicians, but as a marijuana dealer, he earned respect. Very soon the word got around and everyone wanted Mezz to light them up. He became a local hero, an overnight sensation. Like Biro or Hoover, 'Mezzrow' became a ubiquitous name, in this case for a quality reefer, fat and well-packed. Two dictionaries of jive defined the word Mezz as 'genuine', 'sincere' and 'anything supreme'.

Jive was a secret black language, a code with its roots in the plantation life of the South, allowing criticism or ridicule of master or mistress without fear of retribution. The word 'jive' itself appears to have African origins. A variety of African tribes and cultures were herded together on the plantations, 'but the Wolof seem to have played a particularly important and perhaps culturally dominant role in the early slave culture of the Southern United States'.[18] The linguist David Dalby has made some interesting comparisons between Wolof language and American slang closely associated with music:

Wolof	*Slang*
Jev – to talk disparagingly	Jive
Hipi – a person who has opened his eyes	Hip
Degga – to understand	Dig

The linguistic connection between Hipi and Hip was later extended to hippy, a person whose lifestyle is often characterized by the psychedelic search for the inner self, using drugs as a means to achieve self-awareness. The language of drug subculture also fed into black jazz culture; 'hip' has been associated with the opium smoker's habit of lying on his hip in the opium den.

Jive talking among Harlem blacks was impenetrable to those not in the know. Two blacks might have been discussing how to kill the President, and a posse of policeman standing by would have been none the wiser. Whereas Southern plantation code was born out of fear, Northern city jive talk came from a sense of hope and spirit. Dan Burley, editor of Harlem's *Amsterdam News,* called it 'the poetry of the proletariat' and Mezzrow described it as 'jammed with a fine sense of the ridiculous that had behind it some solid social criticism ... a whole new attitude to life.' Except for the honoured few, blacks kept whites out with jive. And as if the language itself wasn't obscure enough, prices and times were often doubled to add confusion. Mezz provides an example of jive and thoughtfully a translation to go with it:

I'm standing under the Tree of Hope, pushing my gage. The vipers come up, one by one.

First Cat: Hey there Poppa Mezz, is you anywhere?

Me: Man I'm down with it, stickin' like a honky.

First Cat: Lay a trey on me, ole man.

Me: Got to do it, slot. [*Pointing to a man standing in front of Big John's ginmill*]: Gun the snatcher on your left raise – the head mixer laid a bundle his ways he's posin' back like crime sure pays.

First Cat: Father grab him, I ain't payin' him no rabbit, Jim, this jive you got is a gasser, I'm goin' up to my dommy and dig that new mess Pops laid down for Okeh. I hear he riffed back on Zackly. Pick you up at The Track when the kitchen mechanics romp ...[19]

Translation:

I'm standing under the Tree of Hope, selling my marijuana. The customers come up, one by one.

First Cat: Hello Mezz, have you got any marijuana?
Me: Plenty, old man, my pockets are full as a factory hand's on payday.
First Cat: Let me have three cigarettes [*fifty cents' worth*].
Me: Sure will, slotmouth [*a private inner-racial joke, suggesting a mouth as big and as avaricious as the coin slot in a vending machine*]. Look at the detective on your left – the head bartender slipped him some hush money, and now he's swaggering around as if crime does pay.
First Cat: I hope he croaks, I'm not paying him even a tiny bit of attention. [*Literally, 'father grab him' means Lord snatch the man and haul him away; and when you 'don't pay a man no rabbit', you're not paying him any more attention than you would a rabbit's butt as it disappears over a fence.*] Friend, this marijuana of yours is terrific. I'm going home to listen to that new record Louis Armstrong made for the Okeh company. I hear he did some wonderful playing and singing on the number 'Exactly Like You'. See you at the Savoy Ballroom on Thursday ... [*That is, the maids' night off, when all the domestic workers will be dancing there.*][20]

Although always a marijuana enthusiast, Mezzrow never tried to push it on people. He dealt mainly to friends and acquaintances; it was a family affair rather than a hard-nosed business deal. Ironically, when he was eventually busted in 1940 after the drug had been banned nationwide, he was caught giving it away.

Mezz was almost an underground national celebrity; visitors to New York sought him out to turn them on and no tea pad or rent party was complete without its stash of best-quality Mezz. Yet something was missing in all this adulation: the music. He was better known as a reefer man than as a musician. Mezzrow saw his marijuana-dealing as virtually a community service. Now, in the early thirties, the white mobsters (who owned many clubs in Harlem) were trying to turn it into a racket, albeit on a small scale compared with the post-war years. Being dragged down to the level of white gangster scum enhanced the sense of inferiority Mezzrow already felt towards blacks.

In this state of rock-bottom self-esteem, Mezz met a drummer named Frankie Ward who reintroduced him to opium. His only previous experience of the drug had been with the mobsters back in Detroit: now he was more than ready to have all his fears and anxieties blotted out. From 1931 until 1935, Mezz spent a large part of his time in a cleaned-out six-foot-square coal bin which served as an opium pad. It had been set up by a dealer called Mike, in the basement of a tenement block where he was caretaker.

Mezz was in trouble. Even the guys whom he smoked with regularly begged him to give it up and not waste his talent as a musician. Like everyone who gets into opiates Mezz believed he could break the habit whenever he wanted to. Some can, and are able to use drugs like opium, morphine and heroin on a 'recreational' basis without ever becoming dependent. Mezzrow was not one of these. He tried hard to give it up and get his music together again. He made an appointment with a big-time radio booking agent to see if it was possible to fulfil his dreams of organizing a racially mixed band. The agent greeted Mezz warmly, but all he wanted to talk about was setting up a marijuana distribution operation. When Mezz did get a contract he was allowed just one black singer. He had a black arranger as well though and everything looked fine until another bandleader poached his musicians: then it was back to the bunker for consolation.

In 1934 he tried again to come off and failed. Louis Armstrong, a long-time friend, offered him the chance of becoming his musical director. He gave Mezz $1,000 to clear his debts and meet his living expenses, but Mezz could not bring himself to tell Armstrong of his addiction. This time Mezzrow knew it was make or break. It is often the way that when there are more reasons for coming off drugs than staying on, a user will go for broke, however unpleasant the experience. And judging by his own description, Mezzrow had a tough time withdrawing from opium over several weeks. But he did it.

> One night I was sitting there listening and then I got up and took my clarinet and locked myself in my room. I put the horn together and looked at it for a long, long time. Then I raised it to my lips and blew. A beautiful, full, round and the note came vibrating out, a note with guts in it, with life and pounding strength. And then I started to cry. I had cried plenty the last four years, but this time my tears were tears of pure joy. I was human. I was awake. I was alive again.[21]

Busted for marijuana dealing in 1940, Mezz did a three-year stretch on Riker's Island. His dealing days were over. Once outside, he carried on as a musician and record producer, and married a black girl. Eventually he moved to Paris, where so many musicians, black and white, have gone into exile and seen their careers reborn among appreciative and receptive audiences. He died there in 1972 at the age of seventy-three.

4

Chant Of The Vipers

With so many musicians using drugs recreationally, it was hardly surprising that they should have written songs about them. In the thirties, the first heyday of songs about drugs, over one hundred containing references to the drug scene were recorded for the American black or 'race' radio-listening audience. In general the songs conveyed their message using the same 'hip' drug/jazz slang that the musicians used between themselves.

One hundred songs may be an underestimate for two reasons. First, after marijuana was banned in 1937, lyrics became increasingly obscure, so it is often impossible at this distance to be certain of the writer's meaning. Secondly, many songs had the word 'high' in the title, but no other lyrical clues in the song. A proportion of these would have been drug-orientated songs, but some writers just cashed in on the fashion for hip slang, to give their songs 'street credibility'. Further confusions arise from commentaries on drug-related lyrics. Charles Winick, a psychologist who has made a study of drug use among jazz musicians, maintains that 'Texas Tea Party' by Benny Goodman (1933) is not about drugs at all, but the opening lines are

> Now, mama, mama mama
> Where did you hide my tea
> Now come on mama mama mama
> Quit holding out on me ...

Who goes to the trouble of hiding a tin of tea?

Marijuana was the drug most often referred to under its many slang names; weed, tea, gage, reefer and muggles, the title of one of Louis Armstrong's most famous recordings. The early 'viper' songs paid homage to the new 'social hero', the man who brought the stuff that people relied on to make their rent parties go with a swing. This was no evil mobster or sinister pusher, but a man like Mezz Mezzrow, regarded with affection and respect. He provided a public service in a city like New York where marijuana had an enormous impact, for not only was it the jazz capital of the thirties, but there were no local ordinances against marijuana smoking.

Musicians sang of the psychological and physical sensations of using marijuana, the illusions when you were high or, as they said, 'walking' tall':

> Dreamed about a reefer five foot long
> The mighty mezz, but not too strong ...
> I'm the King of Everything ...
> If you're a viper.
>
> ('If You're A Viper', 1938)

> You never met the Reefer Man?
> Oh no? You never met the Reefer Man?
> And yet you say you swam to China
> And you wanted to sell me South Carolina
> I believe you know the Reefer Man.
>
> ('The Reefer Man', 1932)

Some of the songs describe effects of marijuana which are totally at odds with the marijuana experience of the sixties. Then the drug was identified with peace, tranquillity and cerebral contemplation. The singers of the thirties related experiences more akin to the contemporary mythology of 'reefer madness'.

> Boy, she's really frantic, the wildest chick in town
> She blows her gage, flies in a rage
> Sweet Marijuana Brown
> In her victory garden the seeds grow all around
> She plants, you dig, she's flipped her wig
> Sweet Marijuana Brown
> She don't know where she's going, she don't care where she's been
> But every time you take her out, she's bound to take you in.
> Boy, that gal means trouble, you ought to put her down
> Get hep, take care, look out, beware of Sweet Marijuana Brown.
>
> ('Sweet Marijuana Brown', 1945)

In the psychology of drug-taking, what the user expects to happen partly determines what actually does happen. This seems particularly true of marijuana. The drug features throughout the history of popular music, experienced differently by divergent subcultural groups: jazz-age swingers, cool beboppers, cosmic hippies and Trench Town roots rockers from Jamaica. Sociologist John Auld has discussed in depth the theory that the effects of marijuana are to a large extent a 'learned' experience, i.e. the novice user has to learn from others what he or she is expected to feel. (This may account for the fact that the first-time user often experiences nothing and wonders what all the fuss is about.) For somebody trying to be part of a social group as 'exclusive' and critical of outsiders as musicians, doing what the others do, saying what they say and feeling what they feel are of paramount importance. To stand a chance of being accepted, one had not only to use marijuana, but to appear to be affected by it in the same way as the others. Moreover, in the thirties, the belief that marijuana drives you mad was so widespread that users may have translated it into their actual experience, or *said* that they did, in order to emphasize their unorthodox outlook on life and consolidate their self-labelled outlaw status.

If the reefer songs reflected subcultural expectations of marijuana, they also reflected the legal response to the drug once it was banned in 1937. Now 'The Man' could mean not only the dealer but the government agent:

> Light up, I know how you feel,
> You find what I mean in any old field,
> Now get your gig going,
> I'll say that's the thing,
> Don't let that man getcha,
> Just puff on your cig and blow those smoke rings.
>
> ('Light Up', 1938)

Of necessity, songs' lyrics became increasingly obscure where drugs were involved. When Julia Lee sang her 'Spinach Song' (1943), she did not have Popeye in mind:

> Spinach has Vitamins A, B and D
> But spinach never appealed to me
> But one day while having dinner with a guy
> I decided to give it a try.

In 1933 Cab Calloway had been allowed to mention reefers in a big-budget Paramount film called *International House.* By the forties, in-joke references to marijuana had to be slipped into Tin Pan Alley songs like 'Tea for Two':

> Do you long for Oolong
> Like I long for Oolong
> Are you gone on Ceylon
> Like I'm gone on Ceylon?

Marijuana found favour with most of the musicians who used it, although songs like 'Sweet Marijuana Brown' (1945) and 'Knocking Myself Out' suggested a downside to the drug and in 'Working Man Blues' (1937), Red Nelson declared 'reefers are made for doggone fools'. About cocaine, there was more ambiguity: several songs said how good it made you feel, but added that there was an eventual price to pay. Even a generally favourable song like Victoria Spivey's 'Dope Head Blues' (1928), has an air of desperation about the first two lines. The advertising for the record announced 'a record that groans with tragedy' accompanied by a suitably woeful drawing of a woman obviously wrecked by drugs:

> Just give me one more sniffle
> Another sniffle of that dope
> I'll catch a cow like a cowboy
> Throw a bull without a rope.
> Just give me one more sniffle
> Another sniffle of that dope.

Less ambivalent was an up-tempo jaunt recorded by Chick Webb in 1938 and sung by Ella Fitzgerald called 'Wacky Dust':

> They call it wacky dust
> It's from a hot cornet
> It gives feet a feeling, so breezy
> And oh, it's so easy to get.

Possibly because most songs were negative about cocaine, writers were less coy about giving the drug its proper name and less often submerged the message in a welter of slang, like 'Wacky Dust'. In 1930 the Memphis Jug Band got straight to the point with 'Cocaine Habit Blues':

> Cocaine habit's mighty bad, it's the worst ol' habit that I ever had.

Cole Porter 'got no kick from cocaine'. Leadbelly and Sonny Boy

Williamson sang blues about it and Dick Justice, Luke Jordan and Lil McLintock all sang a song variously titled 'Cocaine Blues', 'Cocaine' and 'Furniture Man', which further emphasized its perils:

> I call my Cora, hey hey
> She come on sniffing with her nose all sore
> The doctor swore he wouldn't sell no more
>
> Coke's for horses, not for women or men
> The doctor said it'd kill you, but he didn't say when
> I'm simply wild about my good cocaine.

In 1941 'Can't Kick The Habit' was released. This was a decidedly sombre and pessimistic song about the problems of heroin addiction. To some jazz-age hipsters, opium/morphine users were right at the bottom, characters to be pitied rather than respected like the Reefer Man. 'Cokey Joe' and 'Jerry the Junker' were stock characters of death and degradation. 'Cokey' or 'Smokey Joe' turns up in Cab Calloway's 'Minnie the Moocher' (1938), delivered in a slurred, ponderous and tragic tone of voice:

> She messed around with a bloke name Smokey
> She loved him though he was cokey
> He took her down to Chinatown
> Showed her how to kick the gong around.

Smokey was doubly damned – not only an addict himself, but the cause of his girlfriend's addiction too. Hazel Myers' 'Pipe Dream Blues' (1924) is often quoted as sympathetic to opium smoking, but the good times are had only in reverie. When the singer wakes up, all her old troubles and some new ones, picked up through opium, come flooding back:

> Dreamed I had a hot pipe in my hand
> Owned a million dollars down in poppy land
> I burn up ten-thousand-dollar bills
> Everytime I light my pills
> Someone woke me up
> Now I'm crying
> With the mean old pipe dream blues.

As jazz entered the fifties, direct references to drugs of any kind

virtually disappeared. In an era of anti-communist hysteria and draconian drug laws, it was very unwise of any musician to have too high a
profile with the enforcement agencies. Drug references in jazz songs
were largely confined to the titles of instrumentals in the drug slang of
the fifties, like Harold Land's 'Smack Up' made famous by Art Pepper.
You could never be too discreet; walls had ears and every careless word
led back to the G-Man to end them all, the musician's nemesis, Mr
Harry J. Anslinger.

5

Hey, Hey, Harry J. –

How Many Guys Did You Bust Today?

Opium? No! Cocaine? No! The Great American Brain Killer is Dance Music!

Portland Oregonian, 12 June 1932

Jazz... the opiate that inflames the mind and incites to riotous orgies of delirious syncopation.

Harry Von Tilzer, popular song composer

Good jazz can be a wholesome tonic; bad jazz is always a dangerous drug.

Etude magazine, January 1924

For more than fifteen years before the 1937 federal ban on the possession of marijuana, State authorities in the South and West had been lobbying Washington to 'do something' about the drug. In the main, these were areas where Mexican immigrants had initially settled, and the campaign against marijuana was partly a reflection of what the indigenous population thought of the newcomers.

After the Mexican Revolution erupted in 1910, some of the fighting spilled over the Rio Grande. An attack by Pancho Villa on a small military outpost in New Mexico intensified antipathy towards Mexicans, already heightened by the influx of refugees. General Pershing led troops against Villa to the tune of:

It's a long way to capture Villa
It's a long way to go
It's a long way across the border
Where the dirty greasers grow.

Pancho Villa's men had a different battle hymn. 'La Cucaracha' told of a cockroach who couldn't walk any longer because he didn't have any marijuana to smoke. (This song was regularly featured by Edmundo Ros and his Orchestra, a respectable middle-of-the-road dance band frequently heard on British radio in the fifties. Like Musical Youth's No 1 hit 'Pass the Dutchie', this celebration of an illegal drug slipped past the bat-eared radio censors.)

So closely were the Mexicans associated with the drug that, of all the names for it, the authorities and the press adopted the Mexican one, 'marijuana'. The newspapers of the South Western states carried regular stories about Mexicans driven crazy by 'locoweed' and committing assorted atrocities in familiar retellings of the 'cocaine-crazed nigger' scares. Resentment lay behind most of these stories; during the twenties, thousands of Mexicans moved north to Chicago in search of work, but when Depression struck they found themselves like the Chinese before them, in competition with dispossessed white labour.

But antagonism towards Mexican immigrants was not the immediate context in which marijuana became an outlawed drug. Mexicans were blamed for introducing the drug into America, but musicians were cited as the plague carriers, those who spread the disease and infected clean-cut white kids. The failure of Prohibition gave added impetus to the moral crusade against marijuana.

The quotes at the head of this chapter illustrate that drugs and jazz were so closely associated in the public mind that images of one were used to condemn the other. The pre-First World War dance craze brought with it dire warnings in fashionable women's magazines about the dangers of being seduced by stylishly dressed but lower-class 'tango pirates'. The word 'pirate' conjured up an image of an elusive rogue who stole money and virtue from helpless women beguiled by his charms, who 'trapped and tapped the sexuality of women'.[1] Worse than that, he used drugs as part of his arsenal of entrapment. '[Cocaine] ... is the stigma that classes him with the criminal of a lower and less alluring grade.'[2] Telling them the drug was for fun, the tango pirate allegedly inveigled women into sex and into squandering their money. Eliminate him, the reformers demanded, or the traditions of Victorian culture might disintegrate altogether.

It was but a quick two-step from the tango pirate to a new form of social menace, the jazz musician. Jazz was blamed for endangering the morals of young people by encouraging the release of animal passions through sensual dancing, boy-girl contact, the sexual content of jazz lyrics and, of course, the link with drug-taking. In 1922 Hartley Mann's play *The National Anthem* opened on Broadway. The essence of the

46

plot was the debauchery and decadence of youth flying in the face of wise parent counselling. Jazz was implicated as 'modern man's Saturnalia', rhythm without soul. Pseudo-scientific studies purported to demonstrate its evil.

A report from the Illinois Vigilance Association claimed that in 1921-2, jazz had caused the downfall of 1,000 girls in Chicago alone. The leader of the State Hospital in Napa, California declared:

> I can say from my own knowledge that about fifty per cent of our young boys and girls from the age sixteen to twenty-five that land in the insane asylum these days are jazz-crazy dope fiends and public dance hall patrons. Jazz combinations – dope fiends and public dance halls are the same ... where you find one, you will find the other.[3]

Attempts were made to ban jazz from places of public entertainment: some newspapers adopted a deliberate conspiracy of silence, others tried to wish it away by maintaining that jazz was a dying fad. Underpinning most of the objections to jazz was an antipathy to black culture and to the so-called Harlem Renaissance, whereby black artists were fêted (or patronized) by a cross-section of affluent white bohemian society. Laurette Taylor, who played the lead role in *The National Anthem*, summed up the traditionalist viewpoint on jazz: 'Jazz, the impulse for wildness that has undoubtedly come over many things besides music in this country, is traceable to the Negro influence.'[4]

Some people seriously believed that if jazz was allowed to flourish, either the purity of the race would be contaminated by massive miscegenation or the epidemic would infect the sober white population, reducing them to the level of the savage black. No condemnation of jazz was complete without some reference to white kids going out of control to the beat of jungle rhythms.

The drug connection was central to the creation of the jazz (and later, rock) musicians as outlaw figures. From the earliest expressions of concern about marijuana, musicians were implicated. On 21 August 1920, Dr Oscar Dowling of the Louisiana Health Board advised the governor about the increasing availability of the drug. This had come to his attention through the arrest and imprisonment of a twenty-one-year-old musician convicted of forging a doctor's name on a prescription. On 1 July 1928, under the headline 'New Giggle Drug Puts Discord in City Orchestras', the *Chicago Tribune* reported that marijuana addiction was common among local musicians. The paper noted that marijuana 'is an old drug but was generally introduced into the country only a few years ago by the Mexicans. It is like cocaine. In the long run, it bends and cripples its victims. A sort of creeping paralysis results from long use.'[5]

Several states banned the use of marijuana long before 1937. Usually these were in areas of Mexican settlement but, for some still unclear reason, California took the lead in 1915 at a time when there were virtually no Mexican settlers. Louis Armstrong fell foul of this state law in 1931, as he told Max Jones and John Chilton:

> It was during our intermission at this big nightclub which was packed and jammed every night with all sorts of my fans including movie stars. Anyway, Vic [Berton, a top drummer] and I were blasting this joint – having lots of laughs and feeling good, enjoying each other's company. We were standing in front of some cars. Just then, two big healthy Dicks came from behind a car nonchalantly and said to us, 'We'll take the roach, boys.'[6]

Fortunately Armstrong was saved from a possible beating, by the admiration of these two particular cops for his music. They were quite honest, regretting that Armstrong had been unlucky to get caught doing what many others were at. One of the detectives told Armstrong that a rival bandleader had 'dropped a nickel' on him, that is phoned the police to tip them off. Even though the police were sympathetic, Louis Armstrong faced a six-month sentence for possessing a cigarette stub, all that remained when he was arrested.

He spent nine days in the downtown Los Angeles City Jail waiting for his trial. The courtroom was packed and newspaper headlines had Armstrong serving time even before the case had started. In the event, he got off with a suspended sentence and was back playing that night. Movie stars, familiar with morphine, heroin and cocaine on the Hollywood film lots, didn't really know what marijuana was. It was obvious from the comments of some who congratulated Armstrong afterwards that they thought it was Mexican for an underage girl!

It was around the time of Armstrong's bust that the government began to change its mind about marijuana. Up until then, appeals from state legislators and moral crusaders had been ignored. The appointment of a new Commissioner of Narcotic Drugs and the reorganization of narcotics law enforcement heralded the start of a new era in Federal drug policy.

In 1914 a narcotics division was created in the Inland Revenue Bureau of the Treasury Department to collect revenue from opiate sales and enforce the Harrison Act. In 1920 it merged into the Prohibition Unit of that department, which in turn became the Prohibition Bureau in 1927. The Bureau of Narcotics was formed as a separate bureau in the Treasury Department in July 1930.

Prior to the creation of the new bureau, the then Head of the Narcotics Division, Levi Nutt, was removed from office after a scandal involving the major gangster of the day, Arnold Rothstein, and some corrupt Federal agents. Rothstein was murdered in 1928. Among his papers was evidence linking him to Levi Nutt's son and son-in-law, both lawyers. Documents presented to a Grand Jury proved that both had been employed by Rothstein to defend him against the Treasury in tax cases, and one had borrowed money from him. The Jury also heard that the local Federal narcotics office in New York had been instructed by Nutt to boost arrest statistics by falsifying records, and that agents from the same office had colluded with major dealers. Nutt was out, eventually relegated to the Alcohol Tax Unit until his retirement.

...he himself in appearance was a grotesquely ugly man. Frightening. He looked like the Swedish Angel – that wrestler. He was about six feet tall, with the biggest head I've ever seen on a person in my life... completely bald... very large ears.

He had a disposition about him that used to scare the shit out of people who met him wherever he went... Whenever he came to the office, word would spread like word of a plague. Everybody had to be on his toes. He would say very little to any of the people. He just looked at you and he was a scary-looking guy... He had that kind of mystical quality about him and strange manners. I cannot emphasize enough the reverence everyone who worked under him held for him.[7]

On 25 September 1930 Harry Jacob Anslinger, 'the Swedish Angel', took over the newly designated post of Commissioner of Narcotic Drugs. There were narcotics laws, anti-marijuana laws and an albeit localized anti-marijuana campaign before Anslinger came to power (and if that makes him sound like royalty, it's meant to). But it was Anslinger who orchestrated the national campaign against marijuana and determined the drug's image in the minds of the public for the next thirty years. The image changed only when Anslinger changed his tactics. Through a single-minded devotion to the greater glory of his department and to the moral crusade against drugs, Anslinger manipulated politicians at home and abroad throughout his thirty-year reign in the Narcotics Bureau and afterwards as US representative on the UN Narcotics Commission.

Hardly anything is known about Anslinger's personal life. Born in

Altoona, Pennsylvania on 20 May 1892, of dour, upright Dutch parents, he was as enigmatic and secret a figure as his arch-rival, J. Edgar Hoover of the FBI. No biography of him has been written, although he remains the single most influential figure in the history of drugs legislation.

In *The Murderers: The Shocking Story of the Narcotics Gangs,* the second of two books he wrote, Anslinger recalled the incident which decided his destiny:

> As a youngster of twelve, visiting in the house of a neighbouring farmer, I heard the screaming of a woman on the second floor. I had never heard such cries of pain before. The woman, I learned later, was addicted, like many other women of that period, to morphine, a drug whose dangers most medical authorities did not yet recognize. All I remember was that I heard a woman in pain, whose cries seem to fill my whole twelve-year-old being. Then her husband came running down the stairs, telling me I had to get into the cart and drive to town. I was to pick up a package at the drug store and bring it back for the woman.
>
> I recall driving those horses, lashing at them, convinced that the woman would die if I did not get back in time. When I returned with the package – it was morphine – the man hurried upstairs to give the woman the dosage. In a little while her screams stopped and a hush came over the house.
>
> I never forgot those screams. Nor did I forget that the morphine she had required was sold to a twelve-year-old boy, no questions asked.[8]

When war broke out, Anslinger was employed at the War Department Ordinance Division, moving on to become a career diplomat with postings in Holland, Germany, Venezuela and the Bahamas, where he successfully stopped contraband whisky coming to the States from the West Indies. This earned him a transfer to the Prohibition Bureau where he rose to the position of Assistant Commissioner. His career was meteoric; he earned himself a reputation for being hard-working and unflinchingly loyal, with a remarkable flair for investigative work of all kinds. The years in government service had also attuned his skills to the art of the possible. Although a moral idealist, he was also a pragmatic bureaucrat, able to modify his policy when the situation demanded. Just as well, because the course of marijuana prohibition in the thirties twisted and turned like a rattlesnake.

Anslinger came into office decidedly unenthusiastic about a Federal ban on marijuana. When the Bureau of Narcotics was formed, he was allocated only about 300 agents. As a member of the Prohibition Bureau, he had seen the law fall into disrespect not only because it was unpopular, but because lack of resources made it unenforceable. A rerun of that fiasco would kill his Bureau and career stone dead. For most of the thirties, few ordinary people had even heard of marijuana, let alone regarded it as a dangerous drug which should be controlled. It grew wild all over the country, so for all the bluster of state health officials and some newspapers, marijuana was not a public issue.

Anslinger wanted all the states to adopt a uniform State Narcotics Law and then define marijuana as a narcotic. This would mean that marijuana law enforcement would become a local issue, thus taking pressure off the Bureau who were busy enforcing the Harrison Act. Moreover, to define marijuana as a narcotic would establish it as a dangerous drug by linking it with true narcotic drugs like opium, morphine and heroin. In order to pressurize the States, much as they had been pressurizing him, Anslinger began to orchestrate a national anti-drug campaign focusing on the marijuana menace and emphasizing how the drug was supposed to drive men to criminal acts. He whipped up enthusiasm for this campaign by speaking around the country to religious groups, temperance organizations, indeed any organization that invited him.

Although by his own admission the data were suspect, Anslinger built up a case file of crimes which purported to prove beyond a shadow of doubt the evil of marijuana. These cases he gave to newspapers to publish verbatim; nearly all the information on marijuana circulating in magazines and journals in the mid-thirties was supplied by Anslinger's office. The file of gory crimes was brought out at every opportunity and eventually formed the 'scientific' basis for the outlawing of marijuana in 1937. Among Anslinger's favourites was:

> Corpus Christi. Governor of Texas told me of a case he knew about personally, and one which in some measure influenced him to destroy 600 acres of hemp. An oil worker, good character, smoked a cigarette, raped his six-year-old daughter. When his wife returned home in the evening, she found him lying across the bed in a stupor and the little child torn and bleeding. He couldn't remember. Was sentenced to death.[9]

The pick of the crop, however, was the Victor Licata case in Florida. On 17 October 1933, twenty-one-year-old Licata killed his parents, two brothers and a sister with an axe while allegedly under the influence of a 'marijuana dream', as he explained to his arresting officers. This became the standard marijuana horror story repeated by Anslinger and the press time and again. Licata claimed that six months of marijuana smoking had unhinged his mind. Although the police were not convinced that marijuana was wholly to blame, police chief Bush used the occasion to condemn it as a dangerous drug, a theme taken up by the *Tampa Times* which had first reported the story:

STOP THIS MURDEROUS SMOKE

...it may or may not be wholly true that the pernicious marijuana cigarette is responsible for the murderous mania of a Tampa young man in exterminating all the members of his family within his reach – but whether or not the poisonous mind-wrecking weed is mainly accountable for the tragedy its sale should not be and should never have been permitted here or elsewhere... It required five murders to impress the Tampa public and Tampa officials with the serious effects of the habit.

As it turned out, Licata was diagnosed as criminally insane, a condition almost certainly inherited. His parents were first cousins and five close family members, including one of his brothers, were also insane.

Licata remained in the State Mental Hospital until 1950, when he hanged himself. Marijuana was never mentioned in his case notes.

Anslinger's hope that the States would take responsibility for the marijuana issue was not his only reason for launching a scare campaign. A staunch Republican, he had been a Hoover appointee, an appointment not unconnected, some said, with the fact that his wife was the niece of Andrew Mellon, the Treasury Secretary. In 1934, Franklin Roosevelt became President. The Democratic New Dealers took great exception to Anslinger's comments about 'niggers' and how addicts were a menace to society. There were moves in high places to have him sacked, but he hung on thanks to the support of influential Republican Congressmen and of the even more influential Hearst newspaper group, which he assiduously cultivated.

All this meant Anslinger needed to divert attention away from his own right-wing attitudes and to prove the Bureau's worth. He was also anxious to steal some of the limelight away from J. Edgar Hoover and the FBI. The rivalry between the two was intense. Hoover kept his all-American boys away from the sleazy, slightly disreputable world of narcotics enforcement, fearful of corruption which would tarnish the FBI's image. Narcotics work is essentially done under cover; agents have to melt into the criminal background if they are to stand any chance of nailing big-time traffickers. Corruption is almost inevitable where poorly paid officers are mixing with wealthy dealers and the line between police and criminal can become very blurred. So Hoover stuck to 'ordinary' criminals who committed conspicuous crimes like bank robberies and whom he could apprehend with enormous publicity. In the thirties, the FBI netted two big fish, John Dillinger and Pretty Boy Floyd, making all the front pages.

The Narcotics Bureau faced additional problems when the wash of Depression hit it and wiped $200,000 off the budget for 1935 – all the more reason for Anslinger to find every means of demonstrating how well the Bureau was doing. In fact, Anslinger's campaign was bearing fruit. After a slow start, by 1936 thirty-eight of the forty-eight states had adopted the Uniform State Narcotics Law and many had added marijuana to their list of narcotics. In addition, all forty-eight states had enacted some legislation governing the sale or possession of marijuana, completing the process started by California in 1915. So why was there a Federal ban on marijuana in 1937? What was the point?

In the first place, pressure was mounting on the Treasury and thus on Anslinger for the government to ban the drug. In effect, Anslinger's campaign was too successful. The press were saying that if marijuana was that bad, then not only the States, but the Federal Authority itself, had a moral duty to take action and protect citizens. There was little confidence in the idea that marijuana could be controlled locally. Anslinger had to rethink his opposition to Federal action, realizing too that to have control of all illegal drug enforcement was the best way to win the approval of Congress in the light of recent budget cuts. A Federal law against marijuana would do wonders for the Bureau's arrest figures.

The passing of the 1937 Marijuana Tax Act, which effectively outlawed non-medical possession, brought with it a new problem for Anslinger. Again the problem arose as a result of his own campaign. So convinced were people that marijuana use led to crime, that defence lawyers all over the country were pleading insanity and diminished responsibility on behalf of their clients who claimed to have taken the drug. An important weapon in the lawyers' arsenal was Anslinger's own widely circulated article, 'Marijuana: Assassin of Youth', published in the *American Magazine* in July 1937:

> In Los Angeles, California, a youth was walking along a downtown street after inhaling a marijuana cigarette. For many addicts, merely a portion of a 'reefer' is enough to induce intoxication. Suddenly for no reason, he decided that someone had threatened to kill him and

that his life was in danger. Wildly he looked about him. The only person in sight was an aged bootblack. Drug-crazed nerve centres conjured the innocent old shoe-shiner into a destroying monster. Mad with fright, the addict hurried to his room and got a gun. He killed the old man and then later babbled his grief over what had been wanton, uncontrolled murder. 'I thought someone was after me,' he said. 'That's the only reason I did it. I had never seen the old fellow before. Something just told me to kill him!'

That's marijuana!

Once he saw what was happening, Anslinger put the lid on all marijuana horror stories emanating from his office. Furthermore, he set out to discredit other moral crusaders who continued in this vein. This was not only to stop insanity pleas: to have people ranting on about the evils of marijuana would imply that the Bureau was not doing its job – definitely bad for business.

In fact Anslinger was not having much success in pulling off a major drug bust. In a sense, his trouble was that he believed his own propaganda. The drug was *not* in widespread use throughout the country as he claimed, but concentrated both geographically and socio-economically around certain cities like New York, Chicago, Kansas City and New Orleans. Anslinger had also hoped that local police would pick up small-time dealers and users, while the Bureau would grab the headlines by busting the big boys. The trouble was, there weren't any big boys; most of the marijuana dealers were, like Mezz Mezzrow, selling to friends, although there was some mobster involvement in places like Harlem.

So Anslinger adapted his policy once again. Leaving marijuana enforcement to the States, the Bureau concentrated increasingly on opiates, particularly after the war. Nevertheless, Anslinger still hungered after publicity for combating marijuana, and began to pinpoint well-known personalities, film stars, musicians, to extract the maximum exposure for the minimum effort. This became known as the 'star-bust syndrome'.

Anslinger had kept a special file on musicians since the early thirties. A section contained details of musicians arrested for possessing and/or dealing in marijuana. In order to establish musicians as 'public enemies' he made a careful note of every case that came to his attention, however trivial:

1933:

Three Negroes arrived [in Montreal] three days previously from New

York to fill an eight weeks' dancing contract at the Frolics Cabaret, and one of them at least had immediately started in trafficking. In addition to several small buys, one transaction involved the purchase of fifteen cigarettes at a cost of $19.00. Owing to the necessity for not disclosing the agent, it was not possible to charge them with selling, but two of the Negroes, Banks and Burnham, together with the Canadian, Gravel, were found guilty and sentenced to six months' imprisonment with a fine of $200.00, the third Negro being acquitted.

Banks and Burnham admitted using marijuana cigarettes and claimed to secure their supply from a tobacco shop in New York City, but refused to give any further details. They arrived in Montreal by motorbus direct from New York City, and I understand have for some months past been filling dancing contracts in the United States.

The press came to Anslinger's assistance in creating a musicians' 'pogrom' with stories like this from the *St Louis Post Dispatch*, 8 April 1934, headlined 'A drug menace at the University of Kansas':

Everything points to the introduction of the drug [marijuana] into the University by travelling jazz bands that come to play for large university or smaller fraternity and sorority dances. [Narcotics Investigator] Johns says that he has learned that many members of jazz bands not only in this section, but generally throughout the country, often resort to marijuana or some other drug to obscure the monotony of their lives, the ceaseless thumping of jazz night after night. 'They take a few puffs of a marijuana cigarette if they are tired,' Johns says. 'It gives them a lift and they can go on playing even though they may be virtually paralysed from the waist down which is one of the effects marijuana may have.' [No doubt another biochemical insight traceable to the Bureau of Narcotics.]

Lodged in Anslinger's file is a rare cutting from the British music paper, the *Melody Maker*, dated 22 February 1936. It is rare because it marks one of the very few instances when the British music press has made editorial comment about drug use within the industry itself. Britain banned opiate drugs and cocaine with the Dangerous Drugs Act of 1920, adding marijuana in 1928. Statistically, the drug 'problem' in Britain was in decline through the twenties and thirties, not on the increase as the *Melody Maker* maintained. But among the small coterie of the rich and famous, writers, show people and musicians, illegal drugs remained in circulation, hidden from public view. Precisely which drugs were involved is unclear, because 'dope' could involve any or all of the major drugs covered by the legislation. Cocaine was the most popular illicit drug in London, circulating in West End bars and clubs:

> Drug peddling and drug-taking is growing in this country. It can no longer be denied that jazz clubs have been among the haunts of drug pedlars.
>
> It is right that the searchlight of publicity be turned upon clubs of this nature. It is unfortunate that the searchlight should sweep also across the many clubs that are guiltless.
>
> This newspaper has consistently championed the avant garde of dance music and its practitioners. It will continue to do so.
>
> Equally is it determined to stamp upon everything that will hamper the healthy growth of that music whether it be the policy of the BBC, the apathy of the recording companies... or those who would make jazz clubs the market-place of dope...

In America, musicians had been busted for marijuana offences throughout the thirties, but Anslinger himself did not clash with the industry until February 1938, after the Federal ban had been introduced. Two men were arrested near Minneapolis for growing and distributing $5,000 worth of marijuana. The Federal District Supervisor for the area, Joseph Bell, told the *Minneapolis Tribune* that 'Present-day swing music, the Big Apple Dance and orchestra jam sessions are responsible for increasing the use of marijuana both by dance band musicians and the boys and girls who patronize them.' Sidney Berman, editor of the predominantly white *Orchestra World,* fired off a letter to Anslinger complaining of this slur on musicians. Anslinger placated Berman by attributing the comments to those arrested and not to Joseph Bell. But Bell in his report to Anslinger said his own experience confirmed the widespread use of marijuana among jazz musicians and he quoted one of the men he had arrested:

> This person stated that the use of marijuana is quite prevalent among musicians, particularly so-called 'jazz bands', because, under the influence of the drug they seem to acquire a certain talent which they do not ordinarily possess. In the words of the individual I mention, they 'get hot'.

Whether or not musicians actually did 'get hot' was itself a hotly debated issue. For Anslinger, the question was settled by the results of an experiment in 1944 involving marijuana and Carl Seashore's Musical

Aptitude Test. Twelve volunteers were used, all prisoners serving sentences for marijuana offences with a 'mean' usage of about nine years. Of these twelve, only two were musicians, although two had 'musical ambitions', whatever that meant. First they were tested for their responses to pitch, tone, timbre, timing, etc. Then they were administered the drug and tested again. Nine out of twelve achieved poorer scores second time round, although eight *thought* they had done better. According to Anslinger this was conclusive proof that playing better under the influence of marijuana is an illusion. That may well be true, but the test proved nothing of the sort. What about the three who scored better under the influence? How did the two musicians score? Anslinger says nothing about this in his notes. In any case, it was plainly absurd to draw any conclusions about drug use and improvisational jazz playing from an artificial laboratory experiment.

Briefed by Anslinger, lurid press coverage of swing bands' marijuana orgies prompted a bitter response from *Keynote,* the magazine of the Detroit Federation of Musicians, echoing the *Melody Maker's* outburst five years earlier. 'Marijuana – a scourge' was a front page editorial in the January-February issue 1941:

> Marijuana – weed – grass – tea – reefers – call it anything you like – is classed by law and by effect in the same category as narcotics. For some reason or other – and no matter how it hurts, let's face it – the comparatively few musicians who are addicted to its use have gained for the entire music profession a reputation among law enforcement officers, and to some extent among the general public, that is most unsavory, and every day bring disgrace and worse to the good reputation of the great majority who do not use it.

On 15 January 1943 the prestigious jazz magazine *Down Beat* joined the war of words against musicians taking a 'tea break', after some soldiers, musicians and other entertainers were caught in a hotel room with marijuana. The editors faced a classic dilemma: they had previously killed similar stories for fear of bringing jazz musicians into ill-repute, as the mainstream press had done. On the other hand, they felt the need to be seen joining in the condemnation of those musicians who used drugs. So with great reluctance they ran the following editorial:

> This is one of the sorriest messes that we've seen. Immediately after the story broke originally, the *Beat's* New York office was deluged with requests for information... At first our attitude was 'we don't know a thing'; but when the big news weeklies began checking, we

started thinking. And when one of the leaders concerned called up in a panic lest his band be ruined by adverse publicity as being a bunch of 'teahounds', we knew some action was in order... We know that there are musicians who smoke tea... We know that there is a select clique that has been working in the top bands for years who do it, and we know that they are going to get it in the neck if they aren't careful. And if the business as a whole isn't careful, it is going to take a bad rap along with them. Once more the old bogies are going to be floating around. 'Musician' is going to be synonymous with 'weed hound'. The business neither deserves nor can stand a national campaign of this sort... The Narcotics Bureau has the names and facts concerning many of the musicians who use tea. They aren't as interested in jailing these men as they are in finding out the sources of supply and the selling agents. We can only suggest to anyone who uses the stuff: STOP IT NOW, BEFORE YOU GET YOURSELF AND YOUR FRIENDS IN A POTFUL OF TROUBLE! We can only suggest to the AFM [American Federation of Musicians] that it pass a ruling calling for instant expulsion of anyone caught using tea.

Down Beat's attitude represents what is still the attitude of the music business in general to what it *knows* goes on in dark corners. This can be summarized as, 'Don't ask me because I don't know and even if I did, I wouldn't tell you.' This is part studied non-interference, part glamorization through mystique and part fear of attracting the attention of organized crime which runs the trafficking networks.

By 1943, it was clear that Anslinger's 'star-bust' policy had been a dismal failure. His only big-name capture had been drummer Gene Krupa. In July 1943 during one of Krupa's engagements at the Hollywood Palladium and the Los Angeles Orpheum Theatre, Anslinger received information which resulted in Krupa's arrest in San Francisco for possession of marijuana and for sending his seventeen-year-old valet to his hotel room to fetch some reefers. Krupa was found guilty of possession, sentenced to ninety days in jail and fined $500. He was later found guilty of involving the minor in the unlawful transportation of narcotics and sentenced to imprisonment for a period of one to six years, but the conviction was reversed on appeal. Anslinger noted that after Krupa's conviction it was reported in a newspaper column that 'Gene Krupa's well-wishers are setting up a $100,000 fund for a public-relations build-up, so that Krupa's career won't be ruined by his present difficulties.'

In 1959, actor Sal Mineo made a reasonable attempt at playing the drummer in *The Gene Krupa Story*. Krupa is shown turning down reefers left, right and centre until his new girlfriend hands him one saying, 'Be somebody, Gino. Put your miseries out to pasture!' He then gets 'hooked', and when the police find thirty-nine marijuana cigarettes on him, his girlfriend is implicated. After serving ninety days, Krupa is driven out of town, forced to play in any cheap dive he can find. Eventually Tommy Dorsey gives him a break and he finds his way back to the straight and narrow.

Exactly ten years after the film's release, the real Gene Krupa featured in a *Variety* story headlined, 'Gene Krupa Beating Drum Against Marijuana: Warns Youth of Illusory "Highs"'. 'According to Krupa, "I don't think that any person is greater than his talents and if you don't have your full faculties, your technique is not right ... When you play the drums, you try to draw the sound out. When you're on drugs, you pound."[12] He illustrated a drum sound with an even roll as played by a skilled clear-headed skinster, and an uneven sound by a drummer on the weed.' If Harry Anslinger heard about this 'confessional', his thoughts went unrecorded.

Ironically, Tommy Dorsey, 'hero' of the Gene Krupa film, was himself almost netted in 1944. He got into a fight at his birthday party and his opponent started shouting off about marijuana being present. However, when it came to giving a statement to the police, the informant denied ever making the charge and the case against Dorsey had to be dropped.

It was Anslinger's right-hand man, Malachi Harney, who concluded that if the Bureau was to have any success apprehending name musicians, it needed inside information. Anslinger regarded jazz musicians as hardly any better than criminals, notorious 'stoolies' if the price was right or the grudge big enough. He was easily convinced by Harney's argument that a system of informants was the answer. In fact it wasn't. Anslinger had not reckoned on the tightness of the jazz community. Worse still, from his point of view, musicians were blatantly admitting their own marijuana 'addiction' before the Draft Board. In this way, classified as 4-F, unfit for active service, they escaped the war.

To add insult to injury 1946 saw the publication of Mezz Mezzrow's autobiography *Really the Blues*. In an unpublished essay 'Marijuana and Musicians', Anslinger gave vent to his feelings: 'In addition to deriding the dangerous aspects and being a glorification of marihuana smoking and other forms of drug indulgence, the book reeks of filth in general. It seems incredulous [*sic*] that such an advertisement of narcotic addiction could overnight become a sensational bestseller.'[13]

Even without an effective army of informers, the Bureau managed to draw up a list of prominent musicians who were kept under surveillance, including Thelonious Monk. Anslinger also kept a special list of the orchestras containing musicians who had been busted for possessing marijuana. The list read like a pantheon of jazz, including the orchestras of Louis Armstrong, Count Basie, Cab Calloway, Duke Ellington, Dizzy Gillespie and Lionel Hampton.

In the late forties Anslinger tried yet another tactic – enlisting the aid of the unions. He sent the draft of a letter intended for the President of the American Federation of Musicians to his superior, Under-Secretary Foley, for approval. He didn't get it, perhaps for reasons of internal politics. Undaunted by this snub from his boss, Anslinger carried his campaign to the Ways and Means Appropriation Committee in March 1949, where his budget for 1950 was under review. His aim was to establish in the minds of Congress the notion that musicians were responsible for the spread of marijuana among young people:

MR FERNANDEZ: Then I take it there is more widespread use of it [marijuana] in the past two years than there was before the war?

ANSLINGER: I think the traffic has increased in marijuana, and unfortunately particularly among the young people. We have been running into a lot of traffic among these jazz musicians, and I am not speaking about the good musicians, but the jazz type. In one place down here in North Carolina we arrested a whole orchestra, everybody in the orchestra. In Chicago we have arrested some rather prominent jazz musicians; and in New York. It is pretty widespread. The musicians ought to do something about it. I have asked them to do something to see if they can't clean their own house a bit. And we have seized sources of supply from these musicians at different times. We have not made the progress with the marijuana traffic that has been made otherwise. You will notice, however, that in violations reported, our cases year after year seem to be about the same.

By making a distinction between 'good music' and jazz, Anslinger brought down an avalanche of protest letters on the Treasury. With one quote, he had managed to alienate the music industry which he had been trying so hard to cultivate. *Down Beat* made Anslinger's comment the focus of their next editorial after the hearings:

How confused can you get?...

The bad time given to musicians by the daily press in the general run of things is serious enough. But when a government official in a report to Congress divides them arbitrarily into two groups, 'good' and 'jazz', it is going a little too far.

Realizing now that any systematic attempt to enlist the co-operation of any sector of the business was hopeless, Anslinger went back to a more direct approach. He proposed that the Department of State revoke the passports of all musicians who had appeared in court on marijuana charges. Again, he picked on Thelonious Monk. While obviously no fan, Anslinger had noted the significance of Monk for other musicians and fans and this seemed to single him out for special scrutiny. The same applied to Charlie Parker and Billie Holiday. Thelonious Monk was subject to harassment over many years, but he never had his passport cancelled, because again, Under-Secretary Foley refused to back the proposal.

Musicians were at the top of Anslinger's hit list. He tried to get them informed on, kicked out of their union, grounded in the USA and pilloried in the press. He had his victories and probably did more than anybody to establish publicly the link between drugs and musicians. But it was no easy fight; the jazz community closed ranks and his own boss pulled the rug from under his feet on at least two recorded occasions. Yet perhaps the heaviest body blow that 'the Swedish Angel' had to take was dealt by Fats Waller. He was asked to record a song for the troops, a morale booster for 'our boys over there'. The song, an Armed Forces Radio V disc, was distributed by the thousand to all the overseas bases. It began:

Dreamed about a reefer five foot long
Mighty Mezz but not too strong ...

6

Golden Horns, Golden Arms

They can get it out of your blood, but they can't get it out of your mind.

Charlie Parker

We all find ways to try and destroy ourselves. Drugs – it was the rage. It's still the rage. It's the rage when you're not happy, not confident, when you can't deal with life. It's a death wish. I'm speaking from what I know, not something I've read.

Sheila Jordan

The *only* jazz has come out of oppression and drug addiction ...

Archie Shepp

The economic situation in which many black musicians found themselves during the Depression years of the thirties encouraged the younger generation to isolate themselves from the mainstream of white culture. Work was scarce and white musicians were always favoured over black in radio session work. The purge of top-flight gangsters through arrest or assassination closed a number of clubs in New York and Chicago, putting musicians out on the streets. The 'race' record market had been buoyant, but at a time of crippling stringency, 'disposable' income was at a premium and the market declined. So on the air, on the road and in the studio, job opportunities for black musicians were much reduced. In addition, touring bands were playing to increasingly segregated audiences, exacerbating the polarization between black and white musicians.

But the divisions went still deeper; younger black musicians resented and mocked those of an older generation, 'Uncle Toms' who continued to dance to the beat of the white man's rhythm. As pianist Hampton

Hawes put it, 'Our rebellion was a form of survival. If we didn't do that, what else could we do? Get your hair gassed, put on your bow ties and a funny smile and play pretty for the rich whitefolks? We were pilgrims, the freaks of the forties and fifties; our rebellion was a lonely thing.'[1]

The rebellion was bebop, built on the tradition that the black man had to prove that he was *better* than the white man on the white man's own terms, because only by being better could he be accepted. But revolutions need environments to ferment and develop, and perhaps one significant factor in the emergence of bebop and its 'hipster' jazz musician, was that few of the trials and tribulations of the professional black musician applied to those working in Kansas City.[2]

Under the patronage of Mayor Tom Pendergast and his Mafia supporters, every kind of 'public service' was readily available. The booze flowed like water, women were on every street corner and the city was the key drugs-distribution point for the whole of the South Western United States. Prohibition and, to some extent, Depression were events the citizens of Kansas read about in the newspapers. Kansas was a wide-open city with a proliferation of night spots where jazz could flourish as it had done in New Orleans and Chicago. The Pendergast political machine collapsed in 1939, but not before managers, agents and promoters had beaten a path to the city where it was all happening.

New jazz warriors like Lester Young, Walter 'Hot Lips' Page, Ben Webster and Count Basie provided a much-needed injection of freshness and excitement into a music becoming clichéd and clinical with the passage of time. Sax heavyweights like Coleman Hawkins and Chu Berry came to do battle in 'saxophone city'. And hanging over the balcony of the Reno Club intently watching and listening to everything about Lester Young, down to the way he held his sax, was an earnest fourteen-year-old who shouldn't even have been there, as he was under age – Charlie Parker.

Jazzmen of Lester Young's generation were more sophisticated than the early New Orleans/Chicago crowd, but they were not yet ready to fight back against the white establishment. Kansas City may have provided plenty of playing opportunities for black musicians but in every other respect it was a no-nonsense Jim Crow town. So what these musicians tended to do was to bury themselves in an exclusive, bohemian style of living. The stance they adopted was unapproachable, arrogant, non-conformist and inward-looking. Later, the barriers deliberately erected by bebop musicians between themselves and the audience created a romantic, tantalizing image: the street-wise, world-weary Byronic shadow, the Wandering Jew with a saxophone. Central to the creation of this tragic hero and the whole process of cultural isolation was an overpowering need to alter the distasteful reality of everyday consciousness. Lester Young was the first and his isolation tank was full of whisky; but Charlie Parker became regarded as state-of-the-art, because his shield to the outside world was heroin.

Unknown numbers of jazz musicians, black and white, got involved with heroin to a greater or lesser extent in the forties and fifties. It was said that if you wanted to recruit the best band you had to go to the Public Health Service Hospitals at Lexington and Fort Worth, where many narcotics offenders were sent, supposedly to clean up.

Heroin was cheap; even those in the lowliest paid jobs could afford a habit without resorting to crime. The drug came in pharmaceutical No. 5 capsules, ranging from $1 to $3 each. Ten of these capsules contained one gram of heroin. This would constitute a fairly heavy daily habit, but some musicians claimed habits in excess of four or five grams a day. When the Pendergast gravy train ground to a halt in 1939, several musicians moved to New York. Night spots on 52nd Street such as Minton's, the Royal Roost and Smalls' Paradise played host to bebop and to every drug dealer in the city. During the war years, soldiers coming back to base from a night out on the street stoned and/or robbed of their money led the military to put pressure on the city authorities to tighten up law enforcement. In consequence many establishments were closed down and both the music and the drug action became concentrated around just a handful of clubs. After the war the availability of heroin increased dramatically when the Mafia re-opened the supply routes from Turkey and the Far East, via Marseilles to New York, to meet the rising demand from the city's growing black and Puerto Rican communities. Dealers would gather in the men's room at Birdland, openly displaying their wares on the window ledge. Pianist Billy Taylor recalls: 'Around 1948, everything was concentrated on the Royal Roost. I'd come back from Europe in 1947. I thought I was sophisticated, but I stood there with my mouth open. All you had to do was walk behind the bandstand and guys were doing whatever they wanted to.'[3]

For the musicians who became dependent on heroin, including some of the finest players jazz ever produced, the process of dependence involved far more than the physical sensations of being stoned. The pharmacological impact of heroin (or any mood-altering drug) on the person using it is only one part of a complex interaction between the chemical properties of the drug, the physiological and psychological complexion of the user, the user's expectations of the drug and the cultural and social environment in which it is used. Heroin served the symbolic, functional, psychological and social needs of the cool, aloof hipster jazz musician and the whole added up to what might be called the heroin experience. It was this total experience rather than the drug alone upon which musicians became dependent.

Heroin use by black musicians was only the most visible manifestation of what was going on in the black community as a whole in the early fifties. In *Soul on Ice*, Eldridge Cleaver stated that 'prior to 1954, we lived in an atmosphere of novocain. Negroes found it necessary, in order to maintain whatever sanity they could, to remain somewhat aloof and detached from the "problem".' Hampton Hawes was less circumspect: 'All niggers are involved with narcotics ... you had to act a different way around white people and it was all that fear and oppression which made niggers get high. Especially musicians, because if a musician wants to play what he feels, he has to escape all that shit. It's happened to damn near everybody I know.'[4]

The terrible public image of heroin and those who used it made it a perfect vehicle for a trip to the margins of society and confirmed the status of black musicians who, as members of the black community, were already there. Heroin was tailor-made for inducing a sense of emotional distance, a central tenet of the hipster ethic. It remains the most effective physical painkiller ever developed. The feelings are not euphoric or high in the active sense, but cool and detached; some users have likened it to being wrapped up in a huge ball of cotton wool.

If for black musicians heroin symbolized the flight from white society, for white musicians it symbolized the flight *towards* black society. To enter the closed world of the jazz community, white musicians had to transcend the distinct disadvantage (in this one respect) of not being black. Jazz was the music of black society; when the white musicians of Bix Beiderbecke's era, feeling alienated from their own culture, had looked to ally themselves with the jazz/black life, that very act had marked them out as 'social deviants'. In fact for young whites to become jazz musicians was a significantly more deviant act than for blacks. Traditionally, music has been one of the few career options for those in the black community looking to break free from a system eager to condemn them to a life of menial, unskilled labour. Black people have no more 'natural' capacity for making music than Jewish people have for making money. Both aptitudes are consequences of minority status in racist and anti-Semitic communities. Aspiring white jazz musicians often found themselves in an uneasy no man's land, rejected by the society they had turned their backs on, but only very rarely accepted (like Mezz Mezzrow) by the group whose approval they anxiously sought. Many black people thought that whites were attracted to the romantic idea of being black as a political or subcultural statement, without actually relating to black people as fellow human beings. White musicians tried to 'outhip' the real hipsters, to become blacker than black or, in Norman Mailer's terminology, 'White Negroes'. Their self-conscious aim was 'to live with death as an immediate danger, to divorce oneself from society, to exist without roots, to set out on that unchartered journey into the rebellious imperatives of the self ... one exists to be in the present'.[5] Which is a pretty fair description of the heroin experience and part of the reason why many white musicians took up heroin – as the ultimate expression of being hip.

Jazz musicians were faced with a myriad of everyday problems, both personal and professional. Travelling on the road put enormous strains on personal relationships. There were managers, promoters, agents and record companies of dubious integrity to deal with; sometimes hostile or inattentive audiences; ego clashes in the band; the uncertainty of work; declines in popularity, the glare of public attention. For those musicians who found all this too much to handle, heroin provided a functional solution: instead of having to deal with several problems, one problem – maintaining the habit – took over. 'Junk could provide a dream world. The daily process of living was dull and you had to scrounge for an income, when you just wanted to play your horn. Junk seemed to help in a bad time.'[6] (Gerry Mulligan)

This was, of course, an illusion. Heroin might block out the other problems, but its use created more than just one problem. Regular users were often irregular musicians. 'If I had to go to Watts to cop and the cat said "the Man will be here in an hour" and I had to be on the gig in an hour and a half – and the Man didn't get there for two hours – then the arithmetic was simple. I'd be at least a half hour late on the gig. If the Man didn't show, I didn't play ... keeping my ass normal took precedence; everything else had to wait – music, food, home, sleep.'[7]

Those with a bad reputation for reliability had a tougher time finding work than most and could get caught in a downward spiral of using more heroin as finding work became increasingly difficult. Many bandleaders refused to hire 'ex-users' in the belief there was no such thing. Health problems were inevitable in the process of injecting heroin of unknown quality and strength in unsterile conditions, using dirty needles. Personal, domestic and financial problems would escalate and at the end of the line, if you were still alive, came prison. And naturally none of those original problems ever went away; some time or another they had to be faced.

Thus the idea of heroin as a means of collapsing several problems into one was always a chimera. But it did have a more basic functional use – it got the addict musician to work. No musician could play blind drunk, but plenty played well while stoned on heroin. But the belief that you had to have a habit that would fell an ox in order to play like Charlie Parker was the classic mistake many of his acolytes made. What they failed, or chose to fail, to comprehend was that Bird played brilliantly on heroin because he was dependent on it, that was the only time he felt well enough to play normally – i.e. better than anyone else. He wasn't playing better because of heroin; he was just playing normally because he didn't feel sick.

This was borne out by American psychologist Charles Winick in 1954, in the only study ever carried out on the use of drugs by jazz musicians. He interviewed 409 New York musicians and analysed their comments about drugs and their own drug habits: '32% pointed out that if a musician is a regular user of heroin, his musical norm would have to be his behaviour while on drugs. Such a person can only function and play when he is taking heroin.' While 53% regarded the drug as dangerous, there was a view among some that heroin was a 'working drug'; and that's exactly what it was for musicians like Charlie Parker and Hampton Hawes.

Heroin got those already dependent on to the stand to play the gig, but it performed another service which eventually brought several non-addicted musicians to dependency. Musicians are especially prone to colds and flu, moving as they do from freezing tour buses into sweltering club environments and then back out into the night air, for weeks on end. This was a particular problem for singers; if their voices went, the whole gig was in jeopardy – the rest of the band depending on the singer appearing. If you want to stay working in the music business, you cannot ring in sick like other workers. No matter how bad you feel, you've got to be up there. Nobody on heroin gets flu, coughs or colds; the membranes are dried out and the cough reflex suppressed. Eventually, of course, many musicians found they had a heroin habit instead of flu.

Allowing for the pitfalls of attempts at lay psychology, even a superficial examination of the belief systems of musicians seems often to reveal a bedrock of decidedly adolescent attitudes. In those with the strongest adolescent traits these attitudes were served by the use of heroin and other drugs including alcohol. Part of the hipster ethic was founded on control, being strong when everyone else was weak, not becoming a fall-about junkie, seeing how far you could go in order to come all the way back. Those who came back were heroes; those who didn't were legends. Hampton Hawes said of Thelonious Monk: 'If Wardell (Gray) was like my older brother, Monk was my father – and he never interfered in my life or put me down for being strung. But the following year when the shit really got bad, he would be there to reach out a helping hand. If he was using himself, I didn't know it and he didn't show it and that's what being cool is about.'[8] Even the very act of hero-worship has a childlike quality about it, the urge to be like somebody else where a strong personal identity has yet to develop. It is doubtful whether the example of Charlie Parker had much impact on the young black community at large, many of whom had probably never heard of him. But he had an enormous influence not only on the way musicians played, but on the way they lived their lives. The first three notes of 'Parker's Mood' were a signal between users in Los Angeles, a call sign sung outside the dealer's house when they wanted to score in the dead of night.

Paradoxically, those who imagined they were most in control, the prime hellraisers on the jazz scene, often suffered from low self-esteem, a common characteristic of chronic drug users. By his own account Art Pepper, for example, was denied any familial affection. 'I was terrified and completely alone. And at that time, I realized that nobody wanted me. There was no love and I wished I could die.'[9] By his logic, if he was worthless, it didn't matter what he did. Normal restraints were off; he felt, and was regarded as, powerful and potentially dangerous. He ran with street gangs, became a jazz musician, used heroin, committed robberies and had a criminal record.

Although staying in control was the ultimate in cool, the macho test incarnate, it does not appear that credibility was lost by admitting you were *not* in control. Drugs users have a large vocabulary of rationalizations to fall back on. Many musicians blamed the pushers for causing their problems. Ray Charles was more honest. Living in Seattle when the Royal Roost was playing host to all the dealers, Charles had a heroin habit when he was eighteen: 'It happened because I wanted it to happen ... there wasn't no pusher hanging round the back alley ... no white or black cat got me hooked or encouraged me to turn on.' He was young, wanted a piece of any action that was going and in response to warnings about the dangers replied: 'If it's so bad, why are you using it?'[10]

Of course, once a musician had lost control of his heroin use, the 'control ethic' of hipsterdom gave way to the symbol of the doomed hero. Musicians declared they had 'a monkey on their backs', carried like a badge of honour. Where the expression came from is unclear; possibly a reference to the monkey carried around by organ grinders to collect money from passers-by. The monkey demanded money from customers and feeding from its owner – just like the heroin habit for a jazz musician. The status of being a junkie was not something easily surrendered.

Another factor common among children and those indulging in compulsive behaviour is the demand for instant gratification. In many ways the musician 'addict' is just the same as any other 'addict', but writ large, magnified by the pressures and anxieties of being, or not being enough, in the public eye. Some musicians went for the instant gratification of the needle when they realized they were not going to be superstars overnight. For the hipster living for the present who happened also to be a famous musician, a cohort of star-struck acolytes were ready and willing to supply any need the minute it was articulated. This has been taken to ridiculous lengths in the indulgence of rock megastars, but in relative terms the jazz stars of the fifties were similarly fêted.

Richard Freeman, a psychiatrist who treated Charlie Parker, said that but for the music, Parker was just another potential mental patient dumped in a hospital, forgotten by everyone.

> But with Charlie Parker it is the music factor that makes all the difference. That's really the only reason we're interested in him, the only reason his followers are interested in him, the reason we're willing to stop our own lives and clean up his messes. People like Charlie require somebody like that to follow them through life and clean up the shit.[11]

Trumpeter Kenny Dorham played with Bird from 1948-50:

> [Parker] was all music. He needed to have everything. When he played he couldn't play long enough and nothing stopped his playing. The more drugs he took, the more he went on playing. Bird was a high-starred person ... he always had a crowd around him and he gave different jobs to each one. 'You go and get my horn. You get me some pot. You do this. You do that.' And they would jump.[12]

In the 'gimme it now' department, Bird was again fairly unusual. Unlike those of most heavy users of heroin, Parker's other appetites were not in the least diminished. Prior to a gig, he might consume two three-course dinners or two dozen hamburgers, washed down with torrents of whiskey and followed by a gargantuan whack of heroin. After the gig, the women who had taken his fancy that night would follow him to bed. Parker grabbed at every piece of life and stuffed it in his mouth whole.

As well as being a symbol of the urban outlaw, the ultimate test of dues paying, the means to make the gig and the dream ticket out of misery, the social environment of heroin and rituals of its use also fed the demands of musicians for whom the normal support systems within the music community were insufficient. During the fifties that group seemed to be in the majority. One jazz musician has commented anonymously:

> To me, the reason musicians got into drugs so heavily was that, as artists and performers, they wanted to get closer to each other, to communicate as intimately as possible, and at that time shooting up seemed the best way to do this. It became such a habit with so many of them, that it was almost expected for any new man in the band to show his sense of brotherhood by sticking that needle into his arm, just like his buddies would.

The relationships between musicians are probably unique in the world of work. People who would not necessarily be friends, let alone close friends, find themselves incubated together for weeks or months on end in tour buses, hotel rooms, studios and dressing rooms. They can get to know each other better than family or friends. In such claustrophobic environments, relationships can become very intense, volatile and unpredictable, particularly if one or more of the band are heavily involved in drugs. Often the drug users form an inner clique or, as in the case of many jazz big bands in the fifties, represent the majority of musicians.

Bill Harris, trombone player with Woody Herman's Herd, would travel on the band bus for fifty weeks a year out of fifty-two, the only non-user in a band of heroin users. He sat alone on the back seat with his booze reading the paper, books and generally entertaining himself. The rest all sat up front except Herman who travelled alone. Nobody cold-shouldered anybody, it was just that the drinker and the heroin users inhabited different worlds. They had nothing to say to one another.

In the same way that drugs could take precedence over music, so musicians sometimes adopted very different attitudes to each other as professionals and users. As a musician, Hampton Hawes revered the very ground Charlie Parker stood on: 'We'd be willing to do anything to warm ourselves by that fire, get some of that grease pumping through our veins. He fucked up all our minds. It was where the ultimate truth was.'[13] But as a fellow user, he felt he couldn't trust Parker. This was a parallel world where the rules of musicians-in-arms did not necessarily apply:

> [He'd say] the cat's out in the alley, you can cop for twenty-five cents (meaning dollars). I'd say I didn't have twenty-five cents which may

not have been true ... If I said, 'I only need a dime's worth,' he might say, 'Well, I'm low myself, make it two dimes and we'll cow [pool resources]. Of course if I went for that it was unlikely I'd ever see that second dime. It was the survival of the fittest in those days and you had to know where people were coming from.[14]

Nevertheless in most instances addict-musicians felt more at ease with other addicts than with non-using musicians. Art Pepper found self-esteem as a musician, but also as a heroin user. Nothing to do with the physical sensations of the drug, but the social experience of using it. Within the drug-using fraternity he found a ready-made family who understood one another. In their company he was neither terrified nor alone. He took as much pride in being a 'righteous junkie' who did not inform on others to save his own neck, as he did in being a great musician – possibly more so, because like many great artists, he took his talent for granted. 'I've never studied, never practised ... I knew it was there. All I had to do was reach for it, just do it.'

Pepper spent nearly ten years in prison; sadly, he seemed to be most at ease in institutions. Inside, he had no responsibilities, his daily routines were planned out for him. Narcotics offenders had a certain degree of status inside and he could enjoy the adulation of being a famous musician without all the hassles associated with it outside: 'When I started using drugs, I ran into a different kind of person. In jail I found people who had honour. They were real. They said what they thought ... the dope fiends were warm to me and open with me, I felt.'[15]

In the world of jazz, where the daily mundane concerns of 'the squares' were scorned, the addict-musician had nevertheless to establish an elaborate set of routines and rituals in order to ensure continuing supplies of his drug. Connections had to be made, pick-up points arranged, places for fixing organized if home was not possible, followed by the cycle of preparing the heroin for fixing, getting high, then becoming sick or strung out and starting all over again. Nina Simone once said, 'Jazz is not just music, it's a way of life, a way of thinking.'[16] And what did Williams Burroughs say about heroin? 'Junk is not a kick. It is a way of life.' Musicians often had to make the choice during their careers and they didn't always choose music.

The personal investment in the heroin experience can be very strong. The whole routine of heroin use can be a powerful social and behavioural reinforcer. Heroin users have been known to inject warm water when they couldn't afford drugs, just to go through the ritual of fixing up. Ex-users have experienced some of the physical symptoms of withdrawal just by walking past a place associated with their former life.

Art Pepper was 'hooked' on the social rituals associated with maintaining a habit. His description of this may sound sordid and tragic, but to him it represented safety, security, simplicity and order – cocooned in the 'cosy' world of the heroin user. On the road with the Stan Kenton band in the early fifties:

Me and Andy Angelo roomed together for a long time ... and we each had our own outfits. I had a little carrying case, like an electric razor case. I had an extra eyedropper and my needles, four or five of them. I had my little wires to clean the spike out in case it got clogged. I had a little bottle of alcohol and a sterling silver spoon that was just beautiful and a knife to scoop the stuff on to the spoon ... I would set up my outfit next to the bed in the hotel ... I'd wake up in the morning and reach over, get my little knife, put a few knifefuls in the spoon, cook it up and fix. It was beautiful.[17]

The lifestyle of the heroin user and the attendant health risks could sideline a musician from time to time. But just as hazardous to the long-term development of any jazz career in the fifties was a narcotics conviction. Under American law at that time, being a heroin user was by definition a criminal offence. Unlike the system in Britain, it has never been considered legitimate medical practice in America to prescribe drugs to users with the purpose of stabilizing their lifestyle and removing the need to become involved in the black market.

Gerry Mulligan made the point that 'we all started to feel like criminals and had to hide our addiction. After a while, our whole way of life became involved in our habit and we were thrown into contact with people whom we'd usually go out of our way to avoid. Instead, we had to cultivate them as friends.'[18] Addict musicians were vulnerable to unscrupulous gangsters who ran the clubs and controlled the heroin trade. A musician in debt could become much sicker than he ever was on heroin.

Although the number of jazz musicians using heroin in the forties increased, there seemed to be a decline in the *overall* numbers of heroin addicts. In the early years of World War II, heroin use was less of a public issue as the fire of the marijuana debate raged on. Art Pepper's early playing days were around Central Avenue, Los Angeles – 'The dope thing hadn't evolved into what it is now, with all the police activity. I'd never heard of a narc, didn't know what that word meant. Nobody wanted to rat on anybody or plant their car with a joint or with some stuff.'[19]

After the war, addict figures did not rise dramatically even though heroin supplies were resumed – or rather they did not rise dramatically enough for Anslinger. He was anxious to head off any notion that the Bureau might be dispensable.

The figures were actually massaged upwards, the spectre of enslaved adolescents raised once more and demands for stiffer penalties rang in the ears of the judiciary. Since the mid-thirties, Anslinger had held a monopoly over any public information on drug misuse. He could say anything and be believed. He now claimed that heroin was responsible for rising crime because it was used to induce 'dutch courage'. Alcohol or amphetamines can provide such a stimulus, but certainly not dope – the very word is indicative of its soporific effect. Gang-fighting dropped off as young people discovered a new 'high'. Some black commentators have opined that widespread heroin use has kept the lid on the ghettos and so the police have turned a blind eye.

The key plank in Anslinger's anti-heroin campaign was a harsher sentencing policy. In 1951, as a result of Anslinger's testimony to the Kefauver Senate Committee on Organized Crime, Congress passed the Boggs Act. This compelled Federal judges on first, second and third offences for possession to give *minimum* jail sentences of two, five and ten years respectively. From a second offence onwards there would be no parole, probation or suspension. Legal devices which were granted to traitors and murderers were denied to drug users.

The Daniel Subcommittee report of 1955 led to the even more draconian Narcotic Control Act of 1956. Under the Boggs Act, the maximum sentences for first, second and third offences had been five, ten and twenty years respectively. These were increased to ten, twenty and forty years respectively. These sentences applied only to possession, not selling, and applied to *all* drugs, including marijuana. There was a separate penalty of five to twenty years for a first dealing conviction, and ten to forty years for any subsequent conviction. Anyone aged eighteen or over convicted of selling heroin to a minor could expect a minimum ten years with a possible life sentence or even death upon a jury recommendation. Narcotics and customs agents were given guns and could make arrests without warrants. Black jazz musicians were prime targets for harassment. The police hated seeing black and white mixing together, especially if a white girl was on the arm of a black musician. Successful musicians driving new cars could expect regular shakedowns and the sudden appearance of drugs in the car once the officers had done their 'search'.

Perhaps the most extraordinary law passed in 1956 stipulated that not only those who had been convicted of a drug violation but any current non-convicted users had to register with customs and obtain a certificate to *leave* the United States. The certificate had to be surrendered on return and the minimum sentence for failing to register was one year. The law makers actually believed drug users would turn themselves in.

During the fifties and early sixties a number of musicians were arrested on drugs charges (either marijuana or heroin) and some served time in prison. Together they included Gerry Mulligan, Stan Getz, Tadd Dameron, Anita O'Day, Billie Holiday, Art Pepper, Lester Young (a cocaine charge while in the army), Red Rodney, Hampton Hawes, Chet Baker, Thelonious Monk, Miles Davis, Art Blakey, Percy Heath, Phil Urso, Milt Jackson, Elvin Jones, Charlie Persip, Curtis Fuller and Philly Joe Jones.

Amazingly, Charlie Parker was never even *arrested* on a drugs charge, surviving numerous searches and pat-downs. Some of his sidemen were less fortunate. His star trumpet player in the quintet, Red Rodney, copped a maximum five-year sentence for heroin possession after building up a $75-a-day habit. Like Stan Getz and Art Pepper, he had resorted to petty crime in order to raise money when work was hard to come by. He was sentenced in January 1953 to a term in Leavenworth. Under the terms of the Boggs Act he was out on parole in 1955, but with no therapy available in prison he was back on heroin inside two weeks. Coming out of prison and resuming heroin use can be particularly dangerous, because users often go back to the dose they left off when arrested, forgetting or not knowing that the body can no longer tolerate the same amount. Overdosing is common among this group. Rodney survived, however, to commit more burglaries until he was apprehended for parole violations. The rest of his sentence was served out at the US Public Health Service Hospital at Lexington, Kentucky.

Anslinger's informer system did not net the large haul he had hoped for, but a number of well-known musicians were trapped in this way. In 1953 Art Pepper was set up by an unnamed musician and, in the true spirit of McCarthyite America, was pressurized into naming others in exchange for his freedom. His refusal earned him nine months in the Los Angeles County Jail, the first of six spells behind bars. He also spent time in Fort Worth Hospital, the other major public institution housing narcotics offenders. His refusal to inform put him inside when others went free, but not being 'a rat' was an important point of principle for him.

A bass player whom Hampton Hawes named as 'Wally Shade' was an example of a musician who informed on others. Shade was a heavy user who had been busted many times, but who never served time. Ironically, Hawes was entrapped by a Mexican agent named Vince, who got in with Hawes by warning him that Shade was an informer. Vince won

Hawes' confidence and had the luckless pianist buy heroin for him on two occasions. The second time Hawes climbed into Vince's car only to have a ·38 pistol jabbed at his head and a badge flashed in his face.

Because Hawes had been trapped into selling heroin, he was treated like an 'evil pusher' and sentenced in 1958 to a staggering ten years in prison at Fort Worth. In 1960, Hawes started the tortuous process of applying for a Presidential pardon from newly elected John F. Kennedy. Three years later, just ten weeks before he was assassinated, President Kennedy granted executive clemency to Hampton Hawes.

Although Charlie Parker avoided a drugs arrest, he had his New York Cabaret Card revoked from 1951-3, on the recommendation of the Federal Bureau of Narcotics, who always had him high on their suspect list.

During this time, he could not work in New York. Anyone who worked for more than three days where alcohol was being served had to obtain a cabaret card from the division of licenses in the police department. Each applicant was photographed and fingerprinted and charged $2 for the card which had to be renewed every two years. A musician with a narcotics violation record would automatically be denied a card and anyone busted while holding a card would have it revoked.

New York was the world's major showcase for jazz; a musician's out-of-town reputation meant little unless he could win New York. All the best clubs were there and the top money. To be denied the chance to play there was a serious blow to a musician's career from which some never recovered.

Thelonious Monk suffered badly from a vicious system wide open to bribery and corruption. In 1951, a friend accompanied by two other people called at his flat. As the apartment was tiny and his widowed mother bedridden, Monk suggested they go and sit in his car. They were approached by narcotics agents and somebody dropped a small packet of heroin on the floor which was found by the agents. There wasn't enough to charge Monk as a dealer, but he took a sixty-day 'rap' for his friend as a matter of honour. Worse than the sentence, he lost his cabaret card and it took him six years, until 1957, to get it back and only then with the influential help of Baroness de Koenigswater, the jazz aristocrat in whose flat Charlie Parker died in 1955.

Barely a year after his card was reinstated, the authorities got Monk again. He was driving home with the Baroness and tenor-sax player Charlie Rouse, from a week-long engagement at the Comedy Club in Baltimore. They stopped at a motel and Monk went in to ask for some water. He was a large man, six foot tall and over 200 pounds in weight.

His dark presence must have frightened the owner, who called the police. The next minute he was being dragged from the car and beaten up. The police 'found' some marijuana in the car. Even though the possession charge was dropped, Monk still lost his card because he had been *arrested* on a drugs charge. Not until 1967 was the cabaret-card system declared unconstitutional and abolished by Mayor John Lindsay.

How did the jazz community at large react to what many privately thought was a cancer in the body of the music? There was an understandable reluctance to discuss the matter for fear of perpetuating the image of the junkie jazz musician. In the same year that Charlie Parker and Wardell Gray died, Frank Sinatra starred as Frankie Machine in the film adaptation of Nelson Algren's novel *The Man with the Golden Arm*. Dealing as it did with drug addiction, the film needed a Public Control Administration Certificate of Approval (PCA), before it could be shown. After the war, foreign films and television made an increasing impact on American audiences, but were not subject to the same restrictions as Hollywood. Taking a stand for greater freedom, director Otto Preminger released the new Sinatra movie without a certificate. As the film attracted a wide audience, rather than see the code fall into disrepute the PCA amended the regulations, allowing the depiction of drug addiction as long as there was no hint of encouragement, glamour, size of profits to be made out of drugs or any suggestion that the habit could be easily broken. The film caused a sensation, because it showed an addict jazz musician who was white. It probably fused in the public mind for all time (or at least until rock in the sixties) the link between jazz and drugs.

But in this respect the film was not a fair adaptation of the book. Probably because Sinatra was playing the lead, Frankie Machine's musical connections were given prominence, whereas the book hardly mentions them at all. Frankie is basically a hot-shot card dealer. He has a dream that one day he will have a legitimate job as a big band jazz drummer, but it's all a fantasy, constantly pushed out of reach by his heroin habit. (Interestingly, jazz is seen here as the distant 'straight life', rather than disreputably 'deviant'.) Frankie was a classic example of the aspiring musician who used heroin as a rationalization for failure, but in purely dramatic terms the link between jazz and drugs was tenuous.

Similarly, in 1960, Jack Gelber's off-Broadway play *The Connection* was very well received by audience and critics alike. The play had a jazz soundtrack, but none of the users on whom the action focused were musicians. Nevertheless, the same inevitable connections were made.

When it came to illegal drugs, whatever they were, the music industry was caught in a dilemma. The standard response tended to be 'Why pick on jazz musicians when there are far more doctors who misuse drugs?' This may have been fair, but it was hardly going to deflect attention away from the problem or silence the critics of jazz. In any event, a jazz musician arrested for drug possession was news; newspaper proprietors wanted to sell papers, policemen wanted high-profile publicity for star busts.

The industry could not be seen to condone drug use. Cab Calloway was one of the old school; the hipster ethos which embraced heroin was alien to him and he gave vent to his feelings in an article entitled 'Is Dope Killing Our Musicians?' published in the black magazine *Ebony* in 1951:

A spectre is haunting the American music industry; the spectre of narcotics, destroying the talents of many of our finest performers, breaking up some of our best bands ...

Am I overstating the dope menace in music? I think not. As a practising musician for over twenty years, I know the situation as intimately as most members of the profession. I have watched an entire generation of American jazzmen develop during my career and I have seen scores of these promising artists struck down by an evil that is as cruel and relentless as a deep-sea octopus. Some of my dearest friends have been trapped by this insidious habit, which has fastened itself upon them like a plague ... Drugs have caused a disturbing number of good musicians to deteriorate into hopeless has-beens. Many a fine young musician who has switched to heroin to get 'turned on', has discovered to his agony that his entire creative life has been stopped cold by a terrible habit which he cannot control.

In 1953 a half-hearted attempt was made to expel from the Hollywood Local 47 of the American Federation of Musicians any member convicted of drug offences. Fortunately no such action was taken. By contrast, jazz writers were incensed at the savage sentences handed out to musicians convicted of possessing drugs for personal use only. The dilemma was highlighted in the following *Down Beat* editorial of January 1962 on the occasion of Ray Charles' arrest for possession.

THE RAY CHARLES CASE

When Ray Charles was arrested recently in Indianapolis, on a narcotics charge, the singer reportedly told police he had been addicted since the age of sixteen. The arresting officers said they discovered in his room a quantity of marijuana and heroin, plus the paraphernalia used by a drug addict.

There is evidence of another kind in the case, too. Human evidence. Charles is blind and has been since he was six.

So what do you do with a blind man held as a heroin addict? Toss him in jail as a social menace? If he is a law breaker, as the police charge, then the statutes are explicit; he must be punished. Punishment in itself is held by many to be rehabilitative, the premise being that if you are punished for an offence, you may not repeat. But somehow this premise has been proved hollow where the vast majority of addicts is concerned. Besides, Charles had been arrested previously for violation of the narcotics laws.

Now, let's assume for the sake of argument that Charles is not punished if convicted. On compassionate grounds, let's say. Wouldn't this leave us with the question: where do you draw the line? If Charles should be exempted from the usual penalty of the law because of his blindness, why should not other addicts, handicapped in other ways, say by mental or emotional disorders, also be set free? They're sick, too, aren't they?

On the other hand, if Charles is convicted and jailed as an addict, what is the law proving? That it is inflexible and unyielding? Or that it is brutal and blind to the call of compassion? Charles' alleged need for drugs will certainly not be eliminated by serving a jail sentence, just as the craving of thousands of convicted addicts is not allayed by prison terms. Is there, then, a difference between the addiction of Ray Charles, artist, and the addiction of John Doe, car-park attendant? Of course not. Charles' case merely dramatizes in the most human terms one of the crucial problems confronting society. His physical affliction is obvious and inspires sympathy and understanding. In John Doe, car-park attendant, the affliction may not be so readily perceivable or permit of quick understanding, but it exists nonetheless.

In jazz we are prone to feel sympathy and tell ourselves we understand when a musician is jailed for narcotics violations. The empathy between jazzman and a just-plain-lover of the art serves as an excuse here. But too often there exists a tendency among jazzfolk to exempt a musician addict from the strictures of society and from the penalties his addiction incurs. The case of Charlie Parker is probably the outstanding example of this attitude in operation. But this tendency to excuse has deeper and more serious implications when jazz heroes such as Parker and Charles are the objects.

We are tragically familiar with the many literal applications of the faulty syllogism: Bird is a genius of jazz; Bird cannot live without heroin; therefore, heroin is essential to jazz genius. Just as Parker was hailed and enthroned on Olympus in his lifetime, today Ray Charles' music is marketed on record and in person with unstinting employment of the noun, Genius. Whether Charles believes his publicity matters as little as whether Charlie Parker did. The difference between Parker and Charles in terms of general influence, however, should be obvious. Charles is reaching more people with his music and with his personality than Parker ever could. And an astonishing number of Charles-worshippers are kids. It would be tragic indeed if the mass-worship of Ray Charles were to result in just a single literal application of a similar syllogism. Because if one youngster is motivated or influenced to try heroin as a result of the story of Charles' arrest, then what the law may demand of the singer just won't mean a thing.

Industry concern for those musicians who provide the basis of the wealth for the industry, but who also get into trouble with drugs and alcohol, has usually fallen far short of any practical assistance. No doubt the musicians who were paid off in heroin by one small jazz label of the early fifties were eternally grateful, but this hardly constituted a planned response to the problem the industry was facing. In a letter written to *Variety* in March 1954, clarinettist Buddy de Franco called upon all those with connections in the business to start giving serious consideration to the issue of drug use among musicians.

Three years later, despite being strenuously urged to drop the idea, jazz critic Nat Hentoff arranged for a symposium on addiction at the 1957 Newport Jazz Festival. And from that session evolved the Musicians Clinic in New York, funded on a grant from the festival.

The chief psychiatrist was Dr Marie Nyswander, one of the pioneers of methadone maintenance treatment who died in 1986. In 1960, together with psychologist Charles Winick, she presented a paper which examined the progress of musicians who went through the psychotherapeutic regime. In a controlled (clinical) study involving the clinic patients and a group of addict musicians who did not come for psychotherapy, the clinic patients improved significantly over the others in relation to stopping drugs, adjusting to a non-addict lifestyle and getting work. Numbers coming to the clinic in the first year were small; only fifteen musicians came for treatment, whereas in a separate study Winick had estimated that there were probably over 750 regular users of heroin among the New York jazz community.

Outside this one clinic, the narcotic rehabilitation prison hospitals at Fort Worth and Lexington provided what little psychotherapeutic help was available, but notable successes were achieved including Gerry

Mulligan and Red Rodney, who told *Down Beat:*

> I fought it, I didn't want any part of analysis. I even volunteered for narcotics tests. I figured I would get good and high all the time I was in, and ride through the three years. But just before I was to go into the tests, I changed my mind. Maybe I finally realized that I had thrown too much of my life away. But I know that from then on, I began to really live like a human being again.
>
> Analysis is the greatest thing I ever went through. I began to grow up. At first, I lied and told wild stories. Then I wondered, 'Who am I lying to?' The answer, of course, was that I was lying to myself again. When I got straightened out on that score, the analysis began to help me. I saw for the first time how low I had fallen. I was ashamed, more than I had ever been in all my life.[20]

The study done by Winick and Nyswander demonstrated that addict-musicians were constitutionally stronger than the 'typical addict', in that many had withdrawn themselves from heroin on more than one occasion prior to coming for treatment. After a four-year habit during which he sank as low in the gutter as you can get, Miles Davis (not one of the patients) just decided it was too much trouble, sweated it out for twelve days and never went back on heroin. John Coltrane, too, kicked the habit on his own through his strength of purpose, filling the ensuing vacuum not with alcohol as many others did, but with spirituality and music.

Others did not fare so well. Through interviews which appeared at various stages in his disjointed career, *Down Beat* tried heroically to suggest that Art Pepper's troubles were behind him. He had a spell in Synanon, a rehabilitation house which had recorded successes with other musicians, but he could not break his compulsive behaviour. Eventually, in 1982, his body just packed up.

What conclusions can be drawn from the use of heroin by jazz musicians in the post-war era? According to Hampton Hawes, '... the casualty list in the fifties – dead, wounded and mentally deranged – started to look like the Korean War was being fought at the corner of Central and 45th.'[21] Directly or indirectly, long-term misuse of heroin starting in the forties or fifties claimed the lives of – among others – Billie Holiday, Fats Navarro, Sonny Berman (Woody Herman's brilliant trumpet player), pianist Carl Perkins, Wardell Gray, Tadd Dameron, Shadow Wilson, British drummer Phil Seaman and Tubby Hayes. The record books show that by some strange coincidence both Charlie Christian and Jimmy Blanton succumbed to TB in 1942. One jazz musician commented however: 'There are a number of boys who would be living today if not for the pushers – Charlie Christian and Jimmy Blanton, Duke's bass player. They weren't very strong and they allowed bad cats to take advantage of their weakness.'[22]

The need to maintain regular and – for successful musicians – expensive heroin habits, drove some into crazy situations; Charlie Parker actually signed over half his Dial Record royalties to his main West Coast dealer, Emry Bird. Musicians saw their careers ruined by long jail sentences and coming back was not always easy. Street credibility was not much use if you were also regarded as an employment liability. As advances against salaries, gig money got spent before it was earned and many a trusting musician has lent his horn to 'a friend' only to receive a pawn ticket in the post a few weeks later.

Heroin use hurt bebop because many club owners associated the 'new drug' with the 'new music' and banned both. The arrests of Elvin Jones and Tony Williams on drugs charges in Japan in 1966 caused the cancellation of Art Blakey's summer tour of 1967 and with it the loss of nearly $30,000.

But some might argue that all the problems caused by drugs were the price which had to be paid for classic, timeless jazz. Perhaps the same adolescent characteristics that made Charlie Parker a compulsive drug user, drinker and eater gave him the free unself-conscious flights of imagination to produce the music he did. To quote Robert Reisner: 'Bird was a neurotic, but the great strides in art are not made by happy well-adjusted people. Art is a form of sublimation and is created by neurotics and compulsion-ridden people.'[23] Art Blakey observed:

> You do not play better with heroin, but you do hear better. Bird said he wanted to kick the habit so that he could tell people what he heard ... While he is suffering, he cannot produce; but reflecting about his pain, he can create. Musicians who have been junkies and then rid themselves of the habit have sometimes really then come into their own musically.[24]

A good example of this was Miles Davis. Ian Carr, his biographer, noted that the effect of Davis' heroin experience on his subsequent life and work cannot be overestimated. During his years of inactivity, Davis was often to be found on the bathroom floor of Howard McGhee's apartment with a needle in his arm. The chances are that musicians who come out the other side will be stronger, more resilient, more disciplined and able to exploit a major experience for the purposes of artistic creativity. Davis had the talent to capitalize on that; his genius as a musician never deserted him, it just lay dormant.

7

Lady Days

It's like they say, there's no damn business like show business.
You had to smile to keep from throwing up.

Billie Holiday

The dominant psychiatric model of female addiction (formulated largely
by men) has stereotyped women heroin users as natural victims –
passive, insecure, vulnerable, dependent creatures. Their family back-
grounds are characterized as disturbed and chaotic, often containing
episodes of physical or sexual abuse. Such women may get pregnant
several times, as a way of breaking free from an oppressive family
environment and gaining the security of a relationship. If she is 'taken
on' by a man who also happens to be an addict, he will force her into
addiction. For women, this is cited as the most common route to drug
dependency.

Once hooked on heroin, the woman is stigmatized as more 'deviant'
than her male counterpart, because she is seen to be challenging the
status quo by not fulfilling her role as a dutiful wife and mother. But
even if she wanted to fulfil such a role the law has decreed that drug use
and parenthood are incompatible; Billie Holiday was turned down as a
foster parent because of her drug convictions. Recent court decisions in
Britain and America have determined that the unborn child of a
pregnant addict is by definition the victim of child abuse, thus con-
demning the woman as unfit to be a parent. By contrast, the woman
dependent on tranquillizers is not regarded (quite rightly) as beyond the
pale, presumably because her condition is rooted in the 'legitimate'
prescribing practices of respectable doctors, not the outcome of irresponsible hedonism.

In truth, Billie Holiday and the other subject of this chapter, Anita
O'Day, both jazz singers with heroin problems, did fit this model in

part, at a time when the social pressures on women to conform were not counterbalanced by an energetic and well-publicized women's movement. Billie Holiday suffered a highly insecure upbringing away from her mother in the charge of an uncaring aunt. She was subjected to sexual harassment and rape to the point where she became terrified of sex. Aged only ten, she was sent to a Catholic Reformatory after being found guilty of 'enticing' the man who raped her. By fifteen, she was a prostitute. Anita O'Day, dubbed 'excess baggage' by her mother, had to learn to be self-sufficient from an early age, fending off many unwelcome sexual advances. She endured over a dozen abortions, although she was never certain whether or not she was being conned by back-street abortionists, telling her that she had been aborted when she might not have been pregnant in the first place. She spent her middle teen years roaming the dance halls earning money in the notorious dance marathons or 'walkathons' depicted in the film *They Shoot Horses, Don't They?* Not prostitution, but exploitation of the body for money in almost every other sense.

In sociological terms, just by being jazz singers Holiday and O'Day were 'deviant' long before they got anywhere near heroin. But in both women the pull towards tradition and conformity was always lingering in the background; in their autobiographies there are poignant and romantic reflections of the virtues of home, stability, family and children. But however much they might have conformed to some circumscribed image of 'damaged' women, Holiday and O'Day were most definitely not passive souls. Even being a prostitute was a matter of pride for Holiday; she knew she could make more in one night than in a whole month doing laundry and, as she said herself, she was never going to be anybody's maid.

First as professional female singers in the unrelentingly chauvinistic world of jazz and then as heroin users, both women had to cultivate a tough, hard-nosed attitude to business to keep working, obtain drugs and stay ahead of the law. Jazz singers were under particular pressure because the whole band often relied upon their appearance. Nobody would much notice a stand-in drummer or bass player, but the singers were the main attraction and their non-appearance could mean no gig and no money for anyone. Beyond this, however, the circumstances of O'Day's and Holiday's drug dependency differed. Holiday was a star – the dealers came looking for her and there was also a ready supply from the men in her life. O'Day never commanded that kind of status and often had to buy on the streets with all the attendant risks. The other crucial difference, of course, was that Holiday was black and the humiliations and indignities heaped upon her because of her colour were a source of deep bitterness and anguish throughout her life.

Racism threw up many ironies for Holiday; playing in Count Basie's band in 1937, she was actually asked to black up because she looked too fair-skinned under stage lights and house managers were afraid of a riot should the audience think that a white woman was singing in a black band. She joined Artie Shaw the following year, not the first black singer to sing in a white band, but the first in a white band to take the risk of touring in the South. To his credit Shaw took that risk, but not surprisingly Billie received appalling treatment on the road; everywhere there were scenes with sheriffs, hotel and theatre managers. The direst roadside cafés wouldn't serve her even in the kitchen and sometimes promoters or club managers wouldn't let her sing and her place was taken by a white female vocalist. Once she mouthed back 'Motherfuck-er' at a Southern cracker who yelled out 'let the nigger wench sing another song,' and had to be rapidly escorted from the scene before the lynching party could be formed. But the final straw came in the so-called liberal North at the Blue Room of New York's Lincoln Hotel on 43rd Street. The gig was due to be broadcast coast to coast – a golden opportunity for maximum exposure. Claiming as an excuse the high percentage of Southern guests staying at the hotel, the management told Shaw that Holiday could not use the main entrance, travel in the main lift, mingle with the guests or even stay on the bandstand when she wasn't singing. Artie Shaw might have spoken out: he himself had known enough anti-Semitism to understand what Billie was going through, but he decided that he could not sacrifice the prospects of the whole band on a point of principle. As a result Art and Holiday parted company. There was understandable bitterness on the singer's part, although it appeared to mellow with the passing years.

These ignominies were even harder to bear coming in the wake of her father's death in 1937, indirectly another victim of the innate racism of America's white majority. A travelling musician, he caught pneumonia on tour in Dallas, but didn't seek treatment believing that he would never find a hospital that would admit blacks. He was finally persuaded to try, and did succeed in finding one, but by then it was too late. 'Strange Fruit' was the externalization in song of all Billie Holiday's rage about the inhumanity of white towards black.

Despair paved the way for Holiday's entrée into the world of heroin. She had a residency at the Café Society Downtown in New York, but although she was an acclaimed star, she had little money to show for a two-year, seven-nights-a-week engagement and by 1942 she was emo-tionally at a very low ebb. At this point Jimmy Monroe came into her life. Younger brother of Clark Monroe, owner of the Uptown House where Holiday also sang, Jimmy was generally regarded as bad news and Billie was urged not to get involved with him. But she did get involved and eventually married him, a marriage which turned out to be a cruel farce.

Holiday's relationship with men bore a striking resemblance to her love affair with heroin. Both were self-destructive yet compelling and all-embracing – she would move from one 'dependency' to another and back again without missing a beat. It was about as much good telling her not to get involved with somebody as it was to tell her to stop using drugs or getting drunk. Men and drugs seemed to perform almost the same functions in her life, superficially offering safety, security and escape. Social psychologist Stanton Peele has written very convincingly in *Love and Addiction* how similar the two states can be, applying equally to men and women.

Monroe was heavily into opium and Holiday went along the same road, not because he forced her into it, but because if she was going to stay close to him she needed to be on the same wavelength. However, for a touring musician, opium smoking was highly impractical – it was too easily detectable by inquisitive policemen, it made her sick and the smoke affected her throat so that her pre-performance warm-ups were taking longer and longer. So she switched to heroin, altogether more discreet and convenient, and took to wearing long evening gloves to hide the track marks that were evidence enough to get her arrested.

However, it was when Billie Holiday decided to come *off* heroin that her troubles really started. In the immediate post-war years, work in the New York jazz clubs was hard to come by and Holiday took the opportunity to go into a clinic for three weeks at a cost of $2,000. From the moment she came out she had a policeman for a shadow. Back in the 1920s, the clinic had been involved in a deal with the city police whereby the police would threaten wealthy addicts with arrest if they did not go to the clinic for treatment. The clinic then made the appropriate pay-offs. Although the deal had been exposed, it is possible that the connection still operated, or perhaps informers anxious for reward or to keep the heat away from themselves had told police of Holiday's attempts to come off (before then her drug use had not been public knowledge). Only a few weeks after she left the clinic she was arrested, having gone back to using drugs. Assistant Attorney Joseph Hildenberger stated in court that Billie Holiday was a victim of the worst sort of parasite who charged her $100 for a $5 fix, but this did not prevent her from being sent to Alderson Reformatory in West Virginia for a year and a day.

Yet the worst parasites seemed to be those who professed their love for Billie; emotionally and financially, she was robbed blind by all of them. Joe Guy was an addict and Holiday had to take better paying but artistically less satisfying theatre gigs to pay for his habit as well as her own. John Levy, also her manager, had her tied up every which way with deals and contracts and threatened to inform on her ('drop a dime' as the saying went) every time they had an argument. Naturally, after her first drug conviction she lost her New York cabaret card, a serious blow to her attempts at winning national prominence, something she never achieved and another source of despair in her life. Although she never compromised her art if it meant dancing to anybody else's beat but her own, she was desperate to become 'popular' and win *Down Beat* polls. By judicious use of under-the-counter payments, Levy got her cabaret card back, but Holiday was convinced that he also deliberately set her up. One day in January 1949, he gave her some heroin in a hotel room and told her to flush it down the toilet. Just at that moment the police broke in and arrested her for possession. To prove she was clean, Holiday booked herself into a sanatorium to be supervised day and night by doctors looking for signs of withdrawal. She stayed there for four days at a cost of $4,000, but made her point and was eventually found not guilty. Later she saw photos of Levy, taken in the Uptown club, being very friendly with George White, the man who had led the raid.

Anita O'Day was encouraged in her signing by Lord Buckley, the ultimate jazz hipster eccentric, and she also fell for a musician named Don Carter, a brilliant drummer who somehow never made it. Carter taught her a lot about music and at seventeen she married him. She moved in with him and his overbearing mother in their house in Chicago and fought for a year to prise him from his mother's clutches, during which time the marriage was never consummated. Finally it broke up altogether, mother and son leaving home and O'Day moving to the notorious Chelsea Hotel on Twenty-third Street in New York, home to itinerant artists of all kinds and the site where Devon Wilson and Nancy Spungen, the girlfriends of Jimi Hendrix and Sid Vicious respectively, both met their deaths.

Anita O'Day joined the Gene Krupa band in 1941 and began to move into the big time with two hits, 'Let Me off Downtown' and 'Thanks for the Boogie Ride'. That same year she won her first *Down Beat* poll as New Star of the Year and came fourth in the female vocalist section. She maintained her high position in the polls over the next few years and in 1943 married her long time 'on-off' lover, Carl Hoff, a golf pro and jazz fanatic. From Krupa she went to Woody Herman, then had two stints with Stan Kenton. But things were not as well as they seemed; the touring and the pressure from fans took their toll and O'Day hit the bottle in a big way:

> I should have been happy, but I was tired and depressed, drawing on energy I didn't really have ... I didn't eat regularly. But I drank. I even drank a little on the job. But I never thought of myself as looking for booze. On the other hand, I didn't look for food either. I'd never been taught you had to eat. But I should have known I was heading for trouble.[1]

For six weeks in 1945, she suffered a nervous breakdown, spending much of the time in a wardrobe refusing to come out. As someone who felt she was born to fail, she couldn't handle success: 'Maybe I've been too happy ... because I'm not used to that.'

In 1946, Carl and Ray Foreman, an old friend of O'Day's, tried to set up a jazz club in North Hollywood. Either they were incredibly impractical or their lawyer was suspect, because they had no building permits and failed to find out that the site of their proposed club had been earmarked by the city corporation for a water conduit. On top of that there were still restrictions on building inessential structures so that material could be used for the war effort. Not surprisingly, the club did not materialize. Matters took another turn for the worse when Carl was rousted by narcotics agents in March 1947:

> It was a dumb, nightmarish period. If only I'd been lucky enough to have been under contract to a movie studio or a big agency, I'd have placed a call to the head of publicity and he'd have known who to pay off. Around that time the only big movie star who landed in the headlines for using grass was Bob Mitchum, but he certainly wasn't the only one using it. There were lots of others whose drug use mysteriously never made the police records.[2] [Mitchum served a two-month jail sentence in 1948.]

Carl and Anita were released on $1,000 bail pending an appeal. Initially the bust seemed good for business. Crowds flocked to see her at a club in Milwaukee because, as the club manager put it, 'dopers aren't that common around here'. However the appeal failed and O'Day spent ninety days in jail, although she seemed to regard them as a vacation rather than a punishment – for the first time in her life she ate regular meals. But out of prison, aged twenty-nine, she was stuck with a career that didn't seem to be going anywhere. Carl Hoff had another go at starting up a club, this time in Chicago, but it too failed and he and O'Day split up.

O'Day tended now to mix with the bebop crowd. Moving within Charlie Parker's sphere of influence, she was bound to discover heroin. In 1952 she almost shot up for kicks in the company of Stan Getz and Chet Baker, both users at the time. However, Gerry Mulligan was also on the gig and although a heroin user himself, he threatened to beat up anyone who showed O'Day how to fix. In her own words, 'the "Bad Anita" began to take over from the "Good Anita"'.

In October, O'Day and her new lover, a young trumpet player called Denny Roche, were arrested for a second time, suspected of using marijuana. Driving home, they were followed by a police car. The police alleged that they saw O'Day throw a roach (the stub of a marijuana cigarette) out of the car window. She was released on bail; the case took four months to come to trial at the end of which Anita O'Day was found not guilty, because the police could not produce the actual roach she had thrown away. While waiting for the trial, O'Day had her first taste of heroin in the dressing room of Harry 'The Hipster' Gibson, who had a hit record with 'Who Put the Benzedrine in Mrs Murphy's Ovaltine?' but was more famous in the music business as a purveyor of chemicals.

Escaping that marijuana charge and her earlier run-ins with the law made O'Day something of a target at a time when the heat was on musicians and informers were everywhere. It was in fact a musician who set O'Day up for a heroin bust, obviously a more serious charge. A pianist passed her a packet of heroin at the Club Samoa and asked her to hold it for him until the end of the last set. Anita hid it in the ladies toilet, but as she left the stage after the gig she was grabbed by police. Denny was also arrested. The police made reference to the heroin in the toilet and tried to get Anita to admit she put it there. She and Denny were taken away and held on suspicion, during which time they were invited to pay up $2,500 to stay out of court. Anita refused and the hearing was set for 4 May 1953, after one postponement for a singing engagement. After a lot of legal wrangling, the trial eventually got under way on 8 July and dragged on for a month, ending in a retrial with the jury hopelessly deadlocked. Finally on 25 August, Anita O'Day was found guilty and put on probation for five years, on condition that she spent five months in the County Jail on Terminal Island. Again, like Art Pepper, she found that jail was not such a bad place to be – no responsibilities and, as long as you kept your nose clean, no problems either. The only really bad time she had was when her mother died and the prison authorities refused to let her attend the funeral because it was out of State.

The most ridiculous part of the whole business was that apart from an occasional sniff, there was no way Anita O'Day could be described as a heroin user. Yet by virtue of her prison sentence and because there was little distinction made in law or public perception between a heroin addict and marijuana smoker, she was branded as a junkie and faced all the problems of having that label without actually being one. To blot out the reality of her fading career, which was crippled by legal problems and lengthy absences from the stage, she drank heavily. But she had acquired the reputation of a doper, not a drinker, and she resolved, in her own words, 'to play the game, if she had the name'. So it was that heroin came into her life, and with it a new man who became a crucial part of the equation.

For a jazzman, drummer John Poole was an unusual individual. He didn't smoke or drink and because of strong religious convictions he didn't believe in sex outside marriage – but he regularly shot heroin. O'Day and Poole were never lovers, but O'Day pestered him into injecting her. Possibly due to guilt feelings, he never showed her how to do it, but insisted on doing it himself.

As user-musicians on the road trying to find work, O'Day and Poole took enormous risks in order to obtain drugs, trusting unknown connections and even having heroin sent through the post. O'Day stopped drinking, which probably saved her from an early death, but of course injecting heroin brought with it its own potential hazards.

Inevitably, they were busted. They bought 84% pure heroin from an informer who had been supplied with narcotics by government agents. They never got to use it, which was just as well because with the average purity on the streets at that time around 20-30%, a dose that strong would probably have killed them both. Agents raided their room straight after the buy, but Poole put on an act of being completely mad, distracting their attention so that he could push the packet from the table to the floor and out of sight. The police left empty-handed, a very fortunate let-off because it would have meant a second conviction for Poole, after which in the fifties they threw away the key. O'Day would have gone to prison for five years for breaking parole.

Poole and O'Day lost their New York cabaret cards, but they were told that despite their convictions they would both be granted permits if they could pass Nalline tests. Nalline was the trade name for nalorphine, a narcotic antagonist: in other words a drug which reversed the effects of narcotics like heroin. One physical feature of opiate use is a constriction of the pupils in the eye. In the Nalline test, the person was seated in a darkened room, injected with 3mg of Nalline and left for thirty minutes. If after this time the pupils dilated more than 0.5mm, it was taken as proof that the Nalline had found some opiate to antagonize and had proceeded to reverse its action of constricting the pupils. More dramatically, the user would start going into withdrawal, perspiring and yawning. When the subject is clean, Nalline can paradoxically act as an opiate agonist, mimicking rather than combating the effects of heroin. Lenny Bruce took this test when he was off heroin and ended the session high as a kite. O'Day and Poole weaned themselves off heroin using an opiate-based cough medicine called Cosynal, took the Nalline test and managed to pass it. In being given the chance to 'win back' their permits, it might have been significant that both musicians were white.

To say that 1958 was a year of mixed fortunes for Anita O'Day would be something of an understatement. In May she very nearly died and by the end of the summer she was an international star. The turning point was *Jazz on a Summer's Day*, Bert Stern's film of the 1958 Newport Jazz Festival. Stoned on heroin, O'Day was hailed as 'the festival's outstanding act' by *Metronome* and 'the hit' by *Esquire*. Stern included two songs from Anita's nine-tune set in the final cut of the film, 'Sweet Georgia Brown' and a fast version of 'Tea for Two', bringing more accolades from the *New York Times* and *Newsweek* when the film was released. (Ironically, both these songs have drug associations.)

But it could all have been so different; one late afternoon in May that year, Anita had been in a hotel room with John Poole and a guy identified only as a 'very famous jazz drummer' who had a heavy heroin habit. For the first time, she allowed somebody other than John to inject her. But probably because the drummer's tolerance was much higher than hers, he gave her too much and she went out like a light. The drummer immediately shot her full of cocaine and between them, her male companions revived her by walking her up and down the room and showering her with cold water.

Anita O'Day met Billie Holiday only twice. The second time Holiday acted as though O'Day wasn't there, but on the first occasion they had pooled their money to buy heroin:

> I wasn't only in awe of her singing. I was in awe of her habit. She didn't cook up with a spoon. Man, she used a small tunafish can and shot 10cc into her feet. (Later, I understand she ran out of veins all over her body. So she used those on either side of her vagina. One sure thing, no narc was going to bust her for fresh track marks.)[3]

'Later' was 1959. For O'Day, the jazz film paved the way for tours to Europe and Japan, where she was a special favourite. Holiday was in a less fortunate position. In February that year, jazz critic Leonard

Feather went backstage to visit Billie Holiday. What he saw drained the colour from his face. 'What's the matter, Leonard? You seen a ghost?' Feather didn't need to reply: the look in his face said it all. On the afternoon of 31 May 1959, Billie Holiday collapsed in a coma. She was taken to Knickerbocker Hospital in New York and then to the Metropolitan Hospital in Harlem.

The initial diagnosis of a non-lethal heroin overdose was changed to a liver ailment complicated by cardiac failure. She had actually begun to recover when police struck again. They raided the hospital room and claimed they found a small envelope containing heroin. It was pointed out that, wired up to a bank of equipment, Holiday could not possibly have reached where the drug was allegedly discovered. The police ignored this argument. She couldn't be moved, so a guard was placed outside the door as if she was a mafia mobster. Some claimed the drug was planted, others that it was left by a misguided well wisher. Her companion Alice stated in a BBC-TV documentary that the singer had asked for cocaine to be brought in and nurse had noticed traces of it on her lips.

Whatever the truth, it was a blow from which Billie Holiday did not recover. Without her knowledge or consent, the police removed her few possessions from the room and further degraded and humiliated her by photographing and fingerprinting her in her sick bed. Doctors added cirrhosis of the liver to the diagnosis and her condition worsened. She died at 3.10 am on Friday 17 July 1959.

Through the publication of her autobiography *Lady Sings the Blues* in 1956, Billie Holiday became in her own way as much a public campaigner for the humane treatment of drug addicts as Lenny Bruce was for a reform of the laws on obscenity. Her much-publicized views hardly found favour with the police and yet another bust followed the appearance of her book, in which she wrote:

> People on drugs are sick people. So now we end up with the government chasing sick people like they were criminals, telling doctors they can't help them, prosecuting them because they had some stuff without paying tax, and sending them to jail.
>
> Imagine if the government chased sick people with diabetes, put a tax on insulin and drove it into the black market, told doctors they couldn't treat them, and then caught them, prosecuted them for not paying their taxes, and then sent them to jail. If we did that, everyone would know we were crazy. Yet we do practically the same thing every day in the week to sick people hooked on drugs. The jails are full and the problem is getting worse very day.[4]

In his book *The Murderers*, Harry J. Anslinger devoted a chapter to the use of drugs in the entertainment business. He wrote of the perils of being in the public eye: 'Billie Holiday was an example. The harpies were forever after this talented Negro singer. They not only put her on drugs, but would not let her get off ... Despite her addiction, she reached and held a high place in the entertainment world. But only a few years after she reached her peak, she was dead.'[5] Anslinger failed to mention those in authority who killed her career in New York and probably cost her the national acclaim she so desperately craved as well as several thousand dollars in appearance money (to add to the royalties lost to shyster record companies). Nor does Harry J. mention the brave and fearless officers who hounded a sick woman to her grave.

For Anita O'Day, life got worse before it got better. She was an international star, but like Holiday she had little money compared with more commercial singers and as the sixties progressed, she found herself losing out, as many jazz artists did, to the burgeoning pop and rock scene. She described her personal life at that time as a mess; by now heroin was a dominant feature of a life made complicated by affairs with a series of unstable men, including one psychopath who threatened to cut her vocal cords when she spurned him.

By the early sixties, her health had begun to break down – prolonged heroin use, and her lifestyle with its unhealthy diet, interfered with her digestive and intestinal processes and she suffered from severe arthritis in her knees and right arm. She went through a particularly lean spell in 1966; money was tight and she was unable to buy drugs. Her 'hype friend', John Poole, the man who (in her terms) had cared for her for so many years, had given up drugs, got married and moved to Hawaii. She had no option but to try to 'cold turkey', but having been on heroin for fourteen years, she was terrified of withdrawal and the chances of her succeeding with no physical, emotional or financial support were slim. On 4 March 1966, having almost detoxified herself, she took a shot of heroin her body could no longer tolerate and overdosed.

A friend found her with the needle still sticking in her arm and got her rushed to hospital. On arrival she was declared clinically dead, but the staff at UCLA Medical Center managed to revive her. On being discharged she flew to Hawaii where John Poole helped her on the long road back to fitness. She said in her autobiography: 'I finally faced the fact that life was hard. I recognized that I couldn't continue running away from my problems. I realized that I was too old and too tired to do more than make the most of what I had.'[6]

PART TWO

Introduction

The 1950s saw a new generation of disaffected, alienated youth in Britain and America kicking against what their parents regarded as the trophies of victory over the Axis Powers and Japan – peace, safety, security and prosperity. For many fifties youngsters this meant a bland meaningless world where passions were stifled and the pace of life ticked to the beat of the factory clock. Britain was still rather austere and gloomy; rationing did not end with the war, the sights of war damage were inescapable and young people in the early part of the decade did not enjoy the economic freedoms of their American counterparts.

In America, the same stifling cloak of conformity throttled political radicalism in a wave of anti-communist hysteria; 'pinko' was the ultimate insult. In this respect at least, teenagers of all social classes did not demur from mainstream opinion in the fifties. They weren't interested in revolution, because people got killed in real revolution. What they wanted was safe rebellion – weekend unconventionality, crossing on to the wild side on the way home to mom's apple pie or fish and chips out of last Sunday's *Pictorial*.

Adolescent was the jargon of sociologists and psychiatrists – teenage was an entirely different concept, born out of market research and the economics of consumerism. Before the Second World War, those we now call teenagers existed in a demographic wilderness, not quite children, but with adulthood tantalizingly out of reach. A nineteen-year-old whizz-kid from Chicago, named Eugene Gilbert, changed all that. In 1945, he established Gil Bert Teen Age Services, promising hot advertising copy for manufacturers keen to reach this new and affluent market. But it was not until 1956 that the teenager became established as a cultural and commercial force in America. It was the year rock 'n' roll came of age to give teenagers a voice and stance that nobody could ignore. Even so, the phenomenon was not entirely new: like the post-war generation of the 1920s, white kids turned to black music as a vehicle for the release of suppressed emotions and as a statement against cultural and moral 'norms'. But they did not turn to jazz; modern jazz was becoming too introspective, complex and elitist. Moreover, you couldn't really dance to it and as dancing had always been the key to any number of post pubetal possibilities, jazz (and so jazz musicians) tended to be pushed out of the limelight as a source of public outrage at the behaviour of young people.[1] In indeterminate proportions the magic formula of rock 'n' roll mixed black r&b and urban blues with white country and Southern gospel. And the nucleus at the centre of popular music's Big Bang was a truck driver from Tupelo, Mississippi: Elvis Presley.

Much has been written about Presley, but it is worth restating that he was an icon of the new age, the apotheosis of everything that teenagers fantasized about and their parents hated and feared. Thirty years on, when so much has developed out of those early rock 'n' roll records, it is impossible to imagine the impact Presley, Jerry Lee Lewis and Bill Haley had on a generation brought up on Tommy Dorsey, Glenn Miller and Benny Goodman. Here were white country boys not crooning ballads to virginal girls on distant pedestals but singing lyrics to earthy black music whose messages about love left nothing to the imagination. Mainly because of the black influence, rock 'n' roll was condemned in exactly the same tones as jazz had been. Such bastions of free thought as the North Alabama White Citizens Council declared that rock 'n' roll was a racial plot against the white community. Others condemned the music as 'aboriginal' and 'a communicable disease'. There were even Senate hearings on the sexual explicitness of r&b lyrics. However the record companies, RCA above all, were laughing all the way to the bank. 'Heartbreak Hotel' topped the pop, country and r&b charts simultaneously and sixty per cent of RCA's production output was given over to supplying the demand for Presley's music.

Presley also represented the chance for a vicarious experience of 'rebel chic'. Initially at least he was marketed as a new threat to right-thinking Americans whose children would be drowned in the sexual morass of rock 'n' roll. In fact, the dangerous, outlaw rabble-raising image of Presley and Jerry Lee Lewis merely capitalized on their heritage as white Southern boys. There's a long-standing tradition in the American South, in which getting drunk and/or stoned and chasing women and shooting off pistols and racing cars around for the sheer hell of it are normal, every-day male activities, generally accepted with a resigned or amused shrug by much of Southern society.'[2] Through Elvis, the promise of 'Roarin' with the Billies' (as it was called) was served up for kids all over the country; to them, it was young and vital and all the frustrations of being a white teenager in the fifties were heaped on the shoulders of white rock 'n' rollers. Kids rioted when they played; public condemnation became the badge of teenage credibility.

Presley, Brando and James Dean were a new breed of working-class anti-heroes, more potent than the black jazz hipster because they were white and thus embraced and lionized by the media who ensured their bankability whether alive or dead. Their attitude was instantly recogniz-able; the sneer, the curled lip, the slowburn cynicism and the black leather jacket said it all.

Speed informed the philosophy of youth culture; wheels were the essence of the fifties experience in America – bombing up and down in the '49 Ford, the '55 Chevy, the T-Bird and the Studey. Brando rode a bike in *The Wild Ones*, Jimmy Dean drove his way to immortality behind the wheel of his Porsche. But speed meant more than 0 – 60 in seconds and overhead cams. Rock 'n' roll needed high-octane fuel to keep it going – new music and a new generation demanded new ways of getting stoned. To keep the authorities off his back, American D.J. Alan Freed maintained in the fifties that rock 'n' roll was good clean fun. And likely as not, the sea of acned faces out front was consuming nothing stronger than Pepsi Cola; but backstage everyone was wired for sound.

Neither rock 'n' roll, nor the mod or garage bands of the sixties, nor punk in the seventies can be legitimately considered outside the context of amphetamine. The same applies to West Coast rock and acid, and to marijuana and reggae. But this is not to suggest that acid-rock bands used only LSD or that punks stuck only to amphetamine; far from it. Certain drugs influenced the sound and creative context of particular genres more than others, but as the pharmaceutical industry became more competitive and street chemists more sophisticated, so more drugs were added to the music pharmacopeia. There were sedatives, hypno-tics and tranquillizers in a hundred different colours and dosages, notably methaqualone (Quaaludes/Mandrax); a range of synthetic painkillers like Dilaudid; an alphabet soup of hallucinogens - LSD, DMT, PCP, MDA, STP, etc. – and a variety of one-offs like amyl nitrate.

Heroin and cocaine remained for the subterranean jazzman. These drugs figured heavily in the street drug scene of black ghetto areas and so also in the lifestyles of many popular black musicians from Frankie Lymon to Marvin Gaye. These two drugs, supposedly at the heavy end of the drug spectrum, also became seemingly mandatory for the burgeoning white rock elite, as musicians took over from film stars in the early seventies as the new aristocracy. The new stars needed either to be coked up to their eyes to face the microphones and cameras, or to be locked away in heroin hide-aways to enhance their Svengali reputations, ready for the comeback tour and album. They also became the focus of attention for social revenge as the white pop star toppled the black jazzman as public enemy number one.

Then, of course there is marijuana, the drug for all seasons. A mainstay of jazz musicians and beat artists in the fifties, it percolated right through the popular music scene, the drug of relaxation, introspection, political statement and communal spirit, and became most closely associated with reggae once Bob Marley had won international fame.

Finally, alongside the changing nexus of drug/music fashions and the trials and tribulations of individual musicians, sits the interaction between the music business and the traffic in illegal drugs. Taking a wide view, pop and illegal drug use grew up together, parallel developments from the earliest days of New Orleans through Prohibition, the rise of organized crime and its increasing involvement in all leisure industries including popular music. The pathways of drug dealing within the industry are of necessity labyrinthine. At one end of the scale, musicians will deal informally among themselves, going out on the streets to score their own supplies or consorting with small-time dealers in limited amounts of money and drugs. But move up the rock hierarchy and arrangements become more formalized. 'Drugola' has reared its head again – cocaine often replaces women as the social grease of the business when records need to be charted. The Artists Relations personnel within record companies are charged with fulfilling the whims of the company's human assets, whims which are often chemical. And looking up where the air is really thin, drugs can become not only the social grease of the business, but also its currency.

8

Wired For Sound

In Kerouac's *On the Road*, Neil Casady appeared as Dean Moriarty, a composite of the rebel without a cause and the arch villain of Conan Doyle stories. Everything about Casady was 'mad', 'crazy' or 'wild'. He was probably the greatest driver literature has ever seen. Kerouac has Moriarty ripping through the country at ninety miles an hour in search of America. (What he found was Kerouac's *version* of the American Dream. Hunter Thompson, author of *Fear and Loathing in Las Vegas* did no better; at the end of his rainbow were Hell's Angels waiting to beat him up.) But speed meant more to Casady (and Thompson) than a gas pedal jammed on the floor:

> He rubbed his jaw furiously, he swung the car and passed three trucks, he roared into downtown Testament looking in every direction and seeing everything in an arc of 180 degrees around his eyeballs without moving his head. Bang, he found a parking space in no time and we were parked. He leaped out of the car. Furiously he hustled into the railway station; we followed sheepishly ... He had become absolutely mad in his movements; he seemed to be doing everything at the same time. It was a shaking of the head, up and down, sideways; jerky, vigorous hands; quick walking; sitting, crossing the legs, uncrossing; getting up, rubbing the hands, rubbing his fly, hitching his pants, looking up and saying, 'Am', and sudden slitting of the eyes to see everywhere; and all the time he was grabbing me by the ribs and talking, talking.[1]

One could not wish for a more vivid or more accurate description of an amphetamine freak.

Originally synthesized in 1887 by the pharmaceutical manufacturers

Smith, Kline and French, amphetamine was launched on the market in 1932 as a Benzedrine nasal inhaler to relieve the symptoms of colds, hayfever and asthma. Noting amphetamine's stimulant effect, in 1935 the manufacturers launched a campaign promoting the efficacy of the drug in combating a chronic sleeping disease called narcolepsy.

As with other drugs like morphine and cocaine, amphetamines garnered often inappropriate clinical acceptance in the treatment of nearly forty conditions, ranging from radiation sickness and persistent hiccups to, yes you've guessed it, opiate addiction. At the same time there were reports about Benzedrine misuse in the British press and in 1939 amphetamine was added to the UK Poisons List.

Almost as soon as Benzedrine hit the streets, young people looking for new ways to get high discovered the rejuvenating effect of removing the Benzedrine strip from its casing and drinking it in coffee. This was Charlie Parker's earliest introduction to drugs.

Despite some medical misgivings, soldiers in all the fighting forces during the war were liberally supplied with amphetamines to boost morale and fight battle fatigue; seventy-two million tablets were issued to British forces. Kamikaze pilots and German panzer troops went to war with their nervous systems kick-started by speed. Medical records revealed that throughout the war Hitler was being injected with methamphetamine up to eight times a day, which would more than account for his increasingly erratic and unpredictable behaviour, acute paranoia and evermore unrealistic battle plans.

American soldiers continued to use speed during the Korean War, but being in the Far East gave them the chance to try something new. Amphetamines keep you awake and alert, but also very edgy and nervous; in Korea they mixed speed with heroin to smooth off the jagged edges. Thus was born the 'speedball'. Cocaine later replaced amphetamine as the 'up' side of the equation among the *cognoscenti*; according to the coroner, such a concoction killed Meatloaf drummer Wells Kelly in London in 1984.

The function of amphetamines as appetite suppressants enabled the pharmaceutical companies to market speed as diet pills. Those in the public eye anxious to stay trim swallowed amphetamines like sweets, but whether you were using them to stay awake, stay sharp and confident or stay slim, there was always a down side. More than any other drugs, stimulants like amphetamine and cocaine epitomize the saying that there is no such thing as a free lunch.

Stimulants give you energy, confidence, make you talkative and stop you feeling hungry. You feel witty, clever, amusing and powerful. But tolerance builds very rapidly. The more you take, the more you need.

With amphetamine, regular high doses can turn the confident energetic user into a neurotic paranoiac, constantly living on the edge of psychosis. Speed does not in fact *give* you any energy, it *takes* from the body's resources. Stop the drug and a heavy lethargy and depression or 'crash' takes place needing lots of rest and recuperation. But most problematic is the risk that the user will turn to more dangerous sedatives like alcohol or barbiturates to counteract the effects of the amphetamine. In combination such sedatives can be lethal; for example they cost singer Dinah Washington her life in December 1963. She had been desperately trying to get her weight down for an upcoming concert date, using amphetamine diet pills. Elvis Presley took to speed for two reasons – to keep him awake on tour and later to 'help' *his* battle against weight. Again, it was in an effort to counteract the stimulants that he embarked on a chemical grand tour which took him to the farthest reaches of the *Merck* pill index, consuming every painkiller, sedative, hypnotic and tranquillizer that the men in white coats could concoct.

Back home after the war, the American GIs brought their government-issue drug habits with them. Those who could not face the straightjacket of life on the factory floor took to the freeways as truckers, transporting the products of America's post-war prosperity across the country in their beloved rigs. Amphetamine became the trucker's friend. He needed less sleep and less food, while more mileage meant more money. He felt good, too. The redneck Southern truckers, fuelled on amphetamine goodwill, hit the bars and dives of dusty rebel towns like Natchez, Mississippi, to hear country boys belt out their favourite songs and to catch some of the raucous Saturday-night special sounds of this new thing called rock 'n' roll. At the Wagon Wheel in Natchez, Jerry Lee Lewis, then a raw nineteen-year-old, played to truckers who showed their appreciation by tipping him in fifteen-milligram Benzedrine capsules.

Speed stood at the crossroads of early rock 'n' roll and country music, consumed by performers, roadies and audience alike. Johnny Cash got hooked on amphetamines while hanging around the drivers who ferried the Grand Ole Opry stars across the country. At first his performances were pin sharp, his timing excellent and he was confident to bursting point. But before long his voice was shot, he had that lean, hungry, wasted look and his behaviour became violent and erratic. Barred from the Opry, it took a long time to find his way back as a hundred Dr Feelgoods handed out pills on request. Rarely did Cash have to seek illegal supplies in Mexico or through drug thefts. Although a former truck-driver himself, Presley apparently did not get his first taste of amphetamines until a sergeant gave him some to stay awake on guard duty during his army days. Amphetamines were still regular US army issue in the sixties. Between 1966 and 1969 US troops legitimately consumed more amphetamines than British and American troops combined during World War II.

The little magic pills also got rockers to gigs and gave them the confidence to tear places apart. Years before the Who's speed-driven auto-destruction and Hendrix's amphetamine pyrotechnics with a flaming Fender, Jerry Lee Lewis set fire to his piano during Alan Freed's Big Beat tour of 1958. As the fire raged, he bawled at the stage crew, 'I'd like to see *any* son of a bitch follow that!'

Jerry Lee and Elvis became rock 'n' roll models, but they had their own burnout guru in Hank Williams, acknowledged as one of the finest songwriters and performers country music ever produced.

Williams died of a heart attack at the age of twenty-nine, on New Year's Eve 1953. His alcohol and speed intake had been increasing in direct proportion to his meteoric rise to fame, bursting on to the country scene only four years before his death. It was a fame that this semi-literate son of a lumber worker could not handle. As Carl Perkins said about his own drink problem:

> When you're a country boy just a month from the plow and suddenly you're a star with money in your pocket, cars, women, big cities, crowds, the change is too fast. You're the same person inside, but you're a star outside, so you don't know how to act. You're embarrassed about the way you talk, the way you eat, the way you look. You can't take the strain without a crutch.[2]

The timeless quality of his simple, sincere songs of great lyrical beauty meant that Williams did not need an early, tragic death on the backseat of a car to ensure legendary status. But in a sense his life, and the lives of all those to follow who creamed down the fast lane, was defined through its temporal nature. It is difficult to escape the notion entirely that he was ultimately fulfilled at the moment of death.

Hank Williams never made it; Jerry Lee Lewis, Johnny Cash and the Everly Brothers all fought long battles against amphetamine. Cash found religion, but Jerry kept finding John Law round the corner.

When a big bust meant Marilyn Monroe and speed was something the traffic cops got you for, Lewis and his band, the Memphis Beats, were charged with possession of 700 amphetamine capsules after a raid on their motel in Grand Prairie, Texas. In fact, amphetamines were not brought under strict Federal control until 1970, but Jerry Lee and the boys fell foul of existing legislation dating back to 1951, controlling sales of non-prescription over-the-counter drugs. And that's how it went for the next twenty years. Persistent speed-taking made Lewis unpredictable, violent and paranoiac, shooting off guns in hotel rooms and beating up his wife when she flushed his stash down the toilet. On finishing a one-year probationary sentence for possession in 1980, he was busted again at his home in Hernando, Mississippi. Inland Revenue Service agents had to come to seize property in lieu of tax payments and discovered an amount of cocaine. At forty-four, Jerry Lee Lewis was still a marked man.

The history of amphetamines and popular music takes us from the American Deep South to the English South, or more specifically to the club scene in London's West End.

Notwithstanding the *Melody Maker*'s hysterical outburst in 1936 about drug-using musicians, not only was drug-taking in England actually very circumscribed, but the illicit use of drugs in Britain as a whole was not a social issue. Those addicts notified to the Home Office were generally middle-class, middle-aged morphine users, often professionally employed, receiving maintenance prescriptions from their GP. Most (if not all) were therapeutic addicts; that is, they had become dependent on opioids through GP prescriptions for pain. Their numbers were small and falling; from around 700 in 1935 to fewer than 300 in the early fifties. The figures began to rise sharply only in the early to mid sixties, when the addict ranks were swelled by a younger group using heroin rather than morphine and 'recreationally' rather than as a result of a dependence derived from pain relief.

Nevertheless, there was evidence after the Second World War of a drug-using sub-culture which operated mainly outside the network of GPs, involving first marijuana and then heroin and focused around musicians living or working in London. Drugs like opium and marijuana had for years been smuggled into Britain by Chinese and African sailors for use within their own small communities in London and Liverpool. But from 1946–7 drug offences, particularly involving marijuana, jumped markedly, suggesting that the drug was being distributed outside such discrete communities.

Detective Sergeant George Lyle of Scotland Yard described the following incident at a talk he gave in January 1953:

In 1950 complaints began to be received that Indian Hemp was being sold in certain dance clubs in the West End.

On 15 April 1950, at 12.30 p.m. a large force of police, about forty, raided Club 11, a private dance club in Carnaby Street, W1. There were on the premises between 200 and 250 persons, coloured and white, of both sexes, the majority being between 17 and 30. All these people were searched. Ten men were found to be in possession of Indian Hemp. Two also had a small quantity of cocaine and another man had a small quantity of morphine. In addition, 23 packets of Indian Hemp, a number of hemp cigarettes, a small packet of cocaine, a small quantity of prepared opium and an empty morphine ampoule were found on the floor of the club. All the cocaine had been adulterated with boric acid. All were later convicted and fined. The Indian Hemp cigarettes were being sold at 5/- a time and the adulterated cocaine at 10/- a grain.'[3]

The report does not name names, but included in the haul were Ronnie Scott, who already had a cocaine conviction; and the bassist Lenny Bush. The excuses presented in court ranged from, 'I had no idea how the cigarette came to be lying at my feet,' to a plea that the defendant had no idea that cannabis was an illegal drug. Someone claimed that the cocaine found on him was for his toothache. The judge was not impressed. Ronnie Scott's drug conviction was particularly unfortunate because, denied a US visa, he forfeited any chance of a Stateside career.

A second major case of dealing (major for its time, that is) occurred in 1951, when the pharmacy of a hospital near London was raided and large quantities of morphine, heroin and cocaine were stolen. Shortly afterwards, the Metropolitan Police became aware that a man known as 'Mark' was dealing in drugs in the West End. He was arrested and identified as a former employee of the hospital where the break-in had happened. Interestingly enough, of the fourteen people known to have obtained drugs from 'Mark', only two had been previously notified. By the end of 1954, thirty-six people associated with 'Mark', had been notified, twenty-one of whom were musicians.

The first white teenager caught with marijuana in Britain was arrested in August 1952, 'having acquired the habit through frequenting "be-bop" clubs and cafés where addicts congregated'.[4] Marijuana was used most among the jazz and folk musicians and their educated middle-class audience. The heroin users, too, were a literate bunch. Devouring De Quincey, Burroughs and others, they knew more than most doctors about the nature of addiction. The jazz musicians who followed in Charlie Parker's faltering footsteps included two of Britain's finest, Phil Seaman and Tubby Hayes, both now dead.

Until the late sixties, the drug scene was tight, in its geographical location, in its elitist, exclusive attitude and in its numerical strength.

Users knew each other and the Home Office Drugs Inspectors knew all of them, the dealers and the doctors. Amphetamines helped change all that.

Although amphetamines and mods were almost mutually dependent, mods were not the first 'deviant' subculture to start using them. Social workers in the late fifties noted fairly extensive use of Drinamyl, blue triangular-shaped compounds of amphetamines and barbiturates known as purple hearts, among East End prostitutes. Drinamyl, Dexadrine and other amphetamines were so common in the West End in the early sixties that pills were crushed underfoot in the toilets of Leicester Square underground without anyone taking much notice. Speed was also popular among those members of Soho's itinerant teenage population who were gays, lesbians and/or heavily involved in petty crime or prostitution.

Nor was speed exactly unknown among British musicians. Amphetamines in various shapes and colours kept the pop and rock 'n' roll tours moving in the fifties and sixties and Phenmetrazine, marketed as Preludin, was consumed by the handful by bands, most notably by the Beatles, on their trips to Hamburg. Stuffed to the gills with 'Prellies' bought at the chemist, the Beatles played hour after hour seven days a week in the Indra, the Bambi, the Top Ten and Manfred Weissleder's Star Club. Prellies kept them awake, frantic enough to whip up the crowd and free from hunger, which was useful because they had no money to eat. According to Peter Brown, former business manager of the Beatles, 'John was so out of control one night, that when a customer over-enthusiastically approached the stage, John kicked him in the head twice, then grabbed a steak knife from a table and threw it at the man.'[5]

The Beatles discovered what the rock 'n' rollers already knew and the rock musicians of the future would soon find out, that amphetamines were 'working drugs'. Nobody can play blind drunk and those who tried playing on acid often found themselves deep in conversation with microphone stands and speaker cabinets. Speed (and later cocaine) works by giving musicians the courage to get out there and sufficient edge to keep going throughout the performance. But trying to talk to the audience can be a mistake; when Elvis was taking large amounts of speed to trim down for a tour, audiences were subjected to long rambling monologues between songs.

This is amphetamine use in a purely functional role. For the mods, amphetamines were symbolically enshrined at the heart of their subculture, fitting into a discrete universe, a system of magical correspondences in which all objects – clothes, music, scooters and drugs – had a precise relationship with one another. Each item was taken from the

straight world and redefined within a homogenous cosmos; amphetamines were the subcultural adhesive which joined lifestyles and values,
the functional springboard for the frantic activity of staying up, buying
clothes, riding and fixing scooters, and dancing.

'Mod' was a catch-all phrase which encompassed a variety of styles
contributing to a media-created image of 'Swinging London.' It should
have been called 'Speeding London'; the amphetamine-induced arrogance, edginess, narcissism and freneticism of mod culture was reflected
right through the art, music and fashion of the period. London's Pop
Art scene was like a giant Roy Lichstenstein painting – POW!! ZAP!!
But as with all amphetamine 'runs' there came the inevitable crash. Like
the merry-go-round at the end of Hitchcock's *Strangers on a Train* the
scene collapsed and London was probably a duller place for it.

But when it all started, the mods were the upfront ambassadors. By
the time the style had been castrated by the High Street entrepreneurs
for furious but safe consumption, the mods had 'turned neatness into an
art form'.[6] They came from a post-war British working-class attitude to
smartness, best described as 'flash'. The spivs (George Cole as 'Flash
Harry' in St Trinian's films, Arthur Daley as a young man) were
followed by teds, who hijacked a failed attempt by Savile Row to revive
Edwardian elegance for the aristocracy, adding string ties and slick
hairdos to a taste for American rock 'n' roll and the Mississippi
steamboat gambler.

Mods, too, took some inspiration from the States in their musical
taste and their attempt to re-create the sartorial coolness of the black
hipster. However, they looked to the Continent, particularly Italy, for
the clothes themselves.

Amphetamines promote a sense of controlled anger (which is why
they have proved so popular among American footballers). The mod
stance was undeniably uptight. They looked normal, but they weren't.
They made wearing a suit and tie seem aggressive and threatening.
Somehow *too* smart and *too* neat, they caused consternation among 'the
straights', who saw their own conservative dress sense mocked. The
worst thing that could happen to a mod was to have his parents
understand him.

In 1961, 2½% of all NHS prescriptions were for amphetamines. Even
so, Mods made speed their own: it was youthful recreational use of
amphetamines, not over-prescribing by GPs, that caused them to be
controlled in drugs legislation passed in 1964 especially created for the
purpose. Getting blocked on pills at weekends was what separated
'them from us'.

The relentless pursuit of fashion eclipsed everything else; food, drink and women didn't matter because speed killed the appetite for all three, which may account for the fact that the mod cult was predominantly male. Many mods had office jobs, paying around £11 a week, most of which went on clothes and pills. Mod fashion was a microcosm of an industrial society which paid homage to the sacred cow of built-in obsolescence. A mod would spend three weeks' wages having vents put in or taken out of jackets, lapels widened or narrowed, knowing that three weeks later something else would be 'in', and mods would rather stay home than be seen out in last week's fashion. Probably no teenage style has paid such meticulous attention to the minutiae of its uniform; an obsession which had its counterpart in the way amphetamine users can get totally absorbed in mindless and trivial occupations like washing a plate.

For mods, speed also had purely functional applications. First was fighting. The early mods had no time for violence, but the hysterical press reporting of the first major mod–rocker clash at Clacton on Easter Monday 1964 became a self-fulfilling prophecy. This was the first time most people had heard about mods or rockers and the press instantly created a new breed of 'folk devils' to rival teds and razor gangs. The press reports were littered with words and phrases like 'battle', 'attack', 'siege', 'screaming mob' and 'orgy of destruction'. The press exaggerated and distorted every aspect of the confrontation, conveying the impression that the fracas was strictly polarized on mod and rocker lines. In fact initially the clashes were more between rival gangs from London and the Home Counties. Only later, in some of the more bloody disturbances when it had become fashionable to be either mod or rocker, did these battles take on the lines of a clash of subcultures. At that point, the mod underground, a cool, understated bunch of natty dressers, became media darlings. Nothing *really* subversive ever got the *Sunday Times Colour Supplement* treatment. In the hunt for the ideal mod to interview, the *Sunday Times* came up with 'Denzil', who said 'Pills make you edgy and argumentable'; it made them hyper-sensitive to the possibilities of action and generated the desire to go looking for trouble. Having got totally wired up on pills, mods *had* to find trouble to release the frustration of what felt like an arrested orgasm. And after the way the press handled the Easter/Whitsun '64 incidents, it was obvious that any right-thinking mods or rockers out for some free publicity to shock the nation would get together at appointed times and places 'predicted' by the press, in the sure knowledge that the cameras would be ready and waiting.

Denzil had more to say – an average week in the life of the ideal London mod:

Monday night	Dancing at the Mecca, the Hammersmith Palais, the Purley Orchard or the Streatham Locarno
Tuesday	Soho and the Scene Club
Wednesday	Marquee night
Thursday	Washing hair (which *had* to be dried using a dryer with a hood)
Friday	Back at the Scene
Saturday afternoon	Clothes – and record – buying
Saturday night	The All Nighter at the Flamingo

It is unlikely that any mod ever kept up a regime like that for long however much speed he took. It all cost money and although mods were the most affluent teenagers to date, the money had to run out some time. Nevertheless the diary does demonstrate the importance of music and the club scene to all mods, whether 'hard core' or 'weekenders'.

In Britain, the club scene has always provided the main platform for the development of the new genres of musical taste from traditional jazz to punk rock. The only significant competition has been from the college circuit in the affluent late sixties, where many of the underground or 'progressive' bands like Jethro Tull built up their early following. The clubs and pubs also suffered in the early seventies from a vacuum which was left after most British rock bands went to play large arenas in America. Pub bands like Dr Feelgood and Kilburn and the High Roads helped promote a small-venue revival which finally took off with the arrival of punk. With the Beatles, northern clubs like the Cavern in Liverpool and the Twisted Wheel in Manchester, had already carved out for themselves a significant place in rock history, but much of the media and business interest during the sixties focused on London and the Soho club scene. That's where the music was to be found. And the drugs. Dark, subterranean dives, packed with people frantically dancing to loud music were an ideal setting for drug-dealing.

One of the main centres for speed-dealing was the Scene Club, situated in Ham Yard at 41 Great Windmill Street. The club was run by Ronan O'Rahilly, one-time manager of Alexis Korner's Blues Incorporated and a pioneer of pirate radio with Radio Caroline. Although O'Rahilly ran the Scene, it was part of the Nash gang club operation in Soho and hence a dangerous place to be.[7]

The club had an interesting history. Several venues had existed on the site, including the Cy Laurie Club and the Piccadilly Jazz Club, where music entrepreneur Giorgio Gomelsky first saw the Rolling Stones. Back in the forties and early fifties, it was none other than the Club

110

Eleven, where that first London club bust had taken place in 1950. As the Scene, it was the place to *be* seen, as far as Mods were concerned. The DJ was Guy Stevens who had the best American record collection in Britain, chock full of rare soul, blues and r&b discs. He co-ran Sue Records with Chris Blackwell and later produced for Mott the Hoople and the Clash.

O'Rahilly had the walls padded and cushions strewn everywhere, so that those who speeded to exhaustion could crash out. Two cousins who manned the door for a time had a habit of relieving patrons of their pill stash as they entered, pretending to flush them down the toilet and then 'recycling them'. The dealing went on in the club, safe from prying eyes; Drinamyl pills were sold at 1/3d. (*c.* 6½p) each, but were normally bought in fives, tens, twenties, fifties and hundreds.

In March 1967, *Oz* magazine spoke to two twenty-one-year-old dealers called Paul and Cliff. They had a joint income of up to £400 a week and both owned '66 Ford Zephyrs. A third of the money was passed to a godfather figure they called 'Big Sid', and they employed two West Indian 'minders' with whom they shared a twenty-guinea-a-week flat (£21) in Chelmsford:

Starting their work at the Marquee club they sell to a market of thirteen-year-old mods; after a meal they move into the clubs around Greek Street; then to a stand just outside Tiffany's at about one in the morning. When necessary they work a pitch in the Lyon's Cafés around Trafalgar Square; if on Sunday morning they have any pills remaining, they move into Chelsea where apparently tired debs are always a ready market. In conversation with one reporter as to the origin of the amphetamine, they said that some of their pills were knocked off, but most came as a regular supply through London docks – they weren't sure where, but 'Big Sid looks after that end.' In one weekend they never sell less than 3,000 pills and sometimes in excess of 6,000, undercutting other pushers by selling at 1/- each.

Another key club for the speed dealers in the early sixties was La Discotheque in Wardour Street. It was originally called El Condor, and from 1957–61 operated as an exclusive night spot frequented by British royalty. The club was owned by Raymond Nash and Peter Rachman, whose name has since become synonymous with racketeering landlords. Rachman sold the club to Tommy Yeardye and one of Rachman's own protégés, Peter Davies. However, the new club went bankrupt and reopened as the far more downmarket 'Discotheque'; hordes of young people replaced the upper middle class and the smattering of aristocrats.

Rachman and Nash resumed control as joint shareholders. They installed a powerful lighting and sound system. Drinks were 5/- but the place was more awash with cheap amphetamines. A dealer dubbed 'Peter the Pill' forged another link between Rachman and the London amphetamine scene, as he was both a (if not *the*) major dealer in speed *and* one of Rachman's loyal soldiers.

The question of supply during this period is one that has never been fully investigated. Certainly most of the amphetamines in circulation around the clubs were manufactured drugs, not the product of illicit street laboratories. Nor, in view of the huge number of pills involved, could they simply have been spillage from over-prescribing by doctors. Individual youngsters may have obtained some from the medicine cupboard at home, but not dealers.

As these drugs invariably had the manufacturer's name SKF (Smith, Kline and French) stamped on them, those working with chronic amphetamine users in Soho came to the not unreasonable conclusion that vast quantities of drugs were finding their way directly to dealers via SKF employees pilfering from the factory and warehouses. At a meeting of the Society for the Study on Addiction in September 1966, one worker, Judith Piepe, got up and said so in public:

> Extensive security precautions in a factory cost a great deal of money. It is easy for anybody on the production line quietly to take a handful and augment their wages by selling them. The production cost of drugs like Drinamyl are very low and the cost in money to ensure better security arrangements is considered too high by the manufacturers. They do not consider the cost in suffering to young people.

Replying for SKF, a Mr Schrire said:

> In regard to the accusation that tablets are being stolen from the manufacturing companies, I regard this as nonsense. The tablets are manufactured under stringent supervision and it is highly improbably that any quantities could be stolen from the factories in these circumstances.[8]

At about this time, the press reported a Gloucestershire doctor as saying that amphetamines were being made by teenagers with O-level chemistry. He offered no evidence for this and the *Daily Mirror* rang various experts to check the story. One GP, Ian Pierce James, stated that he was sure anyone with O-level chemistry could make amphetamine pills, but wondered how they managed to make the little moulds and stamp SKF on them!

Who were the dealers? To judge from Paul and Cliff's story, the operation was very lucrative and involved some crude dealer hierarchy. At the top may have sat members of Britains' most notorious criminal gangs of the sixties. They owned many of the West End clubs and would be unlikely to allow any profitable side action to be carried out in those clubs without taking some of the profits for themselves. In 1968, the Government introduced a system of NHS clinics supplying drugs to addicts in the hope of preventing organized crime setting up a wide-spread black market in illicit drugs. As we know, at best this system merely postponed the event, but it may have been that the gangs had already staked a claim in the illicit market prior to '68.

The clubs where speed was used and dealt ranged from the world famous to the here today, gone tomorrow. Despite its clean-cut image, the Marquee was a pill palace, catering for a younger mod set who were on the way home to bed, before the All Nighter session at the more sophisticated Flamingo Club got under way. The Flamingo provided mods with a chance to rub shoulders with black American airforce men on forty-eight-hour passes and dance to the black-inspired r&b of Georgie Fame and Zoot Money. Mods frequented the Last Chance, Le Kilt, La Poubelle and the Roaring Twenties, a basement place in Carnaby Street, before the street became fashionable. Originally a failed attempt to persuade Jewish teenagers from the more expensive parts of North London to part with their money on Saturday nights, the club reopened as the Roaring Twenties, a black club where bluebeat first appeared together with pimps, prostitutes and the general mêlée of Soho wide-boys selling stolen watches and dodgy Jags. Tiles was another important venue, providing the meeting place for a lunchtime mod culture which Tom Wolfe called the Noonday Underground.

The Reverend Ken Leech was a well-known figure around Soho in the sixties. He cared for young people in trouble at the Centrepoint night shelter at St Anne's Church, and was a keen observer of life in Soho at the time, trusted and respected by all the disparate and volatile elements that made up the fascinating community.

As you walked up Wardour Street and turned into D'Arblay Street, there was a very small area which you could walk round in ten minutes where there was a very heavy concentration of amphetamine clubs. Within yards of each other you had in 1967, Le Douce, a gay club; directly opposite you had a club which changed its name several times but was most famous as the Subway. Then you had the Coffee

Pot, which never closed (and where according to Richard Neville's *Playpower,* I'm always to be found!) Underneath that was the Huntsman and then opposite, in a smelly cul-de-sac between Wardour Street and Berwick Street, was Wardour Mews with the Limbo Club, the Granada and the Take Five.[9]

And what of the music itself? There was really no such thing as mod music, rather music that mods liked. Mod was originally short for modernists and in musical terms that meant modern jazz. They also picked up on black r&b, soul and Jamaican bluebeat and in the tiny clubs mentioned above, danced frantically to chart stuff from the jukebox. But if any music came to represent the anger, frustration, brashness and arrogance of the mods, it was that of the Who.

Right at the start the Kinks were in competition with the Who to be the mods' living identification, the people's bard, but in the end they couldn't compete with the Who's autodestruction and Townshend's anthems for a teenage wasteland. Nor did they have a Pete Meaden or a Kit Lambert.

Between them, Meaden and Lambert fashioned the Who's mod image; by inclination none of them was a mod. Meaden, a Drinamyl disciple and a face among the faces down at the Scene, became the Who's publicist and began the image-building whereby mods came to identify with the band. His shortlived renaming of the Who to the High Numbers was meant to indicate the state Meaden and the Who were in most of the time. Kit Lambert, who seemed to be able to function only under the influence of uppers or downers, depending on what image he needed to project at the time, completed the process with trips to Carnaby Street and the hairdressers. Townshend later said, 'The mod image was forced on us. It was dishonest.'[10] To keep their credibility intact, the band would watch what dance steps the mod audiences were doing and re-create them on stage, so that another audience would think the Who had invented them. The management of Kit Lambert and Chris Stamp was ideal, as Keith Moon explained: 'These people were perfect for us, because there's me, bouncing about, full of pills, full of everything I could get my hands on ... and there's Pete, very serious, never laughing, always cool, a grasshead ... Kit and Chris were the epitome of what we were.'[11]

The audience responded to the Who on a number of levels. First there was the aggression. 'We were all pillheads,' said Daltrey. 'We were probably the most aggressive group that's ever happened in England.'[12] But the truth was they were not all pillheads to the same extent, Daltrey least of all. The root cause of much of the *frisson* which sparked off fist fights in the band and generated such excitement on stage was precisely Daltrey's anger at Townshend's and Moon's drug intake, which often sent them out of control. But after Townshend had hit his guitar on the ceiling of the Railway Hotel in Wealdstone, Harrow and had to finish the job by wrecking it to save face, being 'out of control' became the Who's trademark – swirling arms, swirling mikes and a demolition derby. On top of that was the immense volume. The fans responded to the physical presence of the Who; shrill, cutting guitar over a raw, open-nerved, tension-ridden pounding and crashing. The Who always had more amplification than anyone else and along with Ginger Baker, Keith Moon pioneered the use in rock of huge double bass drumkits with a forest of tom-toms and cymbals. Then there were Townshend's songs; 'I Can't Explain', in retrospect not the Moon-and-June love song Townshend thought he'd written, but a statement on the inability to communicate much about thoughts and feelings; 'My Generation', with the stutter of an amphetamine freak which Daltrey didn't want to sing at first; 'Anyway, Anyhow, Anywhere' – 'Nothing gets in my way, not even locked doors'; 'Substitute', about all the insecurities beneath the desperate need to keep up appearances and stand behind the image.

The mods were regarded, and regarded themselves, as an army, a unified body which often acted as one. Yet at the same time each mod saw himself as an island; speed gave each individual a razor-edged identity and a pin-sharp sense of his place in the world. And this was the achievement of the Who, the reason why, despite the manufactured image, they symbolized to mods what being a mod was all about, 'the ultimate instance of individuality acquiring its deepest meaning from inter-action with others'. The Who 'balanced the tension between individual vision and collective achievement without ever bothering to conceal the stress it caused – and this became part and parcel of their image.'[13]

Although the Kinks had initially vied with the Who as the mods' band, it was the Small Faces who carried the flame for mod subculture in its death throes, inevitably sucked into the mainstream of sanitized pop. The Small Faces were genuine mods and, just as the Yardbirds took over from the Stones, the Small Faces assumed cult status on the club circuit from the Who. They didn't stay there for long. Their first single, 'What 'Cha Gonna Do About It?' reached No. 14 in the charts in August 1965 and in January 1966 they had a major success with 'Sha La La La Lee'. But from the point of view of this story, 1967 was their most important year. In June 1967, with words like 'hippy', 'joint', 'acid' and 'psychedelic' dropping from everyone's lips, the Small Faces brought out 'Here Comes the Nice', an anthem to the pill-popping heyday of the mod. With the police and the media witch-hunting the Rolling Stones as satanic junkies, the Small Faces calmly strolled on to 'Top of the Pops' with 'Here comes the nice/He knows what I need/He's always there when I need some speed,' the rest of the song being one of the more blatant rhapsodies to the drug dealer as cult hero. Stevie Marriott said later, "Here Comes the Nice" was a drug song, but no one sussed it, the whole point being if they don't suss it, it's cool ... We could do it on "Top of the Pops" and we did it to be rebellious in a way – to see what we could get away with.'[14]

During the same year there was an outbreak of intravenous ampheta-mine (Methedrine) use. The outbreak was not among pill users who had graduated on to the needle, but among the existing group of heroin and cocaine users who had been switched from cocaine to Methedrine by London's most famous (some would say infamous) doctor, John Petro. The Methedrine scene in London at that time had little direct connec-tion with the music business, but it is worth pointing out that Petro was no Dr Feelgood. Misguided he may have been, but he did at least care for his patients. In New York, where intravenous Methedrine use was closely tied in with the music business, the situation was very different.

*   *   *

I don't have a bedtime
I don't need to come
For I have become an amphetamine bum.
If you don't like sleeping
    and don't want a screw
Then you should take lots
    of amphetamine too.

The Fugs' New Amphetamine Shriek

In the mid-sixties, the widespread use of amphetamine pills and injectable Methedrine among New York's artistic community created a highly disturbed environment, where being freaky and strange was 'in'. The focal point for this frantic subculture was Andy Warhol's Factory, located first on East 47th Street and then 33 Union Square, where artists, poets, writers, musicians, fashion models and others vaguely creative in indeterminate ways – groupies, hangers-on, serfs, sychophants and ciphers – foregathered in the desperate hope that Warhol the Wunderkind would give them their allocated fifteen mi-nutes.

They were the mole people, vapid shadow folk seen only at night in *de rigueur* super-cool black, cultivating the elegantly wasted look (later patented by Keith Richard) brought about by a massive intake of speed which diverts blood from the surface blood vessels. Sleeping and eating went by the board. Heroin too, produced the same livid malnourished look with the skin drawn tightly across the face, cheekbones accentuated and eyes sunken.

In truth, however hip, fashionable and 'creative' they were, most Factory folk were damaged, unstable, volatile nonentities speeding like crazy to give them the confidence to project whatever image they wanted. Nobody slept in case they missed something. Everyone talked *at* each other for hours on end about grandiose schemes, fads and whims, forgotten almost as soon as they were uttered. 'Uptight' was the key word; speed made everyone paranoid about their position in the Factory hierarchy – why did Andy seem to like him/her more than me? In fact 'uptight' was very much the key to the whole music business in 1966 – a frenetic jockeying for position, a hunger for publicity. Nobody could see where they were going as they spent so much time watching over their shoulder.

The Factory was just that; people were picked up, processed, marketed to the devouring media (who behaved like the crowd in the story of the Emperor's New Clothes), then tossed aside like empty cans of soup. Some were hounded out or found that their only reality was drug-induced. Stopping speed, for instance, brought unbearable depressions and many hit the bottle or turned to heroin or barbiturates.

Edie Sedgwick was a classic Warhol protégé. Her sad biography tells of a beautiful, doomed, poor little rich girl, speeding through a Warholian maelstrom, 'star' of his movies, crazy for fame and adoration. Factory life went sour for her and she fled to the Dylan camp, where she endured more drug madness and then got dumped. At twenty-eight she was dead from an overdose of barbiturates. Joel Schumacher, director of *The Wiz, Car Wash* and other films, commented, 'She was the total essence of the fragmentation, the explosion, the uncertainty, the madness that we all lived through in the sixties. The more outrageous you were, the more of a hero you became.'[15]

If Warhol was God, then Dr Charles Roberts was the ministering angel. From his surgery on 48th Street, he dispensed shots of Methedrine to the rich, the famous and the not-so-famous. The drug was dispensed indiscriminately for obviously non-medical reasons to whomever had the money. His surgery was packed with actors, models, businessmen and musicians, all lining up for their shots from a doctor who, to quote Schumacher again, 'was stoned all the time'. He had his favourites who could stroll in, sneer at the hordes waiting on the edge of

117

their nerves and see Doc Roberts straight away for speed, debited on a prearranged charge account. Edie Sedgwick was one such favoured client.

Injected Methedrine is a turbo-charged form of oral amphetamine; prolonged use can lead to paranoid schizophrenia-like psychosis, delusions and hallucinations. Chronic users may stay up for days on end, eating very little, using anything up to 5,000 milligrammes a day, when 250 milligrammes can be a lethal dose. After several months' use, it can take several more months to recover from the depressive stage of withdrawal – some never do. But nobody seemed to care much; perhaps it was only an extreme version of what living in New York was like anyway.

Doc Roberts shot up the whole cast of Warhol's film *Ciao Manhattan* to get it finished quicker and on the tapes of the movie, Edie Sedgwick is heard to comment on the simultaneous horrors and delights of speed for her:

> That acrylic high, horrorous, yodelling, repetitious echoes of an infinity so brutally harrowing that words cannot capture the devastation nor the tone of such a vicious nightmare ... [yet] it's hard to choose between the climactic ecstasies of speed and cocaine ... oh they are so fabulous. That fantabulous sexual exhilaration.[16]

Probably the most able interpreters of the swirling vortex of bohemian life which sucked in Edie Sedgwick and others like her, were the Velvet Underground, blessed with the genuine talent of Lou Reed. With their acid-drenched lyrics, the muses of California offered escape and a promise of a better world, full of peace, love and harmony; Lou Reed offered a one-way train ride to hell. With the Velvet Underground there was no escape.

In 1966, a friend of the band, Tony Conrad, found a paperback lying in a gutter in the Bowery, a novel of sado-masochism called *The Velvet Underground*, and gave the band its name. That same year, Andy Warhol wanted to present a multi-media event, a touring show featuring the band against a backdrop of dancing, slides, films and lights. Warhol's most famous actor, Paul Morrisey, recalled sitting around with dancer and poet Gerard Malanga and a Factory figure called Barbara Rubin:

> I picked up a record album with Barbara on the back massaging Bob Dylan's head *(Bringing It All Back Home)*. There were some amphetamine-Bob-Dylan-gibberish liner notes. I looked without

reading and saw these words appear; something 'exploding', something was 'plastic', something was 'inevitable'.[17]

So Andy Warhol's Uptight Show became 'Exploding Plastic Inevitable'. It went on the road during 1966-7. The band made a theatrical impact in their own right; a manic fiddler, a mysterious street-wise punk, a straight-looking guy, a drummer of indeterminate sex, plus for a while Nico, a stunning blonde German singer. They didn't need the light shows and films and deranged dancing. It was OK for the night to create some atmosphere, but all that remains for posterity are the music and demonic writing of Lou Reed. There is a freshness in the songs that is absent from much of the music of that period. The hippy dream is dead, but we are still living Reed's bleak, hopeless view of urban life. Drugs are sickness and love, life and death.

Each Velvet song used a small group of notes that kept battering against one another until feedback – the screech, the amphetamine shriek – was the only place to go. The rhythm never let go, it held you down while the lyrics swamped you with street images. The sound of the band was an aural presentation of the amphetamine experience. That was the band's context, the framework within which they operated; Reed put an amphetamine stutter in 'Sister Ray' to emphasize the point. Against this, Reed sang of a white boy going to Harlem to score heroin ('Waiting for the Man') and of the all-consuming love affair between a heroin addict and his drug ('Heroin'). Despite its title, the song builds up on the crest of a Methedrine wave 'when I'm rushing on my run/And I feel like Jesus' son,' then winds down as the junkie looks for a release from a world where 'I just don't know.' With heroin, he is caught in the ultimate paradox '... Heroin/will be the death of me,' but 'it's my wife/and it's my life.' The maximum shock value of the song was played up on stage; Gerard Malanga would go through the whole fixing routine, heating the spoon, tying off and shooting up, finishing on the floor staring blankly up at Lou Reed.

For writing songs like 'Heroin', Reed got a reputation as the biggest junkie around. His comments on the subject have always been ambiguous, often leaving it at 'just because I write about it, doesn't mean to say I do it,' or words to that effect. On his 1975 album *Metal Machine Music*, the sleeve note read: 'My week beats your year', by the mid-eighties he was saying 'I'm not into dope. I don't smoke grass and I don't like things that everyone sniffs off a table. It is so common.' [18] However, during a particularly low period in his life during the mid-seventies Reed did admit to shooting speed and drugs *have* been a central theme in his music. During this low period he dyed an iron cross

119

in his hair and re-created 'Heroin' in his solo act, complete with tourniquet and syringe. The theme of *Berlin* (1973) was a doomed liaison between two speedfreaks and the title track of *Street Hassle* (1978) told of a young girl whose body was dumped in the street after she had overdosed.

The first Velvet's album was originally rejected by Ahmet Ertegun at Atlantic on account of the drug content. Verve released the album in the United States in March 1967. By the time the album was released in the UK in October that year, Lou Reed's darkest New York subterranean vignettes were surfacing in sunny California. Already degenerating into a seedy tourist attraction, the Haight Ashbury district of San Francisco was witnessing the beginnings of a speed/heroin 'epidemic'. The flower children climbed aboard Jim Morrison's Methedrine crystal ship and slowly the community began to sink.

From this developed the 'Speed Kills' campaign, which grew up on the West Coast. The counter-culture has always tried to look after its own where drugs were concerned; in 1969, some enlightened rock stations put out warnings about adulterated drugs in circulation. The Haight Ashbury Free Clinic, set up to deal with the drug casualties of the area in 1967 (and still going), received $5,000 from the Monterey Pop Festival and rock promoter Bill Graham put on a number of benefit gigs for the clinic when the finances were shaky.

In a strictly clinical sense, speed kills only very rarely, but it was an effective slogan around which to rally support from the music business. A street information service called Do It Now was set up in Hollywood to give out accurate information to drug users. Radio allocated the service slots and musicians would speak on the dangers of drugs. Frank Zappa featured in one slot, saying, 'I would like to suggest that you don't use speed, and here's why: it will mess up your liver, your kidneys, rot out your mind: in general, this drug will make you just like your father and mother.'

To raise further funds, Do It Now knocked on the doors of several record companies, asking them to donate tracks for an album. The record was called *First Vibrations* and among the tracks featured were 'Amphetamine Annie' (Canned Heat), 'The Pusher' (Hoyt Axton), 'Flying on the Ground is Wrong' (Buffalo Springfield), 'Artificial Energy' (the Byrds) and 'Roses Gone' (Peanut Butter Conspiracy). RCA donated 'Somebody to Love', as Grace Slick wanted to tell kids what Jefferson Airplane though about speed. 'One pill makes you larger, one pill makes you small, but if you shoot speed, you won't be here at all,' she said at the time.

Two points to note about the involvement of musicians in the Speed

Kills campaign. First, it was significant gesture on the part of musicians and demonstrated through the release of *First Vibrations* that, contrary to public opinion, most rock songs about drugs took a negative view or at worst a neutral one. This will be examined more closely in Chapter Eleven. Secondly, musicians felt comfortable about being involved in anti-drug campaigns only when the focus was a drug they had never used or had stopped using. The same year as *First Vibrations* was released, Canned Heat were singing about 'Amphetamine Annie' with their guitarist Al Wilson subject to bouts of deep depression and finally overdosing on barbiturates. Grace Slick could take a hard line on speed, knowing that her major weakness was alcohol. This story has been repeated in the recent wave of musicians' statements in Britain about the evils of drugs. Many have made flamboyant anti-heroin statements as representatives of a business literally snowed under by cocaine.

In the seventies, cocaine tended to replace amphetamine as the favoured stimulant among those musicians with sufficient funds to be conspicuous consumers. But for musicians who still considered themselves spokesmen of the not-so-laid-back tradition of American rock, whose music demanded a jagged edge, and certainly for fans who could not afford cocaine, speed remained an important element in the polypharmacy of rock.

Heavy Metal has been home to speed since the days of Blue Cheer, a favourite band of the San Francisco speed-freak scene. For a band like Blue Cheer (whose name actually derived from a reputedly extra-potent strain of LSD) there was no such thing as too loud – legend has it during one gig a dog wandered on to the stage and dropped dead. Led Zeppelin fused the blues-rock initiatives of bands like Blue Cheer and Iron Butterfly and presented the result for an international audience. The atmosphere of a mass Zeppelin gathering was altogether more threatening than the days of peace and love. The Stones at Altamont had set the agenda for heavy metal/heavy rock concerts to come – a brooding sense of violence bubbling under the surface whether or not anybody actually got damaged. To get in touch with the uncompromising, high-energy hurricane of sound, the audiences arrived in various states of chemical readjustment, a sea of working-class long-haired lads in denim mixing speed with booze and showering each other (and unwelcome support bands) with beer cans and bottles.

The Haight Ashbury Free Medical Clinic usually ran a MASH style unit at major rock events and in 1973, they logged an account of two concerts they attended at Kezar Stadium, San Francisco, one involving the Grateful Dead and the other Led Zeppelin. The clinic assembled a team of thirty to deal with the 20,000 crowd that showed up to see the

Dead. The atmosphere was generally warm and mellow, with picnick-
ing, dancing and sunbathing creating a carnival mood. The 55,000 who
came for Led Zeppelin presented an altogether different profile;
'commercialized, bottled and over-sold to a horde of out-of-town teeny
boppers who had never experienced the expectations of a love generation, this crowd seemed curious but sullen.' [19] Harmony and conviviality
were replaced by a mood of restless discomfort. Alcohol and speed were
mixed with a new drug, methaqualone.

Marketed in Britain as Mandrax and in the States as Quaaludes,
'mandies' or 'ludes' were similar to barbiturates in their hypnosedative
effect, but less likely entirely to douse the spirits. 'Luding out' became a
standard rock 'n' roll phrase. Combined with booze and speed at the
Zeppelin concert, ludes produced a tense feeling of repressed anger and
irritation. Of that crowd of 55,000, clinic staff calculated that at least
40,000 had taken some drugs during the day. The preponderance of
sedative drugs, however, kept the lid on actual violence while leaving
vibes which the staff described as 'barbed wire'.

Heavy metal slipped from public view in the mid-seventies but has
enjoyed a renaissance in the eighties on both sides of the Atlantic.
New-wave heavy metal in Britain was spearheaded by Motorhead; SKF
never had a more effective team of travelling salesmen. Everything
about the band is fast; the music, the name (American slang for a
speed-freak) and the leading light, Ian 'Lemmy' Kilminster, bass
guitarist, singer and self-confessed devotee of amphetamine sulphate. It
was this last credential that saw to his exit from Hawkwind. In 1975,
Canadian customs caught him with a quantity of white powder. Fearing
that this would jeopardize their future in America, Hawkwind sacked
him. He came home and put together Motorhead. The album titles
speak for themselves: 'Iron Fist', 'Overkill' and 'No Sleep Till Hammersmith'. Says Lemmy, 'My favourite drug is speed, 'cause it gets me
up on stage in a good mood, but I really wouldn't recommend it to most
people because most people who do it go completely over the top,
given a couple of weeks on it. It's not good for most people, but my
metabolism seems to have adjusted.' But speaking for the band about
heroin, he say 'We hate heroin and always will ... heroin always fucks
people up.'[20]

In England, Motorhead were coming up just at the time when punk
rock was establishing itself and there was a good deal of cross-
fertilization between the two, both feeding off the energy of the other.
Motorhead often appeared on the same bill as bands like the Dammed
and the Adverts. But in eschewing heroin, Motorhead distanced
themselves from a strong tradition of heroin worship in punk, the legacy

of nihilism given to American and British punks by the Velvet Underground. The mantle of outrage passed to Iggy Pop, the MC5, the New York Dolls and Johnny Thunders and the Heartbreakers. Max's Kansas City was joined by CBGBs as host venue to the sound of trash aesthetic.

The New York Dolls best typified the amalgam of the Velvet's urban nightmare, the relentless thud of hard rock, the cult of bisexuality and the wreckless pursuit of doomed intoxication that so influenced punk rock in Britain. Or to put it another way, r&b with make-up and high heels.

The band was formed in 1971 with bassist Arthur Kane, guitarist Johnny Thunders and drummer Bill Murcia, to which were added Sylvain Sylvain on guitar and vocalist David Johansen. It took only a short while for them to become the darlings of the New York club scene, following in the path of Velvet Underground with a stint at Max's Kansas City. In 1972 they received a major boost to their career when the Faces invited them to play Wembley. Tragically, however, on 6 November 1972, drummer Billy Murcia died of an overdose of pills and booze. In an interview with Robert Christgau, Arthur Kane, wearing red lipstick and a sweatshirt over white tights, bemoaned their image as a bunch of 'transsexual junkies'. What also probably slipped his booze-fuddled brain, was that during a song called 'Looking for a Kiss', David Johansen did the old Lou Reed routine with a hypodermic. Meanwhile, backstage, Johnny Thunders and Murcia's replacement, Jerry Nolan, were doing it for real.

Listen to the Sex Pistols and you hear the New York Dolls' basic rock 'n' roll riffs, played hard and fast and overlaid with snarling, sardonic vocals. In fact, it wasn't that much of a coincidence. In an attempt to revitalize a sagging career, the New York Dolls appointed a young Englishman as their manager in 1975. He tried to re-establish their anarchic credibility by spreading a rumour that they were all communists. The attempt failed and the manager, Malcolm McLaren, went back to London to try again.

Malcolm McLaren maintained that there was nothing new about punk: 'I don't see it as a fad, because it's such a simple attitude; it's the same attitude, I think, that Eddie Cochran had, that any real rock 'n' roller had.' Yet the *context* in which punk sprang up was different from those which spawned all previous post-war adolescent movements. The mods in their smart suits and ties were not even pseudo-anarchists; they declared their intention of making it in the world on their own terms, but it was the same world as everybody else's, a world that provided jobs. While Mum and Dad could aspire to fridges, TV and even a car, the media pandered to Junior's tastes in transitory fashions and music.

Britain in the late seventies and early eighties was a very different place. The cut-up punk uniform derived from the throwaway and disposable garbage of a crumbling industrial society with no future. Punks represented to the media the embodiment of Anthony Burgess's vision of an aimless, violent droog army.

Punk *angst* was directed not only at straight society, but at a previous rock generation which in its time had been considered anarchic and subversive. Nothing new there: mods had been equally dismissive of chart dross and men in funny hats playing trad jazz. But what was new for Britain was the explosion of independent record labels providing the only consistent outlet for home-grown three-chord products. As McLaren acknowledged, the music itself was basic rock 'n' roll and the band line-ups – guitars, bass, drums – were equally conventional. Punks had the Sex Pistols; mods had the Who – bands that led the army into the fray. Both subcultural sets had strong affinities with black music and culture – blue beat and soul in the sixties, reggae in the late seventies. The mods looked to the black hipster for sartorial inspiration; punks reinterpreted dreadlocks in spikey gelled mohicans, picking out in them the colours of Jah. However, punk was the antithesis of mod (and seventies disco) designer chic. There was nothing 'flash' about punk dress; it took its cues instead from the sexual ambiguities and fetishes of the Velvet's sado-masochistic vision and the visual drama of glam rock.

Since rock 'n' roll began, the ultimate aim has been to get a reaction, any reaction. Jerry Lee stood on his piano, Elvis wiggled his pelvis, the Who smashed up their gear, Reed and David Johansen shot up on stage, the Stones pissed against walls, the Pistols threw up in airports. Sid spat at the crowd, covered in blood, while Johnny Rotten sneered at the audience, 'ever been 'ad, you fucking idiots?' 'Summertime Blues', My Generation' and 'Pretty Vacant' – all anthems for a caged adolescence banging about through the teen years like balls in a pinball machine. Eddie was too young to vote; Pete seemed concerned about people putting him down; Johnny couldn't give a damn.

And in all this frustration and anger, this frantic effort to validate being young by being outrageous, was speed – a cheap proletarian passport to self-esteem and social mobility. Speed was the subcultural constant linking '56, '66 and '76.

By the seventies amphetamine meant (as it still does) illicitly produced amphetamine sulphate powder rather than pills diverted from doctors, chemists and factories. The effect, however, was the same and Johnny Rotten was the role model of the speed-shot punk: 'Spikey, dyed red hair, death-white visage, metal hanging from lobes, skinny leg strides ... he looks like an amphetamine corpse from a Sunday gutter-press wet dream.'[21] 'Staying up all night in music clubs was back in vogue; to be a Face at the Roxy or the Nashville you needed the appearance of advanced amphetamine psychosis, even if you never went near the stuff.'[22]

But there were plenty of kids who did go near the stuff and plenty more who then switched to more dangerous, but still cheap, barbiturates such as Tuinal to slow themselves down and to take the edge off the amphetamine 'crash'. And for punk rock stars with money to spend there was also heroin. Topper Headon of the Clash and Keith Levine of Public Image Ltd (to name but two) narrowly avoided succumbing to the ultimate rock 'n' roll cliché. Malcolm Owen of the Ruts and Sid Vicious did not.

The *Sunday Times* ran a feature called 'All Dressed Up and Nowhere to Go', about being a punk on the dole. It interviewed 'Keith': 'I was taking acid twice a week and it was making me crazy. I knew what it was like to go crazy.'

LSD was back, not as an artefact of anybody's political ideals, but as part of the self-centred pursuit of getting wrecked. But had it been so different in the sixties?

9

I Had Too Much To Dream Today

The first Prankster rule is that nothing lasts.

Ken Kesey

The real power behind the acid revolution came from the record companies... acid music was album music and an album cost four times the price of a single. If ever a drug was aptly named it was LSD. The pounds, shillings and pence it produced began to affect the industry from top to bottom.

Simon Napier-Bell

But for LSD, the name of Albert Hofmann would have probably remained unknown outside his family, friends and fellow chemists working in the laboratories of Sandoz, the Swiss-based pharmaceutical company.

Hofmann joined the company in 1929 straight from the University of Zürich, in order to work on natural products within the chemical industry. In the early thirties, two Americans had successfully isolated lysergic acid as the nucleus common to all alkaloids of ergot, a fungus found on rye. Most of Hofmann's work up to 1938 was spent investigating the medicinal potential of lysergic acid. He was trying to develop lyserg-saure-diathylamid (LSD) as a circulatory stimulant, but after twenty-five different types of LSD had been synthesized by Hofmann the work was suspended in 1938 as unsatisfactory and inconclusive.

Yet his scientific curiosity would not allow him to abandon the work altogether and in 1943, he again synthesized his last formula, LSD-25. Though meticulous in his laboratory habits, Hofmann allowed his fingertips to come into contact with the chemical and the result became enshrined in annals of drug subcultural lore:

Last Friday, 16 April 1943, I was forced to interrupt my work in the laboratory in the middle of the afternoon and proceed home, being affected by a remarkable restlessness, combined with a slight dizziness. At home I lay down and sank into a not unpleasant intoxicated-like condition, characterized by an extremely stimulated imagination. In a dreamlike state, with eyes closed (I found the daylight to be unpleasantly glaring), I perceived an uninterrupted stream of fantastic pictures, extraordinary shapes with intense kaleidoscopic play of colours. After some two hours this condition faded away.[1]

Concluding that the LSD had been responsible for his bizarre experience, Hofmann took the only course open to a true empirical scientist and ingested some deliberately to see what would happen. He dissolved one thousandth of a gram in 10cc of water and took off on a full-blown acid trip lasting several hours, some of it good, some not so good. Three of his colleagues tried with only one third of Hofmann's dose. The results were the same. Hofmann had stumbled on the most potent mood-altering drug ever known.

A year before Hofmann's momentous discovery and several thousand miles away in Washington DC, a group of American scientists were brought together under the command of the Office of Strategic Services, forerunner of the CIA. Their top-secret brief was to find a speech-inducing drug, a 'truth-drug', for use in intelligence interrogation. As the work progressed, caffeine, alchohol, barbiturates and mescalin were tried and rejected. At one time marijuana looked like the answer, but as with so many mood-altering drugs, the results were too unpredictable. Some OSS operatives who took part in experiments couldn't stop talking under the influence of the drug, others became paranoid in the austere, clinical surroundings of the laboratory and wouldn't say a word. The scientists were faced with a classic testimony of the role of environment and personal expectation in determining the effects of a drug on the individual. For any truth drug to work, the anxiety levels of an enemy agent had to be consistently raised, making him want to talk. Marijuana was dismissed as being ineffective in this way and the research committee wrote a report to that effect. One of the signatories to that report was the head of the Bureau of Narcotics, Harry J. Anslinger, brought on to the committee for his 'expertise' in the drugs field. So at the very time that Anslinger was waging a public war against marijuana as a destroyer of minds, he was signing a report which implied that the most 'psychotic' aspect of marijuana was its capacity to induce uncontrollable laughter in subjects.

The first published reports about LSD began circulating within the international scientific community during 1947. Having read these reports, the scientists working for the CIA (as it was now called), fervently believed that LSD was the drug that they had been looking for: a drug to unlock the mind. A number of secret projects code-named CHATTER, then BLUEBIRD, and ARTICHOKE, had been insti-gated to find a truth drug. Now a mountain of research money was poured into MK-ULTRA to test LSD under operational conditions. The CIA tried out the drug on its own agents with their knowledge and consent, but then carried out unauthorized tests on outsiders without their knowledge. In November 1953, the CIA LSD research team, led by Dr Sidney Gottlieb, dosed the drinks of army personnel at a remote hunting lodge for CIA and army staff in West Maryland. One officer, Dr Frank Olsen, became completely paranoid and a few weeks later crashed to his death from the tenth floor of the Statler Hilton Hotel in New York. It took twenty years for the story to come out along with revelations that the CIA had set up a brothel and paid prostitutes to spike customers' drinks while the CIA watched the results through two-way mirrors. Even today, the full story of the CIA's own LSD experiments has not been told.

But probably the most despicable aspect of the LSD research in the fifties was the work done by scientists whose experiments depended on CIA funding. LSD was tried out on those in no position to resist, such as prisoners and mental-hospital patients. Dr Harris Isbell was given the facility to test hundreds of different drugs on prisoners at Lexington. With heroin and morphine usually the reward for taking part, it is no wonder that the prison had a 90% return rate.

It was through CIA-funded work that Dr Paul Hoch discovered LSD to be a 'psychomimetic' drug – in other words, its action resembled the response of psychosis. Until the drug effects wore off, a doctor might have difficulty distinguishing between an LSD user on a bad trip and a schizophrenic. The CIA were interested in this angle and also in any potential the drug might have as a device for brainwashing.

The army too, got into the act. One army officer devised a scenario whereby an enemy would be bombarded with hallucinogenic gas. While the populace were talking to the trees, in would march the GIs and take over. Nobody would die and what's more, buildings and the national economy would remain intact. Another strain of LSD research theor-ized on the possibilities of the drug not as a weapon of war or counter-espionage, but as a therapeutic device to help those whose psychiatric problems derived from repressed emotions.

Noting, like Hoch, the schizophrenia/LSD comparability, British psychiatrist Humphrey Osmond began working with LSD and mescalin among psychiatric patients in Canada around 1951-2. He also treated alcoholics on the theory that some of them only genuinely try to give up drinking once they have reached rock bottom. LSD was the means to make 'rock bottom' happen. Osmond's work caused great interest in scientific circles and also caught the attention of Aldous Huxley, who had examined the spectre of drug-induced social control in his 1931 novel *Brave New World*. At his home in Hollywood, Huxley experimented with mescalin under Osmond's supervision. The results threw open a whole new vista on LSD, not just a drug with the potential to drive you mad, but one which allowed the existence of alternative or enhanced realities. Writing up his experience in *The Doors of Perception*, Huxley theorized that for the purposes of everyday living, the brain acts as a filter, allowing only essential information to pass through. LSD pushed back this mind screen; it was the key to the doors of perception and once opened, a torrent of sensations, colours, sounds and images flooded in. This, to Huxley, was nothing short of the ecstasies of mystical relevation and he predicted a worldwide religious revival should such drugs become freely available.

The experiments with Huxley also changed the emphasis of Osmond's own work. From Alcoholics Anonymous he learned that one of their major tenets for successful abstinence is a genuine religious experience. If LSD could provide that, then it was more than just a means of provoking a life crisis. This meant also that 'psychomimetic' was too narrow a descriptive term. Osmond first coined the expression 'psychedelic' to move away from the *'psycho'* connotation. He announced his new terminology to a meeting of the New York Academy of Sciences in 1957. By then, a small group of scientists and literary figures had been experimenting with LSD at social gatherings. In a country obsessed by the virtues of psychoanalysis, LSD became all the rage among Hollywood psychiatrists and analysts tending the tortured psyches of the rich and famous. After a course of LSD treatment, Cary Grant said in a widely publicized statement, 'All my life I've been searching for peace of mind. I'd explored yoga and hypnotism and made several attempts at mysticism. Nothing seemed to give me what I wanted until this treatment.'[2]

So what was the LSD experience all about? As we have seen, only minute amounts are necessary for the drug to take effect. This can take anything from thirty minutes to two hours. A feeling of agitation gives way to a sense that the world is slightly out of alignment; weird visions can develop from the most mundane objects. Sensory awareness can be heightened to such a degree that colours are 'heard' and sounds are 'seen' a phenomenon known as synaesthesia. The most banal thoughts can appear profound, random noises extraordinarily knowing.

But the key to the LSD experience during the early stages of the psychedelic journey is usually termed 'ego death'. When experienced either in the company of a guide who has travelled this path before, or in convivial surroundings, or by those whose creative and intellectual abilities already give them a considered view of the world, 'ego death' need not be frightening. Quite the reverse; it stimulates a sense of oneness with the world, as the user lets go of the trappings of his or her ego. Where the user tries to fight the effects of the drug or is dosed unknowingly, the shattering of the ego can produce not beatific visions of 'one world', but the destruction of inner confidence and a feeling that you are losing your mind.

Towards the end of the trip, the user will often become deeply reflective, trying to consolidate the sensory bombardments of the previous hours. It is sometimes during his latter stage that important personal decisions are made. Finally the user will drift off, often into a long sleep.

Some researchers in the fifties, like Dr Oscar Janiger, wanted to explore the relationship between LSD and the creative mind. Volunteers for Janiger's experiments included André Previn, James Coburn, Lord Buckley and Jack Nicholson. (Nicholson later wrote the screenplay of a Roger Corman cheapie *The Trip* [1966], which never received a general certificate in Britain.) Dr Sidney Cohen turned on Henry Luce, president of *Time Life* and an ardent right-winger. His wife, a very influential political figure in her own right, was of the opinion that LSD was fine for doctors and their upper-class friends, but 'we wouldn't want everyone doing too much of a good thing.'[3] James I had uttered similar sentiments about tobacco over 350 years earlier. But while American bluebloods and intellectuals were tripping the light fantastic at cosy dinner parties, a Harvard psychiatrist was waiting to snatch LSD from behind hallowed doors and give it to the people as a panacea for the world's ills.

In 1959, Dr Timothy Leary, aged thirty-nine, author of a standard work of psychology and inventor of the Leary Personality Test (used for recruiting staff by the CIA among others), was undergoing something of a midlife crisis. He was feeling bogged down by university life and two previous marriages lay in ruins, the first having ended tragically when his wife committed suicide. On holiday in Mexico in 1960, Leary, who hadn't even smoked marijuana before, tried some hallucinogenic psilocybin mushrooms. The overwhelmingly religious experience that followed was to change his life.

Back at Harvard, Leary set up a psilocybin research project with Richard Alpert, an assistant professor of Education and Psychology. Together they conducted formal investigations into the hallucinogenic experience, and arranged informal sessions outside the laboratory. Beat poet Allen Ginsberg attended one of these sessions; at the time Leary had yet to try LSD, while Ginsberg had not had a mushroom trip. What seems to have happened is that during the latter stages of the psilocybin trip, Ginsberg had an apocalyptic vision of a new age in which peace and love would pervade the world, ending all war. To achieve this end, Ginsberg decided, all the world leaders had to be turned on so that they would understand and share his vision.

Leary was reportedly not over-enthusiastic at first, while Ginsberg became a one-man psilocybin crusader. Among his closest friends were jazz musicians and it was they rather than rock musicians who first tried hallucinogenic drugs, including Thelonious Monk, Dizzy Gillespie and John Coltrane, who after an LSD trip said he had 'perceived the inter-relationship of all life forms'.

Ginsberg became a conduit through which artists, writers, musicians and poets plugged into Leary's research. From here onwards the LSD story becomes one populated with all manner of eccentric people, literary visionaries, millionaires with time on their hands and money to burn, gangsters, renegade chemists, businessmen, conmen, CIA infiltrators and those who flit about in a shadowland of political intrigue and influence.

One such individual of indeterminate occupation was Michael Hollingshead who came to see Leary from England, toting a mayonnaise jar of LSD – enough for 10,000 doses. Having already initiated jazz trumpeter Maynard Ferguson and his wife, Hollingshead and the new converts turned up at Leary's house. Seeing the look on Ferguson's face, Leary tried some acid and became another instant convert. LSD now became the focus of his psychedelic research.

LSD was not yet illegal in 1962, but Leary's extra-curricular activities aroused the attention of the CIA. Government experimentation was still going on in the early sixties and the CIA were concerned about what they described as 'uncontrolled experimentation', ironic when one considers their own irresponsible testing on unknowing subjects. Leary had already been warned by somebody with CIA connections that he was being watched, since it had become known that he was working with LSD. But a religious fervour had gripped him; religious imagery informed all he felt about LSD. He was a priest of the God Acid; there was a message to preach, souls to be saved, bibles and tracts to be written.

Leary's research was clearly out of step with the psychomimetic model of LSD adopted by all the major government agencies involved in drug research, monitoring and legislation. In 1963 he founded the International Federation for Internal Freedom and, together with Alpert, took a long sabbatical in Mexico to continue his research. He tried to involve both Huxley and Hofmann in his venture but, put off by Leary's blatant publicity-seeking, they refused. It is possible that pressure was put on the Harvard authorities to 'do something about Leary'; amid rumours of campus orgies both Leary and Alpert were dismissed *in absentia*.

Mexico, however, proved untranquil for Leary and friends. The Mexican authorities were unhappy about 'longhairs' hanging around and the researchers were expelled. They were rescued by a twenty-year-old stockbroker millionaire, William Mellon Hitchcock, who in 1964 set up what was now the Castalia Foundation at Millbrook, a sixty-four-room mansion set in massive grounds in upstate New York. Inevitably Millbrook became 'the place to be seen' among New York's bohemian community and many visitors arrived to be turned on, including the walking wounded from Warhol's Factory Scene.

Also in semi-permanent residence were the media. Not only did Leary hype LSD as a short cut to mystical enlightenment, but he guaranteed himself banner headlines by marrying the idea to sex, inventing a concept called 'erotic politics'. Michael Hollingshead showed up again and became a Leary agent in Britain. Following the Millbrook model, he established the World Psychedelic Centre in the King's Road, attracting London's fashionable mid-sixties set including Donovan, the Rolling Stones, Paul McCartney and Eric Clapton.

It was largely through the interest of such trendy luminaries in things hallucinogenic that the mod scene in London dissolved in a haze of LSD and the swirl of marijuana smoke. Hollingshead was something of a drug hog, consuming vast quantities of acid, dope and speed. Eventually he was busted and spent twenty-one months in Wormwood Scrubs where he turned on spy George Blake to LSD that had been smuggled into the prison.

Back in the States, Leary was becoming a twenty-four-carat embarrassment to the political and academic establishment as his media circus rolled on. With his ready catchphrases like 'Turn On, Tune In, Drop Out', Leary became the media-appointed spokesman for anyone under twenty-five, although young people themselves, especially outside America, were not so enamoured of this Harvard academic past forty. Inevitably, Leary was busted on a marijuana charge in December 1965 and from then on Millbrook was subjected to regular police harassment until, virtually under siege, the community broke up in 1967.

Although Leary was a publicity-seeker, he was fundamentally serious about what he was doing. LSD experimentation at Millbrook was a solemn affair, highly ritualistic, accompanied by earnest discussions among participants and meditation on the nature of the LSD experience. Millbrook was a psychedelic seminary. But like the division among academics in the fifties, there was disagreement among the creative spirits about the value of LSD. For acid veterans like Leary and Alpert, LSD was the psychic transporter for the journey into inner space and had to be treated with due reverence. For others, it was a recreational drug, one which encouraged social community and friendship and was, when all was said and done, an interesting way to get wasted.

Ken Kesey was another college boy turned on by Uncle Sam; he volunteered for LSD experiments at Menlo Park Veterans Hospital. Shortly afterwards he got a job as night attendant in the psychiatric ward of the same hospital. There he discovered a treasury of space-age drugs just asking to be lifted. It wasn't long before a select group at Stanford University and Perry Lane, the Greenwich Village-style community that surrounded it, got their first taste of LSD. A psychedelic commune grew up around Kesey and there were frequent takers for his famous acid-laced venison. On the proceeds of his novel, *One Flew Over The Cuckoo's Nest,* published in 1960, Kesey decamped to La Honda, a country home fifty miles south of San Francisco. Like Millbrook on the East Coast, La Honda became something of a point of pilgrimage for a motley assortment of artists, poets, musicians and rootless itinerants.

In many respects, Kesey represented a watershed between the angry 'No' of the Beats who turned their backs on a world they regarded as beyond redemption and the transcendent 'Yes' of the Hippies who believed in a better world attainable through peace, love and chemicals. The Beats had given up on American culture, its redundant materialism – Ginsberg's Moloch – which partly accounts for their adoption of the fatalistic religions of the East. They were also possessed of the old American vision of travel as a means of spiritual discovery, best captured in *On the Road.* But if you live on the West Coast where do you go? The answer for some was India. The Beats lived for any experience which would shut out what they despised; marijuana, booze, speed, heroin and LSD were all indispensable. Marijuana and acid opened whole new vistas for travel – journeys into inner space.

From the individuals gathered at La Honda came the Merry Pranksters, who criss-crossed America through 1964 in a psychedelic thirties' bus driven maniacally by Neal Casady. The Beatles and Dylan blared from speakers, everyone wore funny clothes and was permanently stoned on acid diluted in Kool Aid orange juice. Back in California, Kesey had instigated the Acid Test, forerunner of the 'Be-in', the 'Happening' and eventually the rock festival. Participants, encouraged to dress up as weirdly as possible, paid $1 fr which they could consume as much Kool Aid as they could manage. This formed a stoned backdrop to a totally free-form event; all kinds of musical and film equipment was left lying around for anybody to do what they liked with. A folk/rock band called the Warlocks would usually turn up. Their lead guitarist had been hanging around Perry Lane for the past few years. At the Acid Test, the Warlocks would play only if they felt like it. If they didn't, nobody objected or hassled them. Had they tried that a few years later the reaction would not have been so laid-back, for by 1966 the Warlocks had metamorphosed into the Grateful Dead.

Out on the road the Merry Pranksters hit the East Coast in search of Kerouac and Leary. Kesey envisaged a great meeting of minds, but he was disappointed on both counts. Casady set up a meeting between Kesey and Kerouac, but they had little to say to one another. Kerouac was one of the classic isolationist beats. He had no time for West Coast weirdness, acid sociability and stoned revelations. Burroughs, too, another beat guru, had been scathing about the psychedelic revolution and in *Nova Express* (1964) had warned about the use of hallunci-nogenic drugs as state weapons of social control. No flower children these. Clearly, while the beat poets and writers exerted a measure of influence over musicians, the cultural heroes of the sixties, they had little to say to the masses of ordinary teenagers growing up in that same period.

The Merry Pranksters fared no better at Millbrook. For them, the meditation sessions and earnest discussions about the nature of the psychedelic experience were just plain boring; they dubbed Millbrook 'a crypt trip'.

To extend a comment by David Pichaske in his study of the sixties, the Beats, the acid crusaders and the student radicals desperately wanted everything to mean something. By contrast, the rock audiences were just out for a good time. The musicians went for that, plus the money, which sat easy with establishment businessmen more than happy to finance the indulgencies of rock stars so long as they got their returns.

Another sign that the beat star was on the wane was the break-up during 1962-3 of the North Beach area of San Francisco as a 'bohemian' community. Tourists, hustlers and gangsters combined to drive beats and hipsters to another part of town where a warren of run-down, ramshackle Victorian houses provided cheap accommodation. This was the district known as Haight Ashbury, eventually a state of mind as much as a place, which from 1964, became the new meeting place for all those who felt at odds with America's cultural and political mainstream. And the cornerstone of the Haight's counter-cultural position was rock music.

It would hardly be an exaggeration to say that the music was not just a record of the sixties, it *was* the sixties – not much else remains above the surface. The buildings are gone, the concert halls shut down, some of the best musicians of the era are dead, the fashions are outdated and rather than being expressed openly, the values of the period are locked inside the millions of people who lived through that time. But put on a Doors or Love album and the sixties live again.

In combination, the music and drugs served to bring together many undercurrents from the fifties; feelings against war and nuclear weapons, the growth of anti-establishment satire, poetry and folk music. As part of the youthful love affair with America's ethnic origins, and of the 'back to nature movement' which idolized the American Indians and the time of the early settlers, folk, blues and 'hillbilly' music were very much in vogue. All the major San Francisco bands labelled as purveyors of acid rock had their beginnings playing roots music together in any number of loose permutations.

The Grateful Dead are the premier example of the combination of acid and electricity which brought about a musical revolution on the West Coast. The evolution of the Dead into one of rock's longest-running shows is one of those wonderfully twisted skeins of musical chronology that Pete Frame of *Rock Trees* fame is so adept at unravelling. After dropping out of school at seventeen, going absent without leave several times from the army, guitarist Jerry Garcia settled in Palo Alto along the San Francisco peninsula, home of Stanford University and Kesey's Perry Lane enclave. There he met lyricist Robert Hunter; together they scuffled around coffee bars playing folk songs and sleeping in wrecked cars. Garcia became hooked on bluegrass and in partnership with Hunter toured around the nightspots of Palo Alto, Berkeley and North Beach in a series of folk bluegrass bands like the Thunder Mountain Tub Thumpers, the Hart Valley Drifters (good enough to win the amateur bluegrass section at the 1963 Monterey Folk Festival), the Wildwood Boys and the Black Mountain Boys. Other personnel in these bands included David Nelson (New Riders of the Purple Sage), David Freiberg (Quicksilver Messenger Service and Jefferson Airplane) and Pete Albin (Big Brother and the Holding

135

Company). In 1962 Garcia met drummer Bill Kreutzmann and both ended up working at Dana Morgan's music shop, where budding guitarist Bob Weir often hung around to pick up playing tips. Garcia and several other musicians lived in a pre-La Honda style commune known as the Chateau, to which a blues fanatic harp player named Ron 'Pigpen' McKernan presented himself one day. In 1964, Garcia, Weir and Pigpen conceived the short-lived Mother McGee's Uptown Jug Champions, but then the Beatles redrafted the blueprints for young white musicians and acoustic folk got left behind. The revelation of the Beatles was the fun and profit of playing electric rock 'n' roll. Pigpen took the lead; out went the washboards, in came Kreutzmann to play drums and the Warlocks plugged in. It wasn't long, in the close-knit Bay-Area way of things, for the Warlocks to become involved in Kesey's Acid Tests. Garcia was later to comment, 'The Acid Tests were thousands of people, all hopelessly stoned, all finding themselves in a roomful of other thousands of people, none of whom any of them were afraid of.'

There was no clear chronology to the development of the San Francisco rock scene – all the major bands came together at roughly the same time – but one West Coast band mentioned by many musicians as being a catalyst in the progression towards acid rock were the Charlatans.

Who?

Based in Los Angeles, the Charlatans were one of the first bands to play electric blues and rock 'n' roll smashed out of their brains on acid and magic mushrooms. They had an unlikely residency in 1965 at a rough-house bar called the Red Dog Saloon, Virginia City, Nevada and the Bay Area musicians largely took their cue from this band. Unfortunately, it is often the way that the pioneers of rock music end up languishing in the footnotes of history. So it was with the Charlatans; once 'psychedelia' got under way, they were never able to land themselves a major record deal and disappeared from view.

It was during 1965 that certain individuals saw that all these musicians furiously forming bands were going to need somewhere to play. A would-be rock entrepreneur, Chet Helms, formed a promotions outfit called Family Dog and on 16 October staged the first of a series of highly successful concerts at the Longshoreman's Hall near Fisherman's Wharf. Star guests on that first night were a new band, Jefferson Airplane, named after their guitarist's dog. The Warlocks had already starred in benefit gigs for the San Francisco Mime Troupe (who were being regularly busted for obscenity), organized by the Troupe's business manager and treasurer Bill Graham.

In January 1966, the Merry Pranksters organized what amounted to a three-day acid test called the Trips Festival. Bands on stage included the Warlocks, Jefferson Airplane and Chet Helms' houseband at the Longshoreman's Hall, Big Brother and the Holding Company. Earlier in 1965, Helms had brought a singer, Janis Joplin from Texas, to play the Bay Area folk scene, but he shipped her back sharpish when she became hooked on Methedrine. He brought her back in June to front Big Brother, whose manager he had since become. The Trips Festival grossed $12,500 with few overheads. Two weeks later, Bill Graham started up at the Fillmore Theatre in the heart of San Francisco's black community and from then on every weekend was a Trips Festival. Chet Helms replied with concerts at the Avalon Ballroom on the corner of Van Ness and Sutter. Rock 'n' roll was here to pay.

Inseparable from the growth of the San Francisco music scene and rock in general was the widespread use of marijuana and LSD among the offspring of America's white middle class. If LSD was the icing on the counter-cultural cake, marijuana was its basic ingredient. As well as being central to the jazz scene in the fifties, it was enthusiastically taken up by white musicians on the folk-blues circuit. For those whose folk music was heavily politicized, smoking dope became integral to the protest movement.

The Free Speech Movement started on Berkeley campus in the autumn of 1964 and quickly became a focal point for the rising tide of student activism. Every issue from civil rights to the Bomb was up for grabs. By using an illegal drug like marijuana (LSD wasn't banned in the USA until 1966), cub activists made their first tilt at authority. For many, doing drugs would be their only 'political' statement. Shocking one's parents and teachers was the boundary of most acts of status-quo sabotage. The Left in politics failed to exploit the radical promise of acid, which while communal in its social context, was still far too individualistic and inward-looking an activity for the hardline politicos. The self-obsessed ME generation left outrage to the committed few. When Pete Townshend whacked Jerry Rubin on the head with his guitar as the chief Yippie tried to make an impromptu speech from the stage of Woodstock, the love affair between radical politics and the acid generation was over.

The claims for rock music as a revolutionary force have always been suspect, as protest rock courtesy of major record companies clearly demonstrates. A study which examined the attitudes of young people over a four-year period, from 1966-70, actually showed up rock as a vehicle for social control rather than anarchy. The authors concluded, 'Our study suggests that rock music may have seemed to channel social unrest into a more politically passive direction. By helping to translate revolutionary opinions into rhetorical cant, protest rock facilitated token opposition to the status quo among youth...'[4]

From the early sixties the economics of the drug scene began to change. On the East Coast, for example, marijuana was relatively scarce unless you went to Harlem or bought poor-grade Mafia dope. But as the habit spread through white suburbs and college campuses, a new network of 'hippy' dealers grew up, distributing high-grade Mexican marijuana like Acapulco Gold with the same righteous air as Mezz Mezzrow. Organized crime syndicates like the Mafia gave up on the street marijuana scene to concentrate on drugs like heroin and cocaine, which were less bulky, more profitable, involved fewer dealers and were much easier to control.

But the true Mezz Mezzrow of his time dealt not in marijuana but in LSD. Augustus Owsley Stanley III was once described by a US government agent as the man who did for LSD what Henry Ford did for the motor car. Leary called him God's secret agent and to the hippy in the street he was the King of LSD. Grandson of a Kentucky senator, Owsley was a wayward boy genius of science whose natural home was a chemistry lab. Drifting around the West Coast in 1963, he took up a course at Berkeley and between then and 1965 operated a Methedrine factory, until police swooped and confiscated all his equipment. Fleeing to Los Angeles, Owsley set up an LSD operation which he took back north once the situation had cooled down. From there he began supplying 'Owsley tabs', white at first, then blue and then a whole variety of colours, designed to stay ahead of cheap imitations. Some had designs on them like Batman, others had special names like Purple Haze and White Lightning. All his products were top grade, purer than Sandoz LSD. Owsley had strong connections with the rock scene. Purple Haze was made for Jimi Hendrix: a special double-strength tab with an owl stamped on it. According to Lemmy of Motorhead, who was a Hendrix roadie in 1967, Hendrix bought 100,000 doses from Owsley. Hendrix had an 'acid-taster' to make sure he wasn't being sold bad stuff; but with Owsley acid on offer he didn't need him. Owsley's closest association, however, has been with the Grateful Dead.

Owsley supplied most of the acid for the Acid Tests; here he made contact with the Warlocks, as they still were in 1965. Owsley had a keen interest in electronics and teamed up with electronics wizard Tim Scully, who in turn wished to know more about LSD. Together they supplied acid to the rock community and a mountain of electronic equipment to the Warlocks. The Grateful Dead owed much to Tim Scully for the creation of a sound described by Ralph Gleason as 'rolling thunder'.

Owsley became something of a patron to the band, channelling drugs, money and equipment to them, providing accommodation and even becoming involved in their record production.

Owsley made a fortune from LSD, but like Leary he was an acid missionary, a psychedelic alchemist who probably gave away as much LSD as he sold. He had a 'righteous' view about acid, believing it to be a drug for the people. When criminal gangs tried to corner the Californian market in ergot, Owsley temporarily killed the market in San Francisco by parachuting into the 'Be-In' Festival at Golden Gate Park in January 1967 to give away 100,000 tabs of LSD.

By the time of the Festival, Owsley himself was a criminal as the unlawful manufacture and sale of LSD had been banned under Federal laws introduced on 1 February 1966. In the aftermath of the Thalidomide tragedy, the Federal Drug Administration (FDA) greatly restricted experimentation with new drugs. From 1963, the FDA had to approve all Investigational New Drugs (IND) research in writing for each individual project. LSD was classed as an IND. At first this had limited impact on LSD research but then horror stories about the drug began appearing in the British and American press. The recreational use of LSD was spreading fast; in 1962 Leary estimated that about 25,000 Americans had tried it. A study conducted at the end of 1965 put the figure at nearly four million, of whom 70% were at high school or college. Bad experiences with the drug were inevitable, and not surprisingly the tiny minority of extreme cases made banner headlines; those who flew out of windows or committed murder under the influence of LSD. A heavily-publicized scare about chromosome breakage and deformed babies proved unfounded. One story that was widely reported involved a group of students who, having taken acid, looked into the sun and went blind. The doctor who submitted this story later admitted it was a lie intended to highlight the dangers of the drug. His retraction went largely unreported.

In the midst of all this hysteria Sandoz withdrew their IND application for LSD and took the drug off the market in May 1966 and Sandoz' American office, based in New Jersey, turned over all their supplies to the National Institute of Mental Health (NIMH). The government was now fully committed to the 'psychomimetic' model of LSD; anything else smacked of the dangerous subversion of Leary and his followers. Only those researchers seeking grants to study the adverse effects of the drug had their applications considered.

The Federal law of February 1965 did not outlaw possession of LSD, only its manufacture. But by late 1966 many states, including New York and California, had made possession a felony. Some state laws were

particularly draconian; in Massachusetts, for example, simple possession could land you in jail for up to four years. Persuade someone to
take it and you could be detained for up to twenty-five years. Yet it
wasn't until 1968 that the Federal laws were amended to ban possession
of LSD. That same year saw a reorganization of the drug enforcement
agencies; the Bureau of Narcotics and Dangerous Drugs was created
from Anslinger's old Bureau and the Bureau of Drug Abuse Control
(formerly part of the Health Department). Enforcement of the laws
against psychedelic drugs was also switched from the FDA to this new
powerful drug enforcement agency. The day the laws came into effect in
California, 6 October 1966 (Britain banned LSD the same month), a
large protest-cum-rock event was staged in San Francisco. The bands
played and the counter-culture politicians and poets made speeches.
One immediate impact of the acid laws was dramatically to increase the
appeal of LSD for the 'generation in rebellion'. The Acid Tests petered
out around the time Sandoz took acid off the market; Kesey had already
fled to Mexico in the wake of a marijuana bust. But LSD became a
permanent fixture, backstage and front, of all the major rock festivals of
the sixties in both Britain and America.

The first rock festival to capture the attention of the media was the
Golden Gate 'Be-In' of January 1967. Thousands of people came
together to listen to music, make love, and (courtesy of Owsley's acid
drop), get stoned. There was no trouble and no police. Despite the laws,
the reputation of LSD as a drug of peace and love soared. But the
importance of the concert was blown out of all proportion, possibly
because the nation couldn't conceive that so many young people could
come together to listen to the Devil's music and consume dangerous
drugs without mayhem and disaster. When this didn't happen absurd
ambitions were heaped on 'hippies' (as Herb Caen of the *San Francisco
Chronicle* had dubbed them), as vanguards of the 'new generation',
'saviours of the world' and so on.

The record companies, too, were hailing a new age – of increased
profits. Jac Holtzman, head of Elektra, told an industry conference at
the time: 'To comprehend the music of tomorrow, expand you musical
vistas, sensitize yourself, because the vibrations of contemporary existence cannot be had secondhand.'[5] The dark blue suit gave way to the
Afghan coat, hair cascaded over ears, dope wafted from nostrils and
'man' fell from every corporate lip. Apart from that nothing much had
changed.

The writing was already etched upon the wall at the 'Be-In' of January
1967. Jefferson Airplane, the headlining band, had been signed to RCA
since August 1965, the same month that the Byrds' 'Mr Tambourine

140

Man' was in the British and American charts. RCA wanted their own Byrds and paid out an unprecedented $20,000 advance to secure them. Airplane repaid the debt with acid-drenched chart hits like 'White Rabbit' and 'Somebody to Love'. Grace Slick's brother-in-law, Darby had written 'Somebody to Love' after an acid trip taken to console himself at being dumped by his girlfriend. During the recording of Airplane's 1967 album *After Bathing at Baxters,* which also refers to acid trips, RCA set the band up in a Beverly Hills mansion complete with Japanese houseboy and rifle range, at $5,000 a month. Nevertheless relations with RCA were always strained; the company was only too eager to reap the profits from drug-inspired songs, but there were battle royals over album covers which were too 'psychedelic' for the company's liking.

The Monterey Pop Festival in June 1967 proved to be the launching-pad for a number of other West Coast bands. Some were signed directly as a result of their appearance there, others gained from the international exposure Monterey gave to rock. Backstage was awash with Owsley acid and a new product for the hippy aristocracy, STP, an amphetamine with psychedelic properties. Hendrix, who became a star after Monterey, wrote 'The Stars That Played with Laughing Sam's Dice' as a homage to both drugs. Out front, Janis Joplin impressed Columbia, who already had the Byrds and later signed Moby Grape. Capital paid out $40,000 in advance to Quicksilver Messenger Service and the Steve Miller Band; Vanguard signed Country Joe and the Fish, while Elektra snapped up LA's top acid bands, Love and the Doors.

But what of the Warlocks? During 1966 the band decided that a name change was in order. Talking to Michael Lydon in 1968 Jerry Garcia said,

> One day we were over at Phil's house smoking DMT. He had a big dictionary. I opened it and there was 'Grateful Dead', those words juxtaposed. It was one of those moments, you know, like everything else on the page went blank, diffuse, just sort of oozed away and there was GRATEFUL DEAD in big black letters edged all around in gold, man, blasting out at me. Such a stunning combination. So I said how about Grateful Dead? And that was it.[6]

The name change signified the move away from a rigid folk-blues formula to meandering, free-form rock improvisations. The Dead were probably unique among the acid-rock bands. Many merely jumped on the bandwagon, adopting fashionable psychedelic names and creating a drug atmosphere through judicious knob-twiddling in the studio, but all within the standard three-and-a-half minute format. Even on Jefferson Airplane's most overt drug album, *Baxters,* no track is longer than five minutes. The Dead were more of a touring community than a rock band. They arrived stoned, played stoned and their fiercely loyal fans, 'Deadheads', were stoned along with them. Acid stretched the length of concerts to legendary proportions. They could play five hours and when the promoter pulled the plug on them, they'd set up somewhere else and play for another three. Song structures were at best fluid. About acid, Garcia said: 'It was like another release, yet another opening. The first one was a hip teacher when I was in third grade; and the next one was marijuana, and the next one was music and the next one was LSD. It was like a series of continually opening doors.'[7]

Of those bands signed up prior to Monterey, the Dead held out longer than most against the fluttering chequebook, but finally signed to Warner Brothers in December 1966. Even so, they made acid work for them. Up until then, bands were paid royalties based on the number of songs on an album; if the Dead were going to try and re-create their stage act on record, they would lose out. So a deal was struck whereby royalties were paid per three-and-a-half minutes of music instead of per song.

The Dead played music that was quite specifically aimed at those who used psychedelic drugs and marijuana. Indeed, some of their sixties material is almost unlistenable unless one is in an altered state of consciousness. Similarly targeted was a classic album of the period, the debut offering from Country Joe and the Fish, *Electric Music for the Mind and Body*, with songs like 'Flying High', 'Section 43' and 'Bass Strings':

> Hey Partner, won't you pass that reefer around
> My world is spinning, yeah
> Just got to slow it down
> Oh yes I've sure got to slow it down
> Got so high this time that you know
> I'll never come down – never come down.

The 13th Floor Elevators were an unusual band in that they were the leading lights of a psychedelic rock scene based not in San Francisco but Texas. The Texan acid-rock scene was largely overlooked at the time because of the predominance of San Francisco and, in truth, the music world lost little. But the Elevators' first album, *The Psychedelic Sounds of the 13th Floor Elevators,* released in 1966, is probably the most reverential anthem to acid ever released and certainly left the listener in

142

no doubt as to the source of its inspiration. The sleevenotes read, '...
Recently it has become possible for man to chemically alter his mental
state and thus alter his point of view... he then can restructure his
thinking and change his language so that his thoughts bear more relation
to his life and problems, therefore approaching them more sanely. It is
this quest for pure sanity that forms the basis of the songs on this
album.' The album is full of psychedelic references, both blatant and
oblique. One song called 'Fire Engine' has the line 'let me take you to
the empty place on my fire engine', but 'the empty place' came out as
'DMT place', the dimethylatriptamine under which 'Grateful Dead' was
born.[8] Whatever came out of the 13th Floor Elevators, it certairily
wasn't pure sanity – quite the reverse.

Although the horror stories about acid were exaggerated and most
people suffered no ill-effects, some people took so much acid that, as in
the words of 'Bass Strings', they never really came down. These were
the 'acid casualties'. Their numbers were uncounted, but a disturbingly
large number of people from that period, inside and outside the
business, seemed to know of at least one. Exactly what happened in
these cases is unknown, although the most likely explanation is that the
action of LSD precipitated a latent psychotic condition.

Rocky Erikson, vocalist with the Elevators, finished up in a mental
hospital, where whatever damage had been done by LSD was com-
pounded by the 'Cuckoo's Nest' treatment he received. It took three
years and a court case to get him out. Some years later, interviewed on
radio, Erikson claimed to be interested only in horror and the Devil and
denied ever having been in the Elevators. The band's jug player, Tom
Hall, went the same way. Other notable acid victims included Love's
Arthur Lee, Skip Spence from Moby Grape, Pink Floyd's Syd Barrett,
Mitch Ryder and, it was rumoured, Peter Green of Fleetwood Mac,
while Jimi Hendrix ate acid tabs by the handful.

In 1968 writer Ralph Metzer interviewed David Crosby, then with the
Byrds, for a book called *The Ecstatic Adventure,* a log of chemical
journeys taken by people from all walks of life. Asked about using drugs
while creating music, Crosby said that he had been using LSD since 1964
and had learned to play guitar on speed: 'I don't know any good guitar
players who haven't taken speed... I play most of the time high and I
always write high (on psychedelics or marijuana).'

Crosby once spoke to Bob Dylan about acid and Dylan asked, 'Man,
haven't you done that enough?'[9] The answer went unrecorded, but time
was to reveal that for Crosby there would be no such thing as enough.

Dylan, on the other hand, was speaking from the point of view of
somebody who, by the late sixties, had done it all before. As Michael

Gray observed: 'The attempt to learn from drugs, the attempt to create drug experiences, the rejection of common sense, logic and the acceptance of mystery – Dylan accelerated the awakening to all this.'[10]

Dylan went through some profound drug experiences during 1964-5, taking up Baudelaire's formula for immortality: 'A poet makes himself a seer by a long prodigious and rational disordering of the senses.' He surrounded himself with 'the mindguard' equivalent of Presley's Memphis Mafia and tried just about everything he could to 'open his head' as biographer Tony Scaduto puts it. He talked about recapturing spontaneity and about writing songs that matched his thoughts at the age of ten, which was not going to happen while he was the doyen of protest folk. So he turned his back on politics as marijuana and acid turned him in on himself. Within a few short months the hard-nosed political reality of the 'Lonesome Death of Hattie Carroll' and the 'Ballad of Hollis Brown', gave way to expressions of drug experiences like 'Chimes of Freedom', 'Lay Down your Weary Tune', 'Subterranean Homesick Blues' and 'Mr Tambourine Man'. Michael Gray cites 'Lay Down Your Weary Tune', written in 1964, as Dylan's first acid song, 'the first concentrated attempt to give a hint of the unfiltered world.'[11] In 1964, Dylan refused a request from Ginsberg to lead a peace rally at Berkeley and earned the unbending enmity of singer Phil Ochs, who called him 'LSD on stage'. Dylan reported that Ochs was writing bullshit because politics were absurd and the world was unreal. Dylan took his personal drug-inspired search for freedom and escape through 'Mr Tambourine Man' and 'Highway 61 Revisited', to the ego-dissolution of 'Like a Rolling Stone' and *Blonde on Blonde*. Nevertheless, claims that all references to 'railways' and 'tracks' and capitalized H's on lyric sheets demonstrate that Dylan was a heroin addict or that *'Blowin' in the Wind'* was secretly a song about the wonders of cocaine are probably best left in the more extreme realms of Dylanology.

In the early sixties, sharing the experiences of marijuana and LSD between creative spirits had a missionary zeal about it. Rock writer Al Aronowitz turned both Ginsberg and Dylan on to marijuana; Dylan in turn introduced dope-smoking to the Beatles. They met him on their first tour of America. Dylan was 'anti-chemical' at the time, probably due to a surfeit of amphetamine, and suggested that the Beatles try something more natural. Dylan rolled the first joint and passed it to Lennon, who, too scared to try it, passed it on to Ringo. The episode ended with everyone rolling round the floor in hysterics.

It was during the filming of *Help* that LSD came into the Beatles' lives. A dentist friend threw a dinner party for them at which the conversation focused on a renegade academic called Timothy Leary, whom only John had heard of. The host passed round the LSD with none too beatific results. The Beatles left the party and drove dangerously from night club to night club in a very peculiar state of mind. Driving at 10 m.p.h. they somehow managed to get back to George Harrison's place, by which time neither his girlfriend Patti Boyd nor Lennon's wife Cynthia believed they would ever be sane again. While under the influence of acid, Lennon started drawing and perceived Harrison's house as a big submarine where they all lived.[12] This child-like acid imagery soon grew more pronounced as Lennon became obsessed with acid, taking hundreds of trips which undermined his already volatile personality. Probably acid and a destructive affair with heroin did more to push Lennon and finally the Beatles to the final collapse than any other outside influence.

Like Dylan's, the Beatles' drug adventures soon showed in their music. First *Rubber Soul* (1965) and then *Revolver* (1966) saw the release of Beatles songs in this new context. A concept of love that goes beyond a quick one behind the gasworks appeared in 'The Word', while 'Nowhere Man' examined the inner mental workings of the individual as revealed by psychedelic drugs. 'She Said, She Said' was inspired by a conversation Lennon had with actor Peter Fonda during his second acid trip, and Leary's psychedelic version of the Tibetan Book of the Dead provided the material for 'Tomorrow Never Knows'.

In June 1967 came the release of *Sergeant Pepper's Lonely Hearts Club Band*. Quite apart from being one of the most significant albums ever recorded, *Sergeant Pepper* galvanized the acid subculture and gave LSD an international platform. Whether or not 'Lucy in the Sky with Diamonds' really meant what it looked like is irrelevant; fans looked at the cover, read the lyrics, heard the studio effects and made up their own minds. The BBC also read the lyrics and banned 'A Day in the Life' because of its favourable reference to 'a trip'. In any case, Paul McCartney let the cat out of the bag when he admitted to *Queen* and *Life Magazine* in 1967 that not only had he used LSD, but 'it opened my eyes. It made me a better, more honest, more tolerant member of society.' In the ensuing furore, Brian Epstein tried to salvage the situation by saying that he had been using LSD as well: 'I did have some apprehension, but I took that risk. I think LSD helped me to know myself better and I think it helped me to become less bad-tempered.' In truth, Epstein was not floating through life on a sea of acid, but committing himself to a roller-coaster existence on barbiturates and amphetamines.

The release of *Sergeant Pepper* seemed to accelerate the rate at which the moths of popular culture flapped round the flame of LSD, in a desperate attempt to cash in while it all lasted. If nothing else, LSD brought colour into the lives of many young people, most of whom never touched the stuff. Hippy fashions in ethnic textiles swirled through the streets to the jangle of bells and beads. There were psychedelic films, rock light shows, often unreadable underground newspapers in multi-coloured prints and, of course, the music. Pop co-opted and sanitized acid. The very word 'acid' sounded hard and dangerous, a corrosive element in society; 'flower-power, on the other hand, was safe and innocuous – one of the biggest hits of 1967 was Scott McKenzie's 'San Francisco', with the benign lyric, 'Be sure to wear some flowers in your hair.'[13]

The Beatles also helped to put London on the psychedelic map and there were many attempts to re-create Haight Ashbury in W10 and NW6. For the *Berkeley Barb* and the *Oracle* read *International Times* and *Oz;* the Roundhouse, UFO and Middle Earth for the Fillmore and the Avalon Ballroom; Ally Pally for the Be-In; Pink Floyd, Soft Machine and Cream for the Dead, Airplane and Quicksilver. Cream and Hendrix straddled both continents, representing acid rock on a scale unmatched by any other band, either for power or virtuosity.

In London it was amusing to see r&b artists like Zoot Money and Graham Bond playing the same r&b songs in Hawaiian shirts and calling them psychedelic (or 'psychodalek' as Bond dubbed it). A sign of the times was the opening of the Temple, a seedy rock venue frequented by the capital's acid casualties, on the site of the famous Flamingo jazz club. But acid had a much more profound effect on the music business than the spawning of transitory rock clubs and one-hit wonders like Scott McKenzie. After *Sergeant Pepper*, straightforward 'one for the money/two for the show' rock 'n' roll was brushed aside. Over the next few years albums outsold singles for the first time; there were doubles, triples, boxed sets, concept albums, tracks lasting a whole side, gatefold album sleeves, the album cover as 'art', groups working with orchestras, rock operas and a slew of pretentious and obscure lyrics.

Acid also played a significant part in the development of FM radio in America, in the shape of Tom Donahue. Already a veteran DJ in Philadelphia, Donahue arrived in San Francisco in 1961, worked on KYA for a couple of years and then became involved in concert promotion and record production. As head of Autumn Records, he had eighteen national hits of which two got into the Top Ten. Then in 1966 he gave it all up. His partner in Autumn Records was dying of Hodgkin's disease and not surprisingly had lost interest. Donahue was 'taking a tremendous amount of acid. You know, you're taking acid three or four times a week and it's very hard to talk to thirty-seven

146

distributors and ask them the first day where your money is, the second day what they're doing about your records and the third day where your money is.'[14]

Donahue dropped out for about eighteen months and hung around his apartment doing more acid, trying to conceive where next to go. From his psychedelic musing came the notion of using the FM waveband to play all the 'head' music that AM Top Forty radio wouldn't touch. KMPX started up in the idyllic summer of '67 and became a spectacular success. But although business was good, the acid spirit in San Francisco was already dying. Haight Ashbury was going the way of North Beach, drowning in a sea of tourists, weekend hippies, hustlers, police harassment and bad acid. Injecting Methedrine became popular, serving only to heighten the level of paranoia and suspicion. In London, acid euphoria cooled with the coming of winter. Between August-December, pirate radio stations like Radio London, 270 and Scotland closed down,[15] Brian Epstein died, and the Beatles' attempt to film their own Merry Pranksters trip, *The Magical Mystery Tour*, was a shambles.

Throughout 1968 violence was the new radical pose. Jefferson Airplane said goodbye to the white rabbit and hello to *Volunteers* and 'Up against the wall, motherfuckers'. After the débâcle of *Her Satanic Majesties Request*, the Stones gratefully (and wisely) ditched flower power for *'Street Fightin' Man'*. Woodstock showed it was all still possible, but in December 1969 came Altamont. The Rolling Stones had come to the end of their American tour and Mick Jagger was determined to hold a free concert in California, the home of free concerts, and to release a film of the tour and the concert *before* the Woodstock film was released. A date had been fixed, but only at the eleventh hour could a venue be found – the Sears Point Raceway at Altamont.

Everyone involved knew the crowd would be vast and so it was – at least 300,000 people turned up. To cater for a crowd that size needs time and the careful planning of safety, security, staging and on-site facilities. None of this happened. To compound what was potentially a very serious situation, the site was awash with very poor-quality LSD; the medical team very quickly ran out of Thorazine, the drug used to calm people down on a bad trip. Fights broke out over food, water and in the long queues which formed for the few toilets. In this atmosphere, the appearance of Hell's Angels as security guards for the stage area only served to make matters worse.

At the Golden Gate Park concert in 1967, there was plenty of acid around, the Angels were on duty and there was very little trouble. On the strength of that experience, Grateful Dead manager Rock Scully recommended the Angels to the Altamont concert promoters. This

147

time, however, it all went horribly wrong. By noon, well before the first band came on, the Angels had consumed volumes of alcohol and bad acid thought to have been cut with speed. They were already fighting with members of the audience down near the front of the stage where most of the trouble happened. Nor were the artists safe: Marty Balin of Jefferson Airplane was smashed in the face during their set for trying to stop the Angels beating somebody up.

It was after dark when the Stones finally came on stage. Five songs into the set with fights going on all around him, Jagger had just uttered the first line of 'Under My Thumb', when he spotted a man in the audience waving a gun. He yelled at guitarist Mick Taylor and the music stopped. Holding the gun was an eighteen-year-old black man, Meredith Hunter, who had come to the concert with his white girlfriend. This had angered the Angels; they taunted Hunter and a fight broke out. Hunter was stabbed, but still managed to pull a gun. He was stabbed again and fell to the ground where he was kicked repeatedly. For several minutes, the Angels allowed nobody near him to tend his wounds. Eventually, he was taken to the medical tent, but the promised emergency facilities were not there – there was no equipment and no helicopter to fly Hunter to hospital – and he died.

Meredith Hunter was not the only fatality at Altamont; two people were killed in their sleeping bags by a hit-and-run driver and somebody drowned in a canal during a bad acid trip. The Angels were blamed for everything, but in truth the concert should never have taken place under such shambolic circumstances.

Coming on the edge of the new decade, it was inevitable that Altamont would be played up as a *fin de siècle* for the sixties. Even so, with most of the acid crusaders out of the picture by then, either on the run, in prison or in retirement, it is hard to escape the feeling that as the life ebbed away from Meredith Hunter, the spirit of the sixties went with it.[16]

Acid subculture was bound to dissipate because the whole structure was underpinned by rock music, a business which thrives on instant mass communication and international markets for its survival. In the process, however, LSD did create a new environment for rock to develop; it had a significant impact on already creative and talented minds and it is highly probable that without it the best of sixties rock music would not have emerged. Inevitably, LSD took its toll; with it Hendrix wrote some of the most powerful rock of all time, but it also made him malleable in the face of business sharks.

LSD was and is a drug that demands respect. William Blake knew nothing of it, but he encapsulated its power when he wrote,

To see a World in a grain of sand
And a Heaven in a wild flower
Hold Infinity in the palm of your hand
And Eternity in an hour.

10

Star Wars

If I smoke, will I get caught? Only if you're stupid, unlucky or a pop star.

Richard Neville, Playpower

When I wasn't high, I was in court ... you try saying twenty-five times 'Guilty, your honour' in Marlborough Street and keeping a straight face ... It was a game, nothing to do with justice or law.

Keith Richard, New Musical Express

Getting arrested on drugs charges is as much an occupational hazard for rock musicians as it ever was for the top-flight jazz stars of yesteryear. The context may be different, but the logic of moral outrage remains the same. In jazz's golden days, the spokesmen of 'right-thinking' citizens, the clergy, police, politicians and the press, could conveniently combine their entrenched racism and their disapproval of a delinquent generation by blaming black jazz musicians. If it wasn't for the jungle rhythms of licentious dope-smoking jazzers, young people would obey their parents and not expose themselves to mortal danger and ruin.

But as jazz gave way to rock as a music of mass popularity the moralists were faced with a puzzle; not only was the new breed of musicians white, but the kids were using more drugs than ever. Moreover, a new element entered the analysis: being a long-haired rock star wearing outrageous clothes was bad enough, but the real red rags to the bullish moral establishment were the money and the adoration surrounding the new stars. Some of these yobbos were millionaires, God damn it, their pictures in every paper, on television, the media hanging on to their every word. These publicity-seeking oiks had to be taken down a peg or two. The trouble was that being a teenage idol was not a criminal offence. Taking illegal drugs, on the other hand, was another matter. Busting musicians serves a number of purposes. First, particularly in an era of general public concern over drug use, musicians are an easy target, handy folk devils for the new moral panic. The *London Evening Standard*, for example, ran part of its story about Boy George and his heroin problem underneath a typical piece of unfounded hysteria about the threat of a 'crack' epidemic hitting London (10 July 1986). In the wake of the Boy George revelations, both Baroness Trumpington from the DHSS and Conservative Party Chairman Norman Tebbit railed against 'junkie' pop stars setting a bad example. Mr Tebbit raised the question of whether known drug-using stars should be banned by the BBC, and voiced the opinion that 'twenty or thirty years ago people were perhaps more permissive' (*Oxford Mail*, 5 July 1986). Not necessarily so; or at least, certainly not Mrs D. Baylis of Noss Mayo near Plymouth. The wheel has turned full circle in Britain since 1967 and the *News of the World*'s first 'shock exposé' of drugs in pop. Mrs Baylis then wrote to the paper saying 'Pop stars should be subjected to a system of tests – like horses and greyhounds – before they go on stage.' (*News of the World*, 26 February 1967).

Musicians are also good copy in the propaganda war against drug users, showing that fame and fortune are no protection against drug problems. Indirectly, the bust is a means of exercising unadmitted social revenge and in default of the Mr Bigs, who are rarely apprehended, nabbing Mr Pop Star ensures the police front-page headlines. Attention is thus diverted from the palpable failure in reducing the numbers of people with drug problems, so that the musician in the dock becomes part of the symbolic fight against drugs in lieu of any significant successes in law enforcement, treatment or prevention.

And of course, there's nothing like a good star bust to keep the newspaper proprietors happy. Whoever gets the scoop can be pompously self-righteous in the editorials, while printing a juicy story to sell thousands more copies. It must be said too that musicians are often their own worst enemies in this respect. This was especially so in the 'hang loose' sixties. As Julie Burchill observed, for Traffic to release 'Hole in My Shoe' with the lines 'I looked in the sky/while an elephant's eye/was looking at me/from a bubblegum tree' was tantamount to writing to the drug squad, 'I use illegal hallucinogenic drugs, please arrest me.' And much the same applied to many of those who churned out 'windmills of your mind' acid imagery.

Musicians tend on occasion to be ludicrously careless. While in England in 1968 recording their first album *Children of the Future,* the Steve Miller Band received a box of chocolates sent through the post and stuffed with marijuana. Attached to this box was a customs officer;

151

the whole band were busted and sent home.

On account of two previous marijuana convictions in 1972 and 1973, Paul McCartney had been denied a Japanese visa on a number of occasions. However, under pressure from music promoters anxious to book Wings, Japanese immigration officials relented and on 16 January 1980, McCartney and the band flew into Tokyo airport. Japanese customs are legendary for their scrutiny of incoming musicians – the police are known to follow them around the streets. McCartney was bound to be a target, but there, lying neatly on top of his luggage, was about seven and a half ounces of marijuana. Nine days later, in a flurry of international publicity, he was deported with the loss of the whole tour, £200,000 to compensate the promoters and a further £100,000 in lawyers and sundry expenses.[1]

Because of their high-media profile, musicians are particularly vulnerable to the vengeful impulses of ex-employees, sacked band members, disgruntled former girlfriends and anyone else wishing to bask in the fall-out from chequebook journalism while sticking the boot in at the same time. The police read newspapers too, and arrests have often followed tabloid exclusives. More sinister, there have been examples where it would appear that a musician has been set up by his management to bring an internal row to a 'satisfactory' conclusion.

On 3 May 1969, Jimi Hendrix landed at Toronto airport *en route* from Detroit. Under normal circumstances baggage at airports is searched by customs and if anything untoward is discovered, the individual is escorted into a side office. But on this occasion the Mounties were waiting. They searched Hendrix's luggage as if they knew what they were looking for, duly found some hash and heroin and then began an interrogation in full public view for maximum effect. A heroin charge was serious; at a time when most musician arrests were for possession of marijuana or LSD, Hendrix was one of the first rock stars to be caught in possession of heroin. Yet he had had no need to take such a risk. In the first place, it was usual for other members of a rock entourage, roadies or road managers, to carry any drugs, as they were less likely to be searched. Second, fans were always thrusting drugs on Hendrix wherever he went.

There was a strong feeling among those close to Hendrix that he had been set up by his manager Mike Jeffrey, who at the time was afraid of losing his hugely successful star to his former co-partner, Chas Chandler. Hendrix had been increasingly unhappy about the way Jeffrey was handling his affairs, but if he became embroiled in a drugs case he would need Jeffrey's help. All talk of leaving would cease. If Hendrix got off, he would be grateful. If not, there was still an awful lot of mileage to be made from a rock star out of circulation. Imagine, for instance, the fees for a comeback tour.

It took nine months for the case to come to trial. Hendrix, who was facing a minimum seven years behind bars, was adamant that he did not know the drugs were there and his defence argued a *mens rea* case ('the guilty mind'). In other words, if Hendrix did not know he was carrying drugs, how could he be found guilty of deliberately intending to possess them, or of having them under his personal control? After deliberating for eight hours, the jury returned a verdict of 'not guilty'.

There is an adage in the entertainments industry that asserts there is no such thing as bad publicity. As far as drug busts are concerned, one could indeed take a cynical view of, for example, the intense publicity in 1986/7 exposing Boy George's drug problems and subsequent recovery. Here was a world-famous pop star who had 'over-exposed' himself to the media, had had a flop record after a string of hits, and disappeared from the public eye. George claimed that concert promoters wouldn't let him tour in Britain because of his recent history (*Sunday People*, 19 April 1987). But his first 'post drug' single, 'Everything I Own', went to number one. Boy George did not become addicted for publicity purposes, but tasty headlines like 'Junkie George Has Eight Weeks to Live' (*Sun*, 3 July 1986) didn't exactly harm his prospects. Or consider the revelations in 1984 that Duran Duran were cocaine-crazy: nicely timed, it seemed, to coincide with their attempt to break into the adult album market and gain acceptance as pukka musicians. Nevertheless, drug busts are usually bad news for musicians; great lengths are taken to avoid close encounters of the unwelcome kind.

Many a European concert itinerary has been planned according to particularly lax border checks. One band employed a private detective to scout around the airports of Europe to ascertain which airport staff would cause the least hassle to the passengers of a private jet landing at some remote spot on the airfield. Other musicians would try and bluff their way through. In his less coherent moments, British r&b star Graham Bond, all eighteen stones of him, would shout at the top of his voice going through customs, 'You won't find any drugs up my arse. You can look, but you won't find any!' But often as not, especially where the most famous musicians are concerned, roadies, personal managers and the like will do the carrying, some willingly, others not so. One road manager says 'I have always refused to carry stuff through customs, although some idiots do it, because they get threatened with the sack if they don't.'[2]

Once convicted, international rock musicians can find themselves denied access to countries like America and Japan and lucrative tours will go by the board. Paul McCartney, John Lennon, Brian Jones, Johnny Rotten and Joe Cocker are just a few of the stars who have been inconvenienced in this way. Joe Cocker was lucky first time around; busted at the height of his fame in December 1968, his girlfriend 'took the rap' and charges against him were dropped. However, as his career slumped, his legal problems grew. In 1972 he was busted in Australia and deported; in 1973 he was arrested on marijuana charges in Sheffield; America threw him out on grounds of illegal entry in 1977 and in 1984 he had his collar felt yet again.

In court, defence lawyers use this limitation on touring in appeals for leniency. In 1980, former Led Zeppelin guitarist Jimmy Page was arrested in London for possessing 198 mg of cocaine. By the time the case came to trial in October 1982 his new band the Firm, with singer Paul Rogers, was being launched with projected tours in America and Japan. The defence QC argued that Page stood to lose millions should he be convicted. Moved by this plea on behalf of Britain's invisible exports, the judge conditionally discharged Jimmy Page for twelve months.

The experience of John Lennon showed how a drug conviction can reverberate down the years. In October 1968, John and Yoko were arrested in Ringo Starr's basement apartment after cannabis resin had been discovered in a police raid. Following the famous Rolling Stones bust of February 1967 (of which more later), it was generally accepted around the pop fraternity that the drug squad had targeted those they regarded as big-mouth pop stars who needed sorting out. Most zealous of the boys in blue at the time was Detective Sergeant Norman 'Nobby' Pilcher, who became the scourge of London's drugs/music scene. Several musicians were on his hit list, including Eric Clapton. In 1967, Pilcher led a raid on Clapton's studio flat in the warren of residencies in the King's Road, populated by artists and known as the Pheasantry. Calling out 'postman, special delivery' into the intercom, Pilcher & Co. burst through the door and up the narrow passageway to cries of 'Where's Eric Clapton? Where's Eric Clapton?' Fortunately for Eric, he was out. In fact, despite all his well-publicized drug problems, Clapton has been busted only once. On 20 March 1968, he was arrested in North Hollywood for possessing marijuana in the company of three members of Buffalo Springfield, including Neil Young. Clapton got off, but not before spending a night in jail wearing prison denims and his pink boots, trying to convince his cellmates, Black Panther members, that he had a genuine interest in American blues.

Lennon had been warned that Pilcher was waiting for an opportunity to pounce, and said that he was especially careful not to have drugs in the flat, particularly as the previous occupant had been Jimi Hendrix. (Lennon claimed he went to some lengths to make sure the place was clean.) So it was hardly surprising that Lennon should allege that the resin which was 'found' had in fact been planted. Although never proved, such action would have been in keeping with some of the more suspect methods of the drugs squad at that time. John Lennon testified in court, 'He [Pilcher] said, "If you cop a plea, I won't get you for obstruction and I'll let your missus go." I thought, "It's a hundred dollars [i.e. the potential fine for pleading guilty], it's no skin off my nose." '[3] Pilcher had arrived mob-handed with forty officers. This led to questions in Parliament about why forty policemen were needed to arrest two unarmed suspects and how come the cameras were there first.

In August 1971, John and Yoko moved to New York, where Lennon began to develop more overt links with radical politics. In December he took part in a benefit concert for John Sinclair at Ann Arbor, Michigan. Sinclair was a radical writer, so-called Minister of Information for the White Panthers (formed in 1968) and manager of a politically-orientated rock 'n' roll band called the MC5. He was a wild enthusiast and serious believer in rock as a political force. He wrote a manifesto to accompany the release of the band's first album *Kick Out the Jams* (1969), in which he declared 'We don't have guns because we have more powerful weapons – direct access to millions of teenagers is one of our most potent and their belief in us is another.' Since the mid-sixties, Sinclair had been under the same kind of police scrutiny in his home town of Detroit as Lennon had been in London. He was told to his face on more than one occasion that it was only a matter of time before they would have him 'banged to rights', as London underworld slang puts it. In July 1969, he was sentenced to an outrageous ten years in prison for selling two marijuana joints to an undercover agent. He continued his political activities in jail, but the MC5 split from him because they decided he was too political, while all they really wanted to do was have a good time. Later they signed to Jon Landau who became Bruce Springsteen's manager and Wayne Kramer, the band's guitarist, was to serve a two-year-sentence for cocaine dealing. Sinclair served two and a half years of his sentence, being released only three days after his benefit concert. The FBI duly noted Lennon's involvement and added this to what became twenty-six pounds of documentation on the ex-Beatle.

Nineteen seventy two was election year in the States and there was genuine paranoia in the Administration that Lennon represented a threat to Nixon's re-election chances. Early in February, Republican Senator Strom Thurmond sent a secret memo to Attorney-General John Mitchell, saying that on the basis of Lennon's publicized plans for anti-Nixon rock rallies, 'if Lennon's visa is terminated, it would be a strategic counter-measure'. At the end of the month, Lennon's work visa expired and his application for permanent residence was turned down by the Immigration and Naturalization Service (INS), on the grounds that Lennon's 1968 drug conviction made him ineligible to remain in the States. As mentioned above, drug convictions can make entry into America very difficult. However, the INS can issue discretionary waivers and many musicians have managed to get their HI (work permit) visas on that basis, including John Lennon. Of course, the INS can go the other way, and under political pressure they began the process of forcing Lennon out of the country. Deportation hearings took place in March, April and May 1972. Meanwhile Lennon appeared in anti-war demonstrations in New York and a benefit concert for a mentally handicapped foundation with Stevie Wonder, Roberta Flack and Sha Na Na. This was Lennon's only properly rehearsed concert between the Beatles' final US tour of 1965 and his death in 1980, and it was a great triumph.

Nixon was re-elected in November 1972 and in the same month, back in England, Norman Pilcher was charged with other officers of 'conspiring to pervert the course of justice'. Lennon's defence team, Leon Wildes and Nathan Lewin, entertained the rather fanciful idea that should Pilcher be found guilty, Lennon's conviction would be overturned – even though the background to Pilcher's trial had nothing to do with the Lennon bust – and the INS case would collapse. Pilcher was in fact convicted, but the judicial process in America rolled on and in March 1973 John Lennon was given sixty days to leave the country, while Yoko Ono was granted permanent residency. Lennon appealed against the decision, claiming (correctly as it transpired), that the US government was using the bust to rid themselves of somebody it found politically undesirable. After a long battle which put an incredible strain on John and Yoko's relationship and sent him on another drug binge, the US Court of Appeal overturned the deportation order on 7 October 1975, and in July 1976 John Lennon got the all-important green permanent resident's card.

Presiding Judge Kaufman had ruled against the INS on a very slender point of law, similar to that invoked in Jimi Hendrix's case. Knowledge and intent are important elements in American drug law. At Lennon's trial in 1968, the prosecution could not actually prove that Lennon had intended to possess a controlled drug, merely that both drug and defendant were found together. While that would have been sufficient grounds for a conviction in Britain at the time, it was not enough for Judge Kaufman. As the charge would not have stuck in America, the

INS had no grounds for denying Lennon his resident's status.

Once a drug case involving a musician comes to court, a judicial *pas de deux* is often played out. The defence leads by saying the accused is fully aware of the dangers of drugs and in the intervening period (usually months), between arrest and trial, the contrite musician has given them up. This can be crucial to staying out of jail, but is more often than not an economic rendering of the truth. It formed part of Hendrix's defence, yet he got totally smashed on his way home from court. Judges and juries like to see humility and deference from those who could buy them out many times over – perhaps a power trip for the common man. A frequent conclusion to musician-centred drug trials is the standard homily delivered from the bench on a pop star's responsibility to society.

An early pop bust was Donovan in July 1966, fined £250 for possessing marijuana and told 'I would like you to bear in mind that you have a great influence on· young people and it behoves you to behave yourself.' Pop stars like to think they *are* influential, but where is the actual evidence that young people copy the behaviour of their idols? For youngsters to take specific drugs because a pop musician does, they would have to know about a part of the musician's private life which the musician is normally anxious to keep secret.

Musicians do not snort cocaine on stage, nor do they smoke marijuana in the streets. The illicit nature of the act necessitates secrecy. In addition, musicians who have a drug problem become notoriously unreliable and can find it difficult to obtain work on a regular basis because nobody will take the risk of hiring them or forming bands with them; concert promoters and record companies may be similarly reluctant.

Occasionally the desire to cover up a drug problem can have tragic consequences. Deep Purple guitarist Tommy Bolin was discovered unconscious in a Miami hotel room and put back to bed in the hope that everything would be all right. It wasn't.

In the mid-seventies David Bowie was as popular as ever. His concerts sold out, the audiences dotted with Bowie clones. His records sold by the truckload, his pictures were pinned to countless bedroom walls. But who, outside the business, knew that the Thin White Duke persona on *Station to Station* (1976) was a reflection of Bowie's coke-fuelled existence in Los Angeles? This was revealed only very recently in the flurry of Bowie biographies and by Bowie himself (*Daily Mirror,* 18 March 1983).

Drug lyrics are often quoted in support of the contention that rock music encourages drug-taking. This is the subject of the following chapter, but it is worth saying here that the evidence is again far from conclusive. A similar judicial observation to that about Donovan's social responsibility to society was delivered to Paul McCartney on the occasion of his fourth marijuana charge in 1984 – he was then a forty-two-year-old with a wife and kids. Drug-taking among young people has far more to do with availability of drugs and peer pressure to try them than with the indulgences of a handful of celebrities. It is the press that publicizes use of drugs by musicians, sometimes going to great lengths to do so, and the busts that often follow press stories further publicize these activities.

To reiterate the point from a more recent example: despite the rumours flying round the business and Fleet Street for months, who would have known about Boy George but for the *Sun* and reporter Nick Ferrari? Once the story broke, everyone was looking for George, including the police. Having tracked him down to Meg Patterson via Richard Branson, they allowed him time to complete his treatment before interviewing him. Peter Bruinvels, Conservative MP for Leicester East, was reported as saying it was 'scandalous' that Boy George should be given what he regarded as special treatment (*Daily Telegraph*, 11 July 1986). What he and other MPs *should* have been querying was the appalling legal precedent of charging somebody with *once having been* in possession of a controlled drug. But as he admitted himself in a Radio One interview, by confessing to 'past possession', Boy George saved himself a long drawn-out court case, which in his vulnerable physical and psychological state he was ill-equipped to endure. Presumably the police needed his co-operation in order to bring charges against those accused of supplying him, including his brother Kevin, who subsequently claimed that he was being made a scapegoat for others. In that same radio interview Boy George stated that all his friends were avoiding him, particularly those involved in drugs. Who could blame them? Once the police latch on to a celebrity drug circle, the net widens; early in October 1986, former Culture Club drummer Jon Moss was arrested on a cocaine charge.

The Boy George saga is the most glaring example of the fact that Fleet Street has rediscovered the news value of pop stars – very reminiscent of the late sixties, and of the days of the most famous and intriguing pop drug bust of them all.

In the wake of Donovan's conviction in July 1966, the *Melody Maker* ran an editorial headlined 'Drugs: Is it true what they say about pop stars?' In contrast to its outburst against drug-taking jazz musicians thirty years earlier, the *Melody Maker* this time came to the defence of the beleaguered pop star: 'It is being insinuated in some quarters that drug-taking is widespread among singers and musicians. As a result, the public are being misled into thinking of pop stars and members of beat groups as being addicts or "junkies". This is dangerous, irresponsible nonsense.' The paper admitted widespread use of marijuana, but denied the prevalence of speed, heroin or cocaine. It followed up in November with its own investigation 'Pot in Pop' (26 November 1966) interviewing, among others, Eric Burdon, Eric Clapton, Zoot Money, Brian Auger and Spencer Davis. Everyone agreed that it went on, but nobody would admit to using marijuana themselves. Chris Britton of the Troggs denied ever coming across anyone who smoked!

However, as far as the *News of the World* was concerned, *it* published the first 'exposé' of drug-addled pop stars. The series (devoid of any byline) started on 29 January 1967 with a piece concentrating on Donovan and the use of LSD. This was hardly news of itself, as Donovan had already been busted several months earlier. Ashley Kozak, Donovan's manager, admitted that the singer's number-one hit 'Sunshine Superman' was about LSD. 'Of course,' said the report, 'to the uninitiated, the words are difficult to follow.' Ironically, with Paul McCartney's revelations about his use of acid only weeks away, the *News of the World* stated, 'The leaders like the Beatles derived their success from sheer native genius. But many others in the pop world needed or sought artificial means to gain recognition.' Ginger Baker said he'd tried everything, Pink Floyd and the Move were implicated in the use of acid (Floyd wrote to the *News of the World* two weeks later vehemently denying this). Also mentioned was a house in suburban Roehampton, to the south west of London, rented by the Moody Blues and allegedly visited by musicians to sample acid and other drugs. Pete Townshend and Mick Jagger were among those named. The paper went on to claim that they had tracked Jagger down to Blaises in Kensington, where he freely admitted using hash. Unfortunately the *News of the World*'s intrepid reporters were talking to Brian Jones, not Mick Jagger. Compared with this monumental blunder the fact that the *News of the World* lads confused hash with LSD in their report hardly warrants a mention!

On 5 February 1967, an incensed Mick Jagger appeared on the Eamonn Andrews show, denying everything and announcing he was going to sue the *News of the World*. Two weeks later, on 19 February, the papers carried a front-page story headlined 'Drug Squad Raids Pop Star's Party'. No names or locations were mentioned. Two points of interest arose from this 'exclusive': first, the *News of the World* reported that, 'acting on a tip-off that one foreign national present at the party might abscond abroad, police have been keeping watch at major sea and airports'; second, just prior to the raid, 'one pop star and his wife drove off and so unwittingly escaped the net'.

The key names were Mick Jagger and Keith Richard and the location was Redlands, Richard's house in West Sussex. Richard decided to throw a select party; later he said he wasn't personally involved in sending out invitations, but the guests were Mick, his girlfriend Marianne Faithfull, art dealer Robert Fraser, photographer Michael Cooper, Christopher Gibbs and George and Patti Harrison. Fraser's servant Ali was there, plus two outsiders: a typical pop hanger-on called Nicky Cramer and a Canadian, David Schneidermann. Schneidermann, the 'foreign national', had won instant entrée as the bearer of all manner of psychedelic drugs, including Orange Sunshine, state-of-the-art LSD, produced by Owsley's protégé Tim Scully and another chemist, Nick Sand. The group arrived at Redlands around 6 p.m. on Sunday 12 February 1967, but the Harrisons left shortly afterwards. About ninety minutes later nineteen police officers, led by Chief Inspector George Dineley, turned up armed with a search warrant issued by a Chichester magistrate. Three policewomen were in the party to search the three women who, according to the tip-off, would be found there – Marianne, Patti and Anita Pallenberg. Schneidermann's attaché case, full of drugs, lay in the middle of the living-room floor, closed but clearly visible. Nevertheless the only guest really worried by the police intrusion was Robert Fraser, who had heroin on him supplied by Richard's main dealer Tony Sanchez, plus some hash and speed tablets.

The house was searched and the guests frisked. The police took away for analysis the 'white powder' found on Fraser, marijuana found on Schneidermann and four amphetamine tablets discovered in Jagger's possession (apparently these had been given to Marianne by a French DJ). Keith Richard was warned that should any of the substances turn out to be marijuana, he would be charged with permitting its use on his premises.[5] The police then left.

As the one facing the most serious charge, Robert Fraser was anxious to find a way to 'fix' the police laboratory analysis. Sanchez claimed that £7,000 would sort it out; the money was passed over, but this did not prevent summonses being issued on 22 March, the hearing being set for 10 May at Chichester Magistrates Court.

The charges were as expected and all three pleaded not guilty. They elected to go for trial by jury and to reserve their defence for then. Meanwhile they were each released on £250 bail. As in the Boy George case, there was a snowball effect: the same day as the three defendants were released, Brian Jones was arrested on charges of possessing hash, cocaine and Methedrine. He too was released on £250 bail.

The Redlands bust trial lasted three days, from 27 to 29 June 1967. Defending counsel for Jagger and Richard was Michael Havers (later Sir Michael, the Attorney General). As his clients had pleaded 'not guilty', Havers had to try and convince the jury that Jagger had got his drugs on the authority of a doctor, even though no written prescription could be produced. In Richard's case, Havers had to show that no marijuana had been smoked on the premises, even though it had been in the possession of certain individuals who were his guests. Robert Fraser had his own counsel who advised him to change his plea to guilty.

The cases against Jagger and Fraser were heard first. Both were found guilty. The judge had directed the jury that the phone call which the defence claimed took place between Jagger and his doctor did not constitute a medical prescription. Sentences were deferred until the case against Keith Richard had been heard.

It was during this part of the proceedings that the full story of the bust came out. The main thrust of the prosecution's case was that Miss X (the worst kept secret in legal history), had been smoking marijuana at Redlands. The press were more interested in the allegation that 'Miss X' had been wearing only a rug when the police arrived, which she deliberately let slip in order to embarrass them. A rumour was also circulating, seemingly at odds with the rug story, that Mick Jagger had been interrupted in the act of devouring a Mars Bar inserted between Miss X's legs.

But things really started to warm up when Keith Richard got into the witness box and alleged that the *News of the World* had planted Schneidermann in order to get Jagger convicted on drugs charges, forcing him to drop proceedings against the paper. Until then Malcolm Morris, prosecuting counsel, had managed to keep Schneidermann's name out of the case. Presumably he did not want the jury influenced by talk of a drugs dealer, detracting from the far lesser offence of which Richard stood accused. The matter of the 'plant' was not pursued, no proof being offered. In his summing-up, the judge instructed the jury to disregard the evidence of Miss X that she hadn't been smoking marijuana. The unanimous verdict was guilty. Richard was sentenced to a year in prison with £500 costs, Jagger three months and £200 costs, Fraser six months and £200 costs.

The sentences of Jagger and Richard prompted the famous *Times* editorial 'Who Breaks a Butterfly on a Wheel' (1 July 1967), claiming that the sentence of Jagger was a reflection of who he was rather than what he had done. Interestingly, Keith Richard was not mentioned in this attack on social revenge, presumably because it would have diluted the argument – Jagger was only 'involved' with some amphetamine tablets, while Richard had been linked to cannabis smoking and was thus less defensible morally. So it was rather ironic that, on appeal, Richard's conviction was quashed whereas Jagger's stood, although the sentence was reduced to a conditional discharge.

Was there any truth in Richard's contention that they had been set up by the *News of the World?* Following the allegation in court, the paper printed an editorial headlined 'A Monstrous Charge' (2 July). It was emphatic that there was no connection with Schneidermann, but admitted that it *did* tip off the police after somebody had phoned the paper on Saturday 11 February and then again at 3 a.m. on the Sunday with details of the party. The police moved in around 7.30 that evening. Obviously there must have been collusion; either the police or the mystery voice reported back to the *News of the World* the salient events of the bust so that the paper had its exclusive story ahead of the rest of Fleet Street.

Apparently, some time after the event, Keith Richard concluded that an employee of his had tipped the *News of the World* off about the party. That works as far as it goes, but the paper had reported that 'a famous pop star' and his wife (Mr and Mrs Harrison) had left before the police arrived. There were no minions present at Redlands who could have passed that information back. Indeed it seems that the police had *expected* Patti Harrison to be one of the three women present, because three policewomen were in on the raid. It is that fact which casts doubt on another theory put forward by ex-Beatles business manager Peter Brown in *The Love You Make:* 'Some newspaper accounts intimated that a famous rock star and his wife were at the house all day, but that the Drug Squad had waited for them to leave before raiding the house. This was assumed to be in deference to Brian Epstein's reputation as well as David Jacobs's expertise as a lawyer.'[6] Apart from the fact that the timing is wrong, how could the police or anyone else know that the Harrisons were going to leave, and what would have happened if they hadn't? Would the police let a headlining raid slip away in order to save the image of the Beatles? Unlikely. As for the expertise of the Beatles' lawyer, the Stones were hardly going to rely on a High Street solicitor should they ever appear in court on any charge, let alone drugs, and the police would know this.

Whoever gave the *News of the World* the tip-off and the follow-up story, must not only have known about the party in advance, but have been there at the time. The hanger-on, Nicky Cramer, had his innocence established after a member of the Stones entourage beat him to a pulp, but failed to elicit any confession from him. This brings us back to the mysterious Schneidermann.

Schneidermann was a Canadian who arrived from the West Coast a few weeks before the party, having met Richard in New York several months previously. Apparently he had a number of passports in different names (one being 'English' or 'Britton'), spoke several languages and knew a lot about guns. He may have *used* the *News of the World,* but he doesn't sound like the average grubby informer out for a quick windfall, particularly as he seems to have had ready access to illicit drugs worth thousands.

Two patently suspicious aspects of the raid were that Schneidermann's briefcase was left untouched by the police and the fact that they let him get away. There was some speculation that he was a CIA agent or something of that ilk. This is unlikely, but for lovers of conspiracy theory, it *is* just possible that Schneidermann was working for the Bureau of Narcotics and Dangerous Drugs in Washington. There is no proof of this theory, merely a hypothesis in the absence of any completely satisfactory explanation of how the bust came about. (A key figure, who could have shed much light on this, refused to give an interview).

From about 1967 onwards, links were established between those police units at Scotland Yard involved in drug arrests and their American counterparts based at the European office of the Bureau of Narcotics and Dangerous Drugs in Paris. The British police had little experience of dealing with the widespread use of illicit drugs which had developed only very recently. In contrast, their American colleagues were well versed in drug enforcement techniques like entrapment, paying informers in drugs by under-declaring the amount seized and using a system of 'licensed' or 'favoured' dealers who were allowed to deal with impunity in exchange for information.

In 1973, as a direct result of using such methods, officers of the Drug Squad including the chief, Vic Kelaher, and Norman Pilcher, found themselves in court on corruption charges. Back in 1968, it is just possible that Schneidermann was used either to demonstrate the value of these tactics or merely as an act of goodwill between two groups of police engaged in specialist activities in a climate of developing mutual interest.

The Redlands bust was the first in a long-running saga of police v. Rolling Stones cases that (if you include the publicity over Bill Wyman's affair with Mandy Smith) seems never to have ended. Brian Jones was rousted by Pilcher on two separate occasions during 1967 and 1968, which did nothing for his disturbed mind. Ronnie Wood was allegedly set up for a cocaine bust on the Netherlands Antilles, but was later released and deported, and Keith Richard, of course, has had any number of run-ins with John Law, the most serious being his 1977 arrest in Toronto – almost ten years to the day after the Redlands bust. Anita Pallenberg was arrested at Toronto airport a few days before the arrest of Richard in his hotel room. At first he faced a charge of being in possession with intent to supply, because of the large amount he was carrying to feed his then enormous habit. Eventually this charge was altered to lesser charges of possession, for which Richard was put on probation and ordered to play a benefit concert for the blind.

The Stones weren't the only victims of media/police collusion in 1967. In San Francisco, the police were out to get the Grateful Dead as much as the London Drug Squad wanted to nail the Stones. On 2 October 1967, acting on a tip-off and with the press primed in advance, eight narcotics officers burst into 710 Ashbury without a warrant and arrested Pigpen, Bob Weir, equipment chief Bob Matthews and managers Rock Scully and Danny Rifkin, on marijuana possession charges. They would have had Jerry Garcia, but somebody in the house had seen him coming up the street, leaned out of the window and waved him away. Next day the band held a press conference and issued the following statement:

As you know by now, the San Francisco Police Department and State narcotics officers invaded this house on Tuesday for the unpeaceful purpose of arresting ten persons on charges of possession of marijuana. We have invited you back to our 'way-out pad', as the *Chronicle* calls it, to discuss the meaning of this action. The arrests were made under a law that classifies smoking marijuana with murder, rape and armed robbery as a 'felony'. Yet almost anyone who has ever studied marijuana seriously and objectively has agreed that, physically and psychologically, marijuana is the least harmful chemical used for pleasure and life-enhancement. It is particularly less harmful than alcohol. But the law continues to treat marijuana smokers as felons. The president of a company that makes a defective automobile which may lead to thousands of deaths and injuries can face a maximum penalty of a minor fine. A person convicted of possession of marijuana can be sentenced to life imprisonment. The real danger to society, as well as to thousands of individuals, comes from a law that is so seriously out of touch with reality.

The law creates a mythical danger and calls it a felony. The people who enforce the law use it almost exclusively against the individuals who threaten their ideas of the way people should look and act. The result is a series of lies and myths that prop each other up. Yet all we wish is to be free Americans – endowed with certain inalienable rights – among which, somebody once said, are life, liberty and the pursuit of happiness. Is this so frightening? The Grateful Dead are people engaged in constructive, creative effort in the musical field, and this house is where we work, as well as our residence. Because the police fear and misinterpret us, our effort is now interrupted as we deal with the consequences of a harassing arrest.

The police missed Phil Lesh and Jerry Garcia in 1967, but they caught up with Lesh in January 1973 and Garcia in March 1973 and again in 1984. By then, Garcia was in difficulties with drugs and he was busted on heroin and cocaine charges. He was ordered to attend a drug rehabilitation programme and play some benefit concerts – which he had been doing for years anyway. Talking to *Musician* in 1985, Garcia said 'I got busted under that new thing where they no longer need "probable cause", just this so-called "good faith". That means they can work backwards from what they find.'[7]

Once the police have grabbed one member of a band, others quickly follow – the Stones in 1967-8, the Grateful Dead in 1973, Boy George and friends in 1986. In 1969-70, it was Jefferson Airplane's turn. Jack Casady, the bass player, was first arrested at the Royal Orleans Hotel in 1969 for possessing marijuana. Some months later, other members of the band were caught in a wave of anti-rock hysteria orchestrated by proto-moral majority groups like MOTOREDE – the Movement To Restore Decency. Par for the course was their claim that rock was a communist plot glorifying 'drugs, destructiveness, revolution and sexual promiscuity'.

In May 1970, Marty Balin was arrested backstage at the Minneapolis Auditorium, along with two members of the road crew, on marijuana charges. He was fined $1,000 and given a one-year suspended sentence in the Minnesota Workhouse. The police had no warrant, but the judge refused query of the seizure by Balin's defending counsel. Four weeks later, Paul Kantner was arrested in Honolulu and later convicted of possessing marijuana. Kantner addressed the court: 'I only want to say the verdict and this court is one of the main reasons people have no faith in the government any more.' He then began to argue that the only evidence against him was a marijuana cigarette which vice squad officers *claimed* they saw him smoking at a private party the previous October. At that point his attorney cut him off.

It is the rock-star drug arrests that make the headlines; apprehended roadies and road managers are far less newsworthy. However, these people are often the main conduits for drugs to pass between suppliers and musicians. They can be involved in negotiating deals, collecting supplies and making payments (creaming some profit off the top), as well as carrying drugs through customs and border checks. Lawyers who specialize in the music business are forever defending cases involving roadies and offensive weapons or excessive violence. Few of these cases make the news. One exception was in November 1983, when Michael Houchin, a former Stones road manager, was arrested in Hollywood for dealing cocaine and weapons from his house.

Those who supply drugs to musicians in order to bathe in reflected glory, to curry favour or to stay on the payroll, can come unstuck. Liam Kelly, a former roadie with Thin Lizzy, was sent to prison for two years in October 1986 for supplying cocaine to the late Phil Lynott, who died the previous January. In his defence, Kelly said he had switched Lynott to cocaine to get him off heroin. However, the only reason he was in court at all was because he had been informed on by members of Lynott's family. The *London Evening Standard* quoted a 'close friend' as saying: 'We were disgusted with what happened to Phil and took action to stop it happening to someone else.'

A similar defence was used in probably the most publicized of all roadie drug trials, involving John 'Scooter' Herring and the Allman Brothers in 1976. Even without the trial, which was eventually to help destroy the band, the Allmans must qualify as one of the most jinxed bands of all time. In 1970, their road manager Twiggs Lydon was up on murder charges. Manager Robert Payne was shot by police in March 1971 and in the same month the whole band was busted in Alabama on drugs charges. Seven months later in October, guitarist Duane Allman was killed in a bike accident in Macon, Georgia. (This was followed by a bizarre damages case in which two women claimed to be Allman's widow.) A year later, on the same stretch of road, Berry Oakley, the bass player, also died in a bike crash. Astonishingly, almost on the same spot where Duane Allman died, drummer Butch Trucks broke his leg in a car crash. In 1975, Gregg Allman's marriage to Cher collapsed in a matter of weeks and guitarist Dickie Betts was arrested on drugs charges.

The balloon went up for Scooter Herring in February 1976, when a pharmacist named Joe Fuchs pleaded guilty to a charge of conspiring to possess cocaine with intent to distribute it, for which he was sentenced to ten years in prison. He named Allman Brothers road manager Scooter Herring as his co-conspirator and struck a deal with the District Attorney that other charges pending against him would be dropped if he co-operated in the case against Herring.

So on 23 June 1976 Scooter Herring appeared before the US District

Court in Macon, Georgia, charged on five counts of supplying drugs to Gregg Allman. He was a motor mechanic by trade, but got the nickname Scooter through his acrobatic skills as a child. It was in early 1973 at the garage where he was working that he first met Gregg Allman who had brought his bike in for repair. Said Herring: 'We got to know each other and became good buddies. Our friendship developed and when you get close to someone, you get to know a lot about them.'[8]

At the time, the Allmans were riding high with *'Ramblin' Man'* at No. 2 in the singles chart and a No. 1 album, *Brothers and Sisters*. But Herring soon discovered that all the street rumours about Gregg Allman's drug habit were true: the guitarist was doing heroin in a big way. Although he had no formal links with the band during 1973, Herring hung around with Allman, savouring his tenuous hold on the romantic world of rock. He became involved with Allman's drug intake, somehow rationalizing that he would be doing Allman a big favour by getting him interested in drugs other than heroin – mainly cocaine, but also other opiate-type drugs. In retrospect, however, he admitted that he was really looking out for himself. 'There was no recognition or prestige in being a mechanic ... I know that maybe I didn't have the right feeling in my heart for Gregg, but it was a good shot to make something of myself.'[9]

If Herring was going to provide Allman with drugs, then he needed a supplier. Joe Fuchs, a local pharmacist, became the Man. Herring and Fuchs met at the same garage when Fuchs brought in his '68 Corvette. Herring sold him a number that here was once-in-a-lifetime opportunity to help out a famous rock star. Although initially reluctant, Fuchs too became intoxicated with the idea of being associated with the rock business. A deal was struck whereby Herring told Fuchs what drugs were needed, Fuchs supplied the drugs to Herring, who conducted the transaction, keeping a third of the money for himself and handing over the rest to Fuchs.

Top of the shopping list was pure pharmaceutical cocaine, supplied in bottles by Merck Sharp and Dohme at $22.50 an ounce and distinguishable from cut-street cocaine by its sparkling, fluffy appearance. The other drugs listed in the indictment were both powerful narcotic analgesic painkillers: Meperdine (marketed as Demerol) and a chemically similar drug, Anileridine (marketed as Leritine). Both were supplied to Gregg Allman in injectable form.

All pharmacies are required to keep records of controlled drugs ordered and dispensed. Therefore Fuchs had to devise ways of covering any shortages, should the Drugs Inspectorate arrive to conduct an audit of his stocks. In June 1973 Herring and Fuchs faked a burglary at the store, carried out by Herring while Fuchs was on a flying trip. Other shortages were to be accounted for by altering or forging doctors' prescriptions. A week later, Fuchs and Herring went to the house of another intermediary, Paul Crawford, and sold him one ounce of pure cocaine for $1,200. This was the first of thirty-five separate transactions between then and January 1975 involving the supply of drugs to Gregg Allman, for which he handed over about $10,000.

Once Allman came to know Fuchs, he started bypassing Herring and dealing directly with the pharmacist. Using a prearranged code, Allman would phone Fuchs at his store, Harrison's Pharmacy on Ingleside Avenue in Macon, either to ask him what was available or to order specific items. Allman would then drive to a particular street, Fuchs would follow in his truck and drop the drugs through the car window. No money changed hands – this was still managed by Scooter Herring. Later, at Herring's insistence, the deal reverted to the original arrangement, ostensibly because Allman was consuming too much when he made the collection himself.

It wasn't until the spring of 1974 that Herring was employed to accompany Gregg Allman on his first solo tour, at a time when relationships within the band were very strained, particularly between Allman and guitarist Dickie Betts. By September, Herring was a road manager with the Allmans' organization and had a one-seventh share in the company which employed him, Great Southern. Other shareholders included the band's office manager Willie Perkins, Phil Walden, Gregg Allman's personal manager and boss of the Allmans' label Capricorn Records, and Bunky Odom, vice president of Phil Walden Associates, the band's management company.

All went well until January 1975, when the Drugs Inspectorate turned up at Harrison's Pharmacy and discovered a number of irregularities in the books. In his trial testimony, the officer who actually conducted the investigation, Ronald Byrd, said that they were acting on an anonymous tip-off that Fuchs was dealing in illegal drugs. So who blew the whistle? This was never established in courts, but at least one prosecution witness had a motive.

Janice Allman had married Gregg in February 1973. An admitted cocaine user herself, she testified against Herring under court immunity about collecting drugs from Fuchs for herself and her husband. It was clear from her testimony that she objected strongly to Herring bringing injectable drugs and needles to the house, and largely blamed Herring for the break-up of their marriage in December 1974 just prior to the exposing of Fuchs' drug activities. She knew that Fuchs and Herring worked together. Obviously if Fuchs went down he would try and take

Herring with him, if by doing so he could lighten his sentence. It also transpired that she had discovered that Herring had tampered with her car to allow carbon monoxide fumes to filter through to the driver's seat. This matter was not pursued in court, but would have been reason enough for Janice Allman to have wished Herring behind bars.

There were other wild cards in the pack, like Bobby Wood. At the time of the trial, he was awaiting sentencing for distributing marijuana and like Fuchs, Janice Allman and Gregg Allman, he testified against Herring under an immunity agreement which protected him from any further charges as a result of the trial. In his testimony, Fuchs said that he stopped supplying drugs to Herring in January 1975, when the Drugs Inspectorate came to call. However Wood said that Herring sold him two grams of cocaine from the Great Southern office in August 1975 and that the money had been paid over to Willie Perkins, the office manager. At the time of the transaction, Wood himself was a Great Southern employee, but testified that he was fired in December that year for dealing in cocaine. Despite the twisted logic of such a decision, Wood was unlikely to appeal to any industrial tribunal, so he took his revenge in court.

What it does show is that Herring had sources of drugs other than Fuchs and he may have been using them in addition to Fuchs prior to January 1975. One of these connections could have made the fateful phone call to take Fuchs out of the game. The names of other ex-employees of Great Southern were mentioned in court as drug dealers and the impression was clearly given that although the case focused on just two grams of cocaine plus some painkillers sold to Allman by Herring, there was an awful lot more going on. The Federal Grand Jury hearings which preceded the trial were not just concerned with the activities of a wayward pharmacist and a glory-seeking motor mechanic. This jury had 'been investigating possible local connections with an alleged multi-million-dollar drug ring'.[10] Witnesses had spoken of a conspiracy to supply drugs to musicians throughout the Southern States of America. At the end of the Herring trial, Judge Wilbur Owens said to Herring – 'Now frankly, the Court is troubled by your case and all of its many ramifications. Without going into specifics, your case involves other cases. You know that, your lawyer knows it and the Court knows it.'

It took the jury of nine women and three men two hours to find Scooter Herring guilty on all five counts. Four weeks later, Judge Owens sentenced him to the maximum of seventy-five years, but said he would review the sentence in three months. During that period, the police and drug enforcement agencies were going to be seeking

Herring's assistance in identifying other dealers. The reviewing of the sentence allowed for a deal to be struck.

The dealer is usually portrayed as the 'evil pusher', while the user is the 'victim'. In this case, however, local public opinion as expressed in the press sided with Herring as the scapegoat who had been forced into supplying drugs by Gregg Allman, the powerful and influential rock star. No doubt then, those who were well disposed towards Scooter Herring would have been pleased with the end of the story. Herring was freed on a bond while appealing against his sentence. Finally, in March 1978, the fifth Circuit Court of Appeal ordered a retrial because of a mistake during the original proceedings by Judge Owens. While the trial was in progress, a front-page story appeared in the *Macon Telegraph* stating that Gregg Allman was being protected by four US Marshals round the clock, because of threats to his life if he took the stand. According to the Court of Appeal, Judge Owens should have examined each juror in the presence of counsel, to determine whether the juror had read the article and whether it had prejudiced him/her against Herring.

After the trial, the Allman Brothers broke up; Allman's testimony against Herring had been the final straw. Dickie Betts formed a band called Great Southern, Allman went solo and the rest formed a fusion band called Sea Level, which Herring was road-managing at the time of the successful appeal.

However, Herring was not yet off the hook; he now had to face a re-trial. But possibly because he had something to sell, Herring waived his rights to a retrial and instead pleaded guilty to the much less serious charges of possessing cocaine and using a commercial facility, i.e. a telephone, to distribute the drug to Gregg Allman. On 14 August 1979 Herring stood before Judge Wilbur Owens who by then had definitely changed his tune about the relative culpability of Allman and Herring. Originally he had dismissed any notion that Herring was a scapegoat or in the thrall of Gregg Allman. Now he regarded Herring as a malleable underling and described Allman's influence over him as 'compelling, powerful and awful'. This *volte face* proved crucial for Herring in the final sentencing. Initially he was looking to die in prison, now he was down to thirty months in jail and five years on probation.

Reflecting on past events to a local reporter from his home town of Macon, Scooter Herring said with some conviction that he bore Gregg Allman no ill will. He was more concerned about looking after himself and his future: 'Sometimes I feel I'm reverting to the same old ways, but I'm fighting it ... I want to hold my head up and be who I've wanted to be for a very long time.'[11]

Despite all the media attention given to musician drug trials and the amount of public deprecation heaped on the offending star by politicians and others, judges have been singularly reluctant to send rock stars to prison for anything more than token periods. There may be a number of reasons for this attitude. Certainly most judges, having admonished a rock star for reneging on his duty to society's young, do not then want to make him a martyr in their eyes by putting him away. Others, for more laudable motives, make a specific point of not being influenced by public opinion baying for blood, nor do they succumb to the temptation of administering an unnecessary custodial sentence to make a moral point to someone in the public eye. Some, however, do seem to become star-struck when faced with anybody who has a public reputation – and defending counsel play on this.

Dennis Muirhead is a lawyer (and now rock manager) with a wealth of experience at representing people in the music business and cites the case of drummer Brian Davison in 1974. Davison had been one of Britain's premier percussionists during his days with Keith Emerson and the Nice, but drug problems overtook him and by 1974 he was in serious difficulties. At that time he was in another rock trio, Refugee, with Patrick Moraz (later in Yes) and his bass-playing partner from Nice days, Lee Jackson. Davison was caught with a pound of cocaine – more than enough for a charge of possession with intent to supply and an almost certain jail sentence. Character witnesses included top rock journalist Chris Welch, the conductor Joseph Eger and the late Tony Stratton-Smith, boss of Refugee's record company Charisma. Albums were flashed around with the drummer's name and face on them and much to everyone's amazement, Davison kept his freedom.[12]

John Phillips of the Mamas and Papas also had a narrow escape. Phillips was a multi-drug user for several years and became a significant dealer in his own right to pay for it all, mainly cocaine, but also many thousands of barbiturates, tranquillizers, narcotic painkillers and methaqualone. Like switching on a light bulb Phillips turned anti-drug crusader as soon as the Drug Enforcement Agency caught up with him. Together with his daughter Mackenzie, who also had a serious habit, they turned up on every TV chat show, blaming everything on drugs. It paid dividends. Instead of eight years, he got thirty days, plus five years' probation and a promise to do 250 hours of anti-drug campaigning in the following year. Hugh Cornwell of the Stranglers was not so lucky – he wasn't nearly so famous, didn't do any breast-beating chat shows or have big guns to speak up for him to dazzle the bench.

Travelling back from a Stranglers gig in Cardiff in November 1979, Cornwell was stopped by a routine police traffic check on Hammersmith

Broadway in West London at about 3 a.m. To the police, the girls travelling with Hugh and Paul Loasby looked under-age. All the occupants were searched and from Hugh the police extracted a gram and a half of cocaine, 90 milligrams of heroin (about one syringe-full), half an ounce of hash and some marijuana. The cocaine was in two separate packets and taken with the other drugs made a total of five counts of possession. Paul Loasby was charged with possessing fifteen milligrammes of coke, a minute amount.

The case was heard at West London Magistrates' Court in January 1980. Both men pleaded guilty and the respective defending counsels went on at length about their previous clean record and impeccable behaviour. The fact that Hugh Cornwell has a degree in biochemistry was mentioned. Unfortunately all this backfired, as the magistrate remarked, 'All this good character stuff makes your behaviour more despicable. You should have known better if you are that intelligent.' Apparently this particular magistrate was usually quite fair, but when a drugs case came before him, something snapped. Loasby got two weeks for an amount of cocaine you could hardly get under your fingernail while Cornwell got two months in Pentonville, of which he served six weeks, fourteen days longer than John Phillips.

Cornwell wrote up his jail experiences in *Inside Information*, published by the Stranglers Information Service in 1980. His account of the stupidities and injustices inherent in the prison system is extremely sharp-witted. The magistrate made it clear that he was out to make an example of Cornwell – 'Young people today look to you for guidance,' were his exact words. And Hugh Cornwell's conclusions? 'If they wanted to teach me a lesson by sending me down, they've failed. They ended up spending £140 a week keeping me in there, whereas they could have made me pay them money which would have crippled me a lot more. Actually, you could even say I benefited from it publicity-wise.'[13]

Coming up to date and at the other end of the drug-possession spectrum, first the American and now the British government have recently launched new drugs enforcement initiatives. These involve the seizure of any money or property from convicted traffickers unless they can prove that it was not obtained through the proceeds of their dealing activities. In British law, as enacted in September 1986, any property obtained up to six years prior to conviction could be confiscated. Similar laws were passed in the States in 1985, under the provisions of the Comprehensive Crime Control Act, and it was the music business that felt the early weight of this landmark legislation.

In September 1985, the Plant Studio in California was impounded by Federal agents after the owner Stanley F. Jacox was arrested on drug-manufacturing charges. The studio shut down for two months and reopened under a contract with the US Marshal's office in San Francisco. This was done to maintain the value of the property and offset the cost of maintaining it pending the trial. Business carried on as usual with Uncle Sam paying the bills. First through the door when it reopened was Carlos Santana. A Deputy US Marshal was quoted as saying, 'The studio is interesting, but we're not experts in the rock 'n' roll business. It's not our line of work.'

What is definitely their line of work is going after dealers, and there could be big problems ahead for musicians in the habit of carrying around large amount of drugs for personal use. Should a charge of possession with intent to supply actually stick, any musician in that position now stands to lose a lot more than a tour of Japan.

11

One Step Over The Line

Name me one rock group that doesn't have in its repertoire hymns to LSD and marijuana.

Timothy Leary

I ask Congress to give thoughtful consideration to legislation entitled appropriately, the Banana and Other Odd Fruit Disclosure and Reporting Act of 1967. The target is those banana-smoking beatniks who seek a make-believe land ... as it is described in the peel puffers' secret psychedelic marching song 'Puff, the Magic Dragon'.

Congressman Thompson of New Jersey
Congressional Record 19.4.1967

Between July 1969 and July 1971, rock suffered its first and arguably most significant losses to drugs. Barbiturates are potentially the most lethal of all mood-altering drugs in both overdose (particularly when mixed with alcohol) and withdrawal (during which users have died of convulsions). It was these drugs that were primarily implicated in the deaths of Brian Jones (3 July 1969), Al Wilson of Canned Heat (3 September 1970) and Jimi Hendrix (18 September 1970).

A few weeks after Hendrix died, Janis Joplin overdosed on heroin mixed with Tequila and Valium. Heroin and booze were also possibly implicated in the most mysterious of all rock deaths, Jim Morrison's on 3 July 1971. Only his wife Pamela and an unidentified doctor saw the body before it was buried in a Paris cemetery. Officially, Morrison died of a heart attack in his bath; retrieval of the body from a bath could also suggest an attempt to revive him from an overdose. Morrison's drinking and to a lesser extent his drug use were legendary. In the event, Pamela Morrison took the secret to her grave. On 24 April 1975, she died of an overdose of heroin.

Together, this spate of major rock deaths, the musician-inspired 'speed kills' campaign, the anti-rock publicity of the post-Altamont period and the rising levels of adolescent drug use fed conveniently into a systematic attempt by the US government to generate public hysteria over heroin. In his twilight years, Anslinger was no doubt proud of his legacy. The impetus for the campaign came from Nelson Rockefeller, Governor of New York State.

At the 1964 Republican convention, Rockefeller was ditched in favour of Barry Goldwater. Thereafter, Rockefeller latched on to the· drug issue as a means of toughening up his law-and-order image with Republican hardliners, while at the same time appealing to moderates by promising a reduction in street crime. His campaign got under way in 1966 and from then till 1973, in the time-honoured tradition of American drug law enforcement, 'the size of the addict population proved to be conveniently flexible.'[1] In New York, the figure swung between 25,000 and 200,000, depending on whether Rockefeller was trying to justify more judges or demonstrating that he had the 'heroin disease' under control. Rockefeller's 'finest hour' came in 1973, with the enactment of the most draconian drug laws ever passed in America. These laws 'made it mandatory that anyone convicted of selling or possessing more than a fraction of an ounce of heroin (or even amphetamine or LSD), would be imprisoned for life'.[2] Life was also mandatory for anyone ingesting a 'hard drug' up to twenty-four hours before committing any one of a whole list of (mainly petty) crimes. The laws proved unworkable and a later evaluation proved that they had virtually no impact in reducing either the level of drug use or crime in New York,[3] but as a political exercise to show that Rockefeller was 'tough on drugs' they served their purpose: under Nixon he became Vice President of the United States. While Rockefeller was preparing the groundwork for his reign of terror against users in New York, the Bureau of Narcotics was undergoing a reorganization. By amalgamating other drug agencies, including Anslinger's office, a Bureau of Narcotics and Dangerous Drugs (BNDD) was created in 1968. That drugs had become a law-and-order issue rather than one focused on revenue, was emphasized by the transferring of responsibility from the Treasury to the Justice Department. Also, much to the chagrin of the customs service, the BNDD was allowed to operate overseas: it was Bureau agents who broke up the 'French Connection' – the Far East– Marseilles–New York trafficking route for heroin.

Under its new director James Ingersoll, the Bureau grew dramatically in strength. Prior to 1968, there were never more than 330 agents on the payroll nor a budget greater than $3 million. By 1971, 1,500 agents were being paid out of a budget in excess of $43 million. Like Rockefeller, Ingersoll had a vested interest in the public regarding drugs as 'public enemy number one' and this inevitably meant massaging the heroin addiction figures upwards. An astonishing jump in the national statistics from 69,000 in 1969 to 560,000 in 1971 was achieved by the simple but fraudulent expedient of calculating a notional figure of those users who did *not* come forward for treatment and presenting this as an accurate count of the numbers of addicts. Congress swallowed it whole and agreed the appropriations.

The third and most crucial factor in the equation was President Richard Nixon. The anti-communist platform on which he had built his reputation in the fifties was on the wane, while much unwelcome attention was being focused on issues like civil rights and the Vietnam War. Once Nixon received the Republican nomination for President in 1968, he took his cue from Rockefeller and made the 'war against drugs' the key issue on which to fight the election. But what started out as a law-and-order electioneering strategy become something very different once Nixon took office in 1969. Gradually, under the guise of an unimpeachable battle against a social evil, the White House laid the foundations for acceptance by the people of a new all-powerful internal enforcement agency operating almost entirely outside the constitution. This evolved into the Office of Drug Abuse Law Enforcement (ODALE), established by Nixon in January 1972 without consideration or approval by Congress. The hope was that nobody would dare oppose Nixon for fear of being branded 'soft on drugs', an act of political suicide for any politician anywhere in the world. (ODALE and BNDD were both subsumed in July 1973 in a new superagency, the Drug Enforcement Administration, which remains the major American agency for drugs law enforcement both at home and abroad. Probably only Watergate prevented the DEA becoming Nixon's personal shock troops.) As soon as he was installed in the White House, Nixon immediately sought the help of the media in putting his message across, especially to young people. A special meeting was called of the country's leading disc jockeys; among those who attended were Murray the K and Cousin Brucie Morrow. The reception of some DJs was decidedly lukewarm, seriously doubting whether they could exert any influence over young people other than perhaps their listening habits. Others, however, like Bruce Morrow, became ardent enthusiasts. He began working with the National Institute of Mental Health, touring around schools to speak out against drugs. WWRL, a black soul station in New York, flooded Harlem with 'Help a Junkie – Bust a Pusher' badges; WKYC in Cleveland went on the air with a recorded suicide note from a nineteen-year-old addict, which WFMJ in Youngstown, Ohio, distributed around the schools, and there were similar radio campaigns from coast to coast. However, the Administration had been putting most of its anti-drug campaigning efforts into television advertising, slots in chat shows, etc. This upset the National Association of FM Broadcasters, who wrote complaining to the President that as broadcasters of rock music, FM radio stations could play a particular role in spreading the anti-drug message.

What happened next, began a process of claim and counter-claim which rumbled through the US justice system for three years. The Federal Communications Commission (FCC) is the government's broadcasting licensing body. On the 10 September 1970, FCC commissioner Robert Lee sent a note to Senator Frank Moss with a list of songs 'that would appear to be eulogizing the use of narcotics'. The list was apparently produced by an advertising agency and 'does not have any government sanction'. The list of songs was as follows:

'Happiness is a Warm Gun'	Beatles
'Everybody's Got Something to Hide Except Me and My Monkey'	Beatles
'With a Little Help from My Friends'	Beatles
'Cold Turkey'	Plastic Ono Band
'19th Nervous Breakdown'	Rolling Stones
'Let's Spend the Night Together'	Rolling Stones
'Don't Bogart That Joint'	Fraternity of Man
'White Rabbit'	Jefferson Airplane
'The Acid Queen'	Who
'Mr Tambourine Man'	Byrds
'Rainy Day Women'	Bob Dylan
'Cocaine Blues'	Johnny Cash
'The Trip'	Donovan
'Cloud Nine'	Temptations
'I Like Marijuana'	David Peel and the Lower East Side
'The Alphabet Song'	David Peel and the Lower East Side
'Walking in Space'	cast of *Hair*
'Heroin'	Velvet Underground

Each song title was accompanied by some indication of how successful

177

the song had been, plus sample lyrics. It is a curious list, to say the least, ranging from the obvious pro-drug material like David Peel's songs and 'The Trip' by Donovan, to the equally obvious anti-drug songs like 'Cocaine Blues' and 'Cold Turkey'. Note, too, the legalistic and pejorative use of the term 'narcotics' in Lee's note to Senator Moss referring in part to drugs which have no narcotic action.

Four days later, Vice President Spiro Agnew, speaking at a Republican dinner in Las Vegas, criticized rock-music lyrics for glamorizing and promoting drug use, citing all the songs from the list which had 'no government sanction'. In what seemed like an answer to the FM Broadcasters' complaint, Agnew went on to suggest that television had a far greater role in drug reform than radio could ever have. Perhaps too the powerful pharmaceutical industry lobby had been at work, as the speech coincided with the leaking of new National Association of Broadcasting guidelines aimed at curbing the exaggerated claims of non-prescription drug advertisements.

Surprisingly, the initial counterblast to Agnew's speech came not from the radio bosses, but from a dissenting voice within the FCC itself. In a speech before foreign service officers of the US Information Service, Commissioner Nick Johnson cited several other songs like 'Amphetamine Annie' by Canned Heat and 'The Pusher' by Steppenwolf as examples of anti-drug messages in rock. He went on to attack television for promoting alcohol and prescription drug misuse and further noted that Agnew refrained from attacking those whose support was important at election time, like the beverage alcohol industry and other large corporations like Ford and TWA who were at the time using the imagery of illegal drugs in their advertising.[4] Finally, Johnson rounded on the tobacco industry: 'There are a lot of kids who are being exposed to drugs because of the deliberate efforts of greedy immoral television and tobacco company executives to hook 'em on nicotine – executives who are revered as the pillars of our society and whose activities are sanctioned by the Federal Government – than there are those who get pot "with a little help from their friends".'[5]

The presidential campaign moved up a gear when seventy radio station owners and managers were called to the White House on 14 October 1970 for a carefully stage-managed conference 'to urge increased drug education programming and to curb pro-drug music and jargon of disc jockeys'.[6] To add weight to the conference, Dean Burch, chairman of the FCC, agreed to speak. Burch opened the proceedings by suggesting the FCC would look favourably on licensees who provided more airtime for anti-drug commercials. Nothing was said about the FCC's attitude towards those it felt were promoting drug use by playing certain records. For the rest of the day, the station managers were treated to the same show put on for the TV producers six months earlier – shock films, sniffer-dog demonstrations and a display of law enforcement techniques. As before, John Ehrlichman, presidential adviser on domestic affairs, announced dramatically at lunchtime that the dogs had actually discovered some marijuana during the demonstration. And again as before, Nixon addressed the meeting, not as part of the officially announced programme, but as if it was an eleventh-hour decision on the part of the President himself to grant the station bosses a special audience to emphasize the importance of his mission. Said Nixon (in apparent contradiction of his Vice President), 'No one is in a better position than you to warn our youth constantly against the dangers of drugs.'[7]

Nixon's Presidential adviser on Federal law enforcement and internal security, Egil Krogh, had told Nixon that there would be no press coverage of his remarks to the conference. However, *Billboard* magazine reported that Nixon had urged the broadcasters to screen the lyrics of all rock records to ensure that no songs favourable to drug use were given air time.[8] In the light of subsequent events, it was highly significant that Nixon should add that although the government (through the FCC) were the broadcasting licensers, it would never become involved in the programming content of a station.

The next step in the 'war' against drugs and rock came from within the music business itself. Early in November, Mike Curb, President of MGM Records, announced that eighteen allegedly drug-orientated bands were being dropped by the label. 'I'm not looking to go on a witchhunt,' said Curb, 'and we are not asking any acts to roll up their sleeves [but] MGM will not be used to further the use of drugs.' Curb was also seeking the support of broadcasters to ban songs with drug-related lyrics. Nixon praised Curb's actions, as did some record-company bosses. Others were more sceptical of Curb's motives: Gil Friesen, Vice President at A&M, and Columbia Records boss Clive Davis both accused Curb of exploiting recent rock-star deaths and making a 'grandstand play', as Davis put it, to rid MGM of unprofitable acts. And there is a deal of substance to this allegation.

Back in the late sixties, MGM tried to cash in on the San Francisco sound by trying to hype Boston as the new rock capital of America. They spent around $4m launching the 'Bosstown Sound' with a bunch of local no-hopers like Beacon St Union, Chameleon Church, Orpheus, Puff, Kangaroo and the marginally better Ultimate Spinach. The project was a disaster; MGM sacked the whole A&R department and brought in Mike Curb to try and salvage something from the mess. Curb was in favour of a new breed of record company for the seventies. Rock was getting a bad name after the 'anything goes' sixties and many of the true company hedonists of that period found themselves on the streets. Too many people were stoned and self-absorbed and spending company money as their own. Curb's move against drugs was thus partly symbolic of a new mood of austerity within the business which rebelled against excess and overindulgence. MGM lost a reported $18 million in 1968–9; Curb's job was to put that right. Eric Burdon was one MGM artist who was not dropped, despite the release of drug-related songs like 'Girl from Sandoz' and 'San Francisco Nights'. Truth was, Burdon was still a good earner for MGM and his retention is perhaps the best indicator that Curb's motives were financial rather than moral. Eric, on the other hand, was supposed to be somewhat insulted that he was not considered druggy enough to be dropped. Burdon eventually did leave MGM, which became a label for good, clean family acts like the Cowsills and the Osmonds. Yet despite paring down the roster of artists, the company barely broke even in 1970 and 1971. Curb was the last President of MGM before it was sold to Polygram. Quite possibly, he had one eye on his political career in supporting Nixon's drug campaign: when he finally left MGM in 1973 he became Reagan's right-hand man in California, as Lieutenant Governor of the State.

As well as criticizing Mike Curb, Clive Davis led a spirited defence of the music industry, flatly denying that rock music encouraged drug-taking: 'Music is a reflection of a culture – a footnote to the events within a society.'[9] He was supported in this view by Dr David Smith, medical director of the Haight-Ashbury clinic, who explained in a *Billboard* article how much rock bands had done to raise finds for his clinic, and then went on to say: 'I consider the current attack on youth culture and rock lyrics as not being an expression of concern over the tremendous problem of drug abuse [but] a political tactic, playing off the hysteria of the dominant culture in this area.'[10]

But the White House was not going to be diverted from its course by minor inconveniences such as the total lack of empirical evidence of a causal link between rock music and drug-taking. Nixon's special plead-ing to the radio station owners and the presence of the FCC Chairman at the same meeting, were the warning lights that sooner or later the question of stations playing 'drug songs' would become a licensing issue.

Sure enough, on 5 April 1971 the FCC issued a Public Notice which it claimed resulted from the receipt of a 'number of complaints' about the lyrics of some records being played on the radio. The FCC required stations to pre-screen all records before playing them on the air, work out what the lyrics meant and determine whether or not it would be in the 'public interest' to play the record. There was no further explanation of phrases like 'language tending to promote or glorify' drug use, nor was it at all clear how far stations should go in making 'reasonable efforts' to determine lyrics and their meaning. The sting in the tail, however, was unmistakable. Failure to adhere to these nebulous, ill-defined guidelines, would 'raise serious questions as to whether continued operation of the station is in the public interest'. So much for presidential reassurances about non-interference. One has only to remember the list of songs sent by the FCC Commissioner to Senator Moss, to realize that the FCC had a very clear idea as to which songs it regarded as unacceptable (i.e. *any* song that mentioned drugs). However, it saw fit not to relay this to those who depended on FCC licences for their livelihood.

There were many appeals for the FCC to reconsider its position and on 16 April the Commission issued what it called a Memorandum Opinion and Order. The FCC reiterated that it was not trying to censor radio playlists, merely that station owners should know whether or not any song tended to glorify drug use and if it did, make a decision against playing it. Again, requests that licensees should act 'reasonably' and in 'good faith' went unexplained.

Attached to the original Public Notice in March, came a highly publicized minority statement by Commissioner Nick Johnson, who had previously attacked Vice President Agnew. Johnson called the FCC Notice 'a brazen censorship move' which breached the First Amendment of the Constitution on Freedom of Speech and threatened the livelihood of radio station employees. He pointed to all the songs which glamorize drinking and again emphasized the heavy advertising of non-prescription drugs on television. In all this, Johnson saw a thinly veiled attempt by the Nixon Administration to attack the anti-establishment stance of American youth culture through its music and divert attention away from the real social evils of the day – racial prejudice, unemployment, poverty, urban decay, the Vietnam War and so on. He cogently argued that to expect licensees accurately to decipher which songs were pro- or anti-drug (or neutral), was ridiculous, particularly as the FCC refused to define its terms sufficiently. He made the obvious deduction that no licensee was going to risk getting it wrong, which meant that any drug song was likely to be banned from the airwaves; by any definition this was censorship. Undeterred, the FCC issued a second memorandum on 18 August 1971 refusing to clarify previous statements, on the basis that a fuller explanation 'would not appear to be useful'.

How did the music industry itself react to the rubics from the FCC?

As *Rolling Stone* succinctly put it, 'Rock stations, AM and FM are scared shitless.'[11] One of the first songs to suffer was Brewer and Shipley's 'One Toke over the Line'. Jeff Kaye, programme director of WKBW in Buffalo, told *Rolling Stone*, 'I frankly didn't know what "toke" was. So we did a street survey and 90% of the kids said it had to do with marijuana.' So just as the song was beginning to climb the charts, it was dropped by WKBW and several other Top 40 stations, along with 'White Rabbit', 'DOA' (Bloodrock), 'Monkey Man' (Stones) and 'Eight Miles High' (Byrds). WDAS-FM in Philadelphia also reacted swiftly by dropping 'I am the Walrus', 'Let It Bleed', 'One Toke over the Line', 'Small Circle of Friends' and 'Needle and Spoon' (Savoy Brown). A major row broke out at WDAS-FM. One DJ, Steve Leon, defied the order and played a number of drug songs on a particular show. His brother-in-law, Station Manager Robert Klein, pulled the plug on him. Leon stormed into his office, dangled his privates in Klein's face, and got fired.

By not giving clear guidance the FCC were in fact playing a very clever game which attacked rock music in general, not just drug songs, because of the very subjective nature of song lyrics. As Commissioner Johnson predicted, no station boss was going to take chances with the station's licence. Therefore any song, whether containing intentional drug references or not, was liable to be axed. A song with the word 'high' or 'trip' in it, was an obvious target; station managers relied heavily on second-hand knowledge of drug slang to make decisions on records where they themselves were often completely ignorant. One owner banned *all* Bob Dylan songs because he couldn't understand any of the lyrics, and there were demands that lyric sheets be included in every album.

The FCC also relied on the fact that should any station take the FCC to court, even if the station won, it could be crippled by legal costs, absence of staff while giving evidence, and so on. However, a number of stations and individual DJs did decide to pursue the matter through the courts, represented free of charge by an ex-aide of Commissioner Johnson, Tracy Western. She declared to *Rolling Stone*: 'This is an insidious and underhand form of censorship, because the FCC has not had to guts to come out and say what they really mean. They are trying to scare private stations into doing censorship themselves and avoid the rap.'[12]

From the US District Court, the petitioners went to the Court of Appeal in March 1972. They accused the FCC of devising a policy that was deliberately vague and unconstitutional. Furthermore, based on affidavits received from many station, they set out to prove that the policy was unworkable. Specifically they stated:

1   With most stations having libraries of up to 7,000 albums and receiving around 200 new albums a week, it was impossible to expect DJs to listen to every lyric on every record before playing it.
2   The lyrics of many modern songs were indecipherable.
3   Where the lyrics could be understood or were printed, there was still the job of determining meaning.
4   Having done that, the licensees still had to decide whether or not the lyric actually promoted or glorified drug use.

The petitioners also asked the Court of Appeal to rule on the FCC's refusal to adjudge whether or not the uncensored musical programming of Yale Broadcasting Station, WYBC, would pass muster with the Commission. The station had actually asked the FCC to check its playlist, as a way of forcing it to issue specific instructions, rather than vaguely worded notices.

In January 1973, a three-judge panel upheld the FCC policy of requiring licensees to screen lyrics prior to broadcast and threw out any claims that the wording was vague and an infringement of free speech. The Court said the first Public Notice was confusing, but ruled that the follow-up Memorandum clarified the issue. The Court was of the opinion that the FCC were merely requesting licensees to be aware of the drug situation and know what they were putting on air and could see no threat, implicit or explicit, not to renew licences. They further made the point that if a lyric was completely indecipherable, it was largely irrelevant as to its subject matter and would therefore fall outside the Commission's ambit. All that was required of a licensee was that he should know what he was allowing to be broadcast.

However, the story did not end there; while Tracy Western was planning an appeal to the Supreme Court, the Chief Appeal Court Judge, David L. Bazelon, in an unprecedented action, issued a warning, calling into question the legitimacy of the FCC policy on drug lyrics. The judge wanted the case reheard by the full nine-member Appeal Court, saying the case raised many questions about censorship and possible political pressure on broadcasters. He disagreed with his fellow jurists that there was no implicit threat in the FCC pronouncements and felt particularly strongly that the court had dismissed the fears of broadcasters simply because nobody had yet lost their licence over the issue. Judge Bazelon went public with his views after failing to secure another hearing.

The broadcasters used Judge Bazelon's published opinions in their own submission to the Supreme Court in May 1973, that FCC policy contravened the First Amendment of the American Constitution. However, in a seven to two vote the following October, the Supreme Court refused to review FCC policy on drug lyrics. Of the two dissenting votes, Judge Douglas was particularly critical of the majority verdict: 'The Government cannot, consistent with the First Amendment, require a broadcaster to censor its music any more than it can require a newspaper to censor the stories of its reporters. Under our system, the government is not to decide what messages, spoken or in music, are of the proper "social value" to reach the people.'[13]

FCC policy on rock and drug songs was based on the generally accepted premise that listening to such songs directly affects the decision of young people to use illegal drugs. What about songs like 'Lucy in the Sky with Diamonds' or 'Purple Haze'? Surely this is all the proof that is required to demonstrate the role of idolized pop stars in glorifying and encouraging teenage drug abuse. Certainly the argument seems very persuasive. Here you have the world's most popular rock musicians singing favourably, it seems, about the psychedelic experience at a time of increasing drug use among those most heavily committed to rock music.

But this casual link has yet to be established, something neither the White House nor the FCC attempted, presumably because the readiness of the public to assume such a link existed was all that was required for the Government's political purposes. In fact, a number of independent studies have been carried out and they all come to the same conclusion, that there is no empirical evidence to indicate that a pro-drug message will promote drug use among those who hear it.[14] If any link does exist it is probably symbiotic rather than casual, and even then it is probably confined to situations where the social environment is an important part of the drug experience, such as in the smoking of marijuana.

In 1977–8, a study was conducted to discover the facts about the 'Woodstock Generation's' drug use ten years previously. Forty-three per cent of the 1,000-person sample believed that much of the music of the sixties could only really be understood by those who had gone through the drug experience. The majority stated that their initial marijuana cigarette had been in the college dorm with a group of friends, with Dylan or Led Zeppelin playing in the background.[15]

Sociologist John Auld has tried to explain the interaction between music and drugs in this very common type of social setting. He has described how the suspension of normal communication in marijuana-smoking groups together with the redirection of attention to expected changes of mood, creates a 'space' for introspective concentration on the music that would otherwise be regarded as bad manners. In return, the music provided a focus and rationale for such introspection. The smoker is thus saved the embarrassment of sitting in strained silence with a group of other smokers waiting for something to happen.

As I stated earlier, marijuana smoking does appear to be a learned behaviour; among young smokers in any given group, the majority will be uncertain as to how they are supposed to react or how they appear to the supposedly 'drug-sharpened' perceptions of their friends. In this scenario, the relationship between drugs and music is symbiotic – interdependent elements giving the listener-user 'permission' to exist outside normal goal-orientated behaviour and thus the normal social pressures. And of course the music could be entirely instrumental or with minimum lyrical content or with lyrics which have nothing to do with drugs. Furthermore, in a truly symbiotic relationship, one could equally argue that drug-taking encourages people to listen to rock music!

Another fault in the anti-rock argument was the assumption that all rock songs about drugs project a favourable image, a point raised by Commissioner Johnson and others in defence of the industry.

A study conducted in 1972[16] examined the lyrics of several songs and classified them as pro, anti, descriptive or conjectural. This last meant that there were no explicit drug references, but interpretations had been imposed on the song (e.g. 'Lucy in the Sky with Diamonds'). (There were also categories for 'Alcohol' and 'Drugs' – not included here.) The results were as follows:

	Pro	Anti	Descriptive	Conjectural
Marijuana	43	7	29	21
Heroin	0	67	23	10
Cocaine	11	50	35	4
LSD	16	16	34	33
Amphetamines	1	4	3	1

What the lyrics of many of these songs showed was that they reflected the personal experiences of the singer whose opinions about drugs were not necessarily consistent. Country Joe McDonald, for example, could write songs like 'Bass Strings' which was obviously favourable to LSD, but also 'Here We Go Again' with the lines, 'Crystal got my woman/ dope's driving her insane/she used to be so pretty/Now she can't remember her name.'

Dion, who had a string of hits in the sixties including 'Runaround Sue' and 'The Wanderer' acquired a bad drug habit as his career began to decline. Coming out the other side he found religion and recorded 'Your Own Backyard', probably the most personal and straightforward song about drug problems ever released:

> Since I've been straight
> I haven't been in my cups
> I'm not shooting downs
> I'm not using ups
> You know I'm still crazy as a loon
> Even though I don't run out and cop a spoon
> Thank the Lord I've had enough.

Songs like this, Neil Young's 'Needle and the Damage Done' or James Brown's 'Heroin' are often meant to serve as anti-drug warnings as well as personal statements. All that can be said about them is that they prove the existence of anti-drug songs in popular music. There is no evidence whatsoever that they are any more effective in warning young people off drugs than pro-drug songs are in encouraging experimentation.[17] The truth is that no form of drug education, be it pop song, TV advertisement, poster campaign, shock film or pure information-giving, has ever been shown to be more or less effective in preventing drug misuse than any other. Take the shock film for example, much-loved by drug squad officers going into schools: those who will be genuinely shocked probably wouldn't try drugs anyway, while for some kids the dangers involved in drug-taking are precisely what makes it attractive. And for those who are tempted but put off by seeing a film, how much impact does it have three weeks later? How many people give up smoking for good after seeing an isolated documentary about lung cancer?

By now the issue of whether rock encourages drug-taking should be dead and buried. However, the recent emergence of 'moral-majority' style anti-drug parent groups in America has brought the whole debate back on to centre stage. The National Federation of Parents for Drug Free Life wants to force record companies to print all song lyrics on the record sleeves 'so parents will know the glamorization of the drug culture that some music represents'. Already some companies are feeling pressured enough to put stickers on records warning about the lyrical content, in much the same way as films are rated.[18] The American Parents Music Resource Centre wants to 'clamp down' on subversive pop. In support of their crusade, they use a paper called 'The

Hurried Child' by David Elkind, a professor of child studies at Tufts University, Massachussetts. The following interpretations are seriously proposed by Professor Elkind:

'Hey Jude':
> Jude is the Judas who betrayed Christ under the guise of friendship. Heroin at first seems a friend until it betrays the user. McCartney's song 'let her into your heart' means the drug.

'Bridge Over Troubled Waters':
> [Elkind claimed that in a survey of teenagers, 15% thought the narrator was a drug pusher] Silver girl is slang for the hypodermic and the line 'your time has come to shine' clearly suggests a drug trip. 'If you need a friend/I am sailing just behind', indicates that the pusher is always there when another fix is needed.

These are only more extreme examples of what is still a generally accepted viewpoint.[19] In the final analysis, it's all in the ears of the listener. Perhaps the best example of that comes from the pages of America's bible of the drug subculture *High Times*. The author of an article in the August 1982 issue was at a party where some premium-grade marijuana was being passed around and the subject of 'great songs of the dope culture' came up. The question was posed: 'What is the ultimate dope song, the single song that best captures the spirit and soul of the smoker?' The list of songs to choose from could be long indeed, but the author finally picked on a song which has no drug references in it whatsoever. He cast his mind back to a marijuana 'safe house' in Greenwich Village, where people could smoke the finest Colombian Gold. The proprietor of this 'den' played one song over and over again until the grooves wore out and an assistant was sent to buy another copy. The song was an old Elmore James number made famous by Eric Clapton called 'Key to the Highway'. The author, pseudonamed 'K', was enamoured of this song not for any super subliminal messages about the drugs experience, but because 'that song has an undeniable appeal to a certain type of personality attracted to outlaw, adventurist intrigue ... the true all-time inside smuggler song. What it's really about is moving. It's a classic road song. A driving song. A-driving-long-distances-for-forty-eight-hours-with-a-truck-full-of-trouble-if-you're-ever-stopped song. Majestic.'

12

Redder Than Red

Whereas jazz and rock often reflect an amphetamine frenzy,
reggae tunes in to the slowness of ganja.

New Statesman, 8 July 1977

... you can dance with ganja rock/grab your chance with ganja
rock/jump and prance with ganja rock...

'Ganja Rock', Benjamin Zephaniah

The significance of ganja in Jamaica is not simply a matter of the
massive financial worth of the crop. It is as much a question of who
controls that money and what cultural significance the plant
possesses on the island.

Tim Maylon, *Big Deal: The Politics of the
Illicit Drugs Business*

It is always a dangerous game to credit any popular protest music with
the capacity to propose serious political alternatives to the situation
about which it is protesting, let alone actively to promote tangible
change. More than most protest music, reggae has been over-
romanticized in this way by gushing white journalists at the height of
Bob Marley's fame (and in subsequent deifications), without making
sufficient distinction between those artists who protested from the solid
foundation of an organized philosophical or political structure (like
Rastafari) and those who were merely 'bandwaggoning' as Rasta
saxophonist Cedric Brooks put it. Writing in the *Kingston Daily Times*
(27 March 1977), Trevor Fearon stated that distinctions had to be made
between 'political protest' and 'social reportage' and pointed up the
lack of principle among singers who cease to protest once their own
place in the system has been improved by a successful career in music.

188

However, given these caveats, reggae did become the strident voice of Jamaica's impoverished majority, venting in 'dread songs' the cultural predicament of a country caught between poverty and a lack of national identity born of years of imperial control. Reggae attempts to resolve this predicament with anthems to the beliefs of Rastafari, the vision of the black redeemer and the Back to Africa Movement, and with public protest against political violence, poverty and hunger, the duplicity of politicians in the pocket of Jamaica's ruling families and the Americans, police harassment and the laws against marijuana or ganja.

The relationship between ganja and reggae is probably the most complex drugs–music nexus to be discussed in this book, going beyond the *prima facie* interreaction between a musician and drugs to encompass many of the significant events of Jamaica's cultural, political and religious history. The first point to make is that ganja is neither reggae-nor even Rasta-specific; it was introduced into Jamaica around 1845 by indentured East Indian workers brought in to work on the sugar-cane plantations which had lain mostly idle since the abolition of slavery in 1830. The etymology is a little confused, but ganja is a Hindi word possibly derived from bhang or bhanga, the common word for marijuana in India. Other Hindi words which have become part of the lexicon of ganja include chillum (the pipe used for smoking ganja) and kali (a variety of ganja, nowadays rendered as colley or colly). The term ganja itself is now so closely associated with Jamaica that it has become enshrined in the language of Jamaica's drug legislation.

Together with their labour and language, the workers brought with them the cultural baggage of centuries of ganja use among India's rural communities. Ganja rapidly diffused into Jamaica's black working class where it has remained endemic ever since. Studies carried out in the seventies estimated that between 60% and 70% of the population used ganja in one form or another.

Like opium in nineteenth-century England, ganja became something of a universal panacea in working-class culture. Either smoked, drunk as tea, cooked in food or applied as a poultice, ganja is a multi-purpose drug – social relaxant, an aid to work, to sleep, to calming fractious infants and (according to one seventeen-year-old interviewed in a study) to success in sex and cricket.

To complete the 'ganja vision', it constitutes an important vehicle for the rites of passage of male adolescents and is, of course, the sacred herb of Rastafari. The hallucinatory effects of ganja are not usually sought by working people, who tend to eschew its hedonistic functions in favour of social and practical uses. Among Jamaica's middle classes, smoking ganja is very much frowned upon, associated as it is with the unruly mob of 'violent' Rastas. Discrete sipping of ganja tea behind closed doors is more acceptable, but among the young well-to-do smoking ganja has the vicarious thrill of the forbidden. Divorced from the long-standing cultural context of ganja in Jamaica, these sophisticates look more to the American experience of the drug which is almost entirely hedonistic; for them, 'getting out of it' is the key to the whole adventure.

History is replete with examples of how the authorities respond punitively to the use of a certain drug by working people where it is seen either to be a debilitating agent undermining the efficient working of the labour force or as a threat to law and order. In this the colonial power in Jamaica was no exception; as early as 1913 Jamaica had anti-ganja laws on its statute book, making it one of the first countries to do so and beginning an internal process whereby increased penalties for ganja possession, sale or cultivation followed hard on the heels of any explosion of social or political dissent. In the words of one academic: 'Outlawing a popular custom is also a very convenient control device. The ganja legislation in Jamaica is very clearly like the legislation against illegitimate children or against obeah, a particular form of lower-class religion. It can be used by the elite to control the lower classes with no loss in world opinion.'[1]

In 1937, the Jamaican government was bombarded by propaganda from Washington to promote America's Marijuana Tax Act. At the time Jamaica was in deep economic depression and there were many bloody encounters between workers and police, the most serious being the sugar-cane cutters' strike. On the premise that the troubles were inspired by a psychopathic minority driven crazy by ganja, in 1941 the government revised its 1924 Dangerous Drugs Law and introduced mandatory imprisonment for any first ganja conviction under the law. As the Rastafari movement grew in strength from this time on, the so-called 'mad few' and the Rastas became as one in the eyes of the authorities and so the war against ganja became synonymous with the war against Rastafari.

Out of the protests of 1937-8 came the Jamaican trade union movement, and from the two largest trade unions evolved the two political parties which have dominated the country ever since: the Jamaica Labour Party (JLP) founded by Alexander Bustamante, representing middle-class business interests, and Norman Manley's People's National Party (PNP), which gleaned most of its support from Jamaica's urban and rural poor. In 1960, following an abortive Rasta-inspired uprising led by the Reverend Claudius Henry and his son Ronald, a Detention Powers Bill was passed providing for the detention of

190

suspects without trial. The laws against ganja were further tightened as a means of clamping down on the Rastas, who were increasingly viewed by the middle class as the vanguard of revolutionary conspiracy. The PNP were in power at the time and were, ironically, condemned by the JLP for failing to present any evidence to support their allegations of a link between ganja and crime. Ironic, because when the JLP took office in 1963, penalties were increased still further in the wake of unrest following independence in 1962. Arrests for possession shot up by 300% through the sixties as political violence increased. It wasn't until the PNP regained control in the early seventies that fines replaced imprisonment for a first offence.

In 1974, Norman Manley's son, Michael, now leader of the PNP and Prime Minister of the day, brought in the Drug Enforcement Administration to try to end the ganja trade with America. Violence on the island had escalated to unacceptable levels as a consequence of the ganja-for-guns business that had been going on between the two countries. The purpose of Operation Buccaneer was a top-to-bottom assault on everyone from the farmers in the hills to the dealers in the towns and the smugglers in the air or out at sea. Dealer groups were to be infiltrated, air and sea patrols were to stop ganja reaching America and crops were to be destroyed where they grew. The exercise was a success. It took about three years for operations to start up again; but start up they did. A Congress study mission to Central America and the Caribbean reported in 1985:

The Government of Jamaica has taken some positive steps in narcotics control. These include enactment of a new civil aviation law aimed at narcotics traffickers, agreement on a modest US assistance program, signature of an extradition treaty, some significant seizures, an aerial survey of marijuana fields, and eradication of more than ten per cent of its estimated marijuana production. Nonetheless, these efforts have had minimal impact on illicit production in or trafficking from Jamaica.

Jamaica is caught in a bind. It has treaty obligations to combat the marijuana trade and is forfeiting valuable American aid so long as cultivation and selling goes unchecked. However, like many Third World drug-producing countries, Jamaica's ganja brings in millions of dollars, helping to maintain the country's fragile political and economic stability. In 1980, the government were seriously considering legalization to cope with Jamaica's foreign exchange difficulties. Tentative estimates put the annual export value of ganja at $200 million, roughly equivalent to the net deficit in foreign reserves at that time. As Prime Minister Edward Seaga made clear the same year: 'It [ganja] supplied black-market dollars which were then used by industrialists and other persons in the economy who wanted to import raw materials for which they could not get Bank of Jamaica dollars. On that basis they were able to avert a lot of closures and substantial lay-offs.'[2]

In fact Seaga is still in a position to play the 'ganja card' should he so wish. The Americans want his support because he is virulently anti-communist and supported the US invasion of Grenada. In Somoza's Nicaragua and in Burma, the CIA have supported drug-trafficking activities to keep anti-communist factions in power. Seaga can in effect say to the Americans 'pay up or we legalize ganja,' for if Washington pushed too hard on eradication and Seaga fell, America would lose an anti-communist bulwark in the Caribbean.[3]

Ganja cultivation is a poor person's enterprise which fits well into the island's pattern of mixed cropping. In a typical farming community, at least a quarter of all households cultivate ganja ranging from a small crop ('roots') for personal household use up to large-scale cultivation for commercial sale in Kingston. What this amounts to is about half a million small farmers earning most of their cash income from growing ganja. And some of them are doing very nicely.

Any general eradication of ganja trading or use seems impossible so deep is the drug embedded in Jamaica's economic and social founda-tions; even so no opportunity has been lost to use the drug laws to harass in particular one sector of the island's population, the Rastafari.

Often regarded as the conscience of the country the Rastafari movement came together in the 1930s at the confluence of several developments in Jamaica's religious and political history which can be sketched only briefly here. In 1655, the Spanish released a group of slaves who fled into the hills. Dubbed the 'Cimarrons' or 'Maroons' ('the fierce ones'), they waged a guerrilla war against the British which lasted from 1729-39 when the occupying army was forced to sue for peace. The black people of Jamaica never accepted their fate as slaves. The Maroons were the spiritual ancestors of the Rastafari and began a tradition of slave and plantation worker rebellions which flared up intermittently right until the last war, then metamorphosed into the popular protests of the post-war period.

In the Afro-Christian religious sects which proliferated in nineteenth-century Jamaica, there was a particularly strong rememberance of Africa. Drawing on this and his alleged Maroon ancestry, Marcus Garvey kindled a fire of Pan Africanism and black consciousness which found its most potent expression in Rastafari. Garvey was born in 1887 near St Anne's Bay in the north of the island, where the Garvey of his age, Bob Marley, was born nearly sixty years later. He went to London in 1912 and returned two years later with a deep interest in African history. He founded the Universal Negro Improvement Association (UNIA) whose purpose was to unite 'all the Negro peoples of the world into one great body to establish a country and government all their own'. To further his aims, Garvey spent the years 1916-27 in America. There he set up the Black Star Line, a shipping company which was an important symbol in the vision of a return to Africa, and the Negroes' Factories Corporation. An unyielding enthusiast for his ideals, he even went to the Ku Klux Klan for money to send black people home. This appalled prominent black leaders and white liberals in America and hostility towards him grew. Garvey was an inspirational leader, but he was no businessman and all his ventures collapsed. He was deported back to Jamaica in 1927 on being convicted of selling stock in the shipping company after it had gone bankrupt. Back home and later in London, Garvey's other enterprises to promote black self-awareness also failed and he died penniless in West Kensington in June 1940.

Garvey is best remembered for perceiving that black people could not fulfil their destiny while they remained displaced persons. They had to return to Africa, under the guidance of a black redeemer who would be crowned King in Africa. Although this prophecy was actually uttered by one of Garvey's associates, James Morris, at a UNIA convention in 1924, this was forgotten in November 1930 when Ras Tafari Makonnen was crowned Emperor Haile Selassie of Ethiopia. The coronation made front-page news in Jamaica; many regarded Garvey's prophecy as fulfilled, a feeling strengthened when Ethiopia repulsed the forces of Mussolini in 1935.

A further impetus to the development of Rastafari was the inspiration of two preachers, Charles Goodridge and Grace Jenkins Garrison. In 1925, they founded the Hamatic church in Jamaica and introduced a bible called the Holy Piby, compiled between 1913–17 and written in Amharic, the language of Ethiopia. Allegedly the Holy Piby was closest to the very first version of the Old Testament.

On the run from religious persecution, Goodridge and Garrison fled into the bush in the forties to be joined by other key leaders of embryonic Rasta groups, most notably Leonard Howell. Howell was imprisoned in 1933 for selling one-shilling postcards of Haile Selassie to Kingston's slum-dwellers and telling them they were now the proud owners of passports back to Africa. In 1935, the year Howell was released, the fledgling Rastafari movement received some bad publicity when it was linked to an allegedly secret society called the Niyabinghi

Order, headed by Selassie and, according to the *Jamaica Times*, dedicated to the death of all black and white oppressors.

In consequence Howell formed the Ethiopian Salvation Society and took several hundred of his followers into the bush to an abandoned estate called Pinnacle. Because of the Niyabinghi scare and the general campaign of harassment through the ganja laws, the commune came under constant police surveillance. Howell spent another two years in jail for growing ganja and on his release he formed the Ethiopian Warriors, dreadlocked guards who patrolled the Pinnacle estate with dogs. The commune survived the hurricane of 1951 which flattened Trench Town and all but wiped out the ganja crop, but finally succumbed to intense police action in 1954.

Deriving fundamentalist interpretations from the Holy Piby, the Rasta preachers constructed a worldview in which Africa was Zion or the Promised Land and the world of oppression was Babylon. They formulated strict dietary laws ('Ital') and rules against cutting hair, both of which bore a striking resemblance to the tenets of orthodox Jewry. Alcohol and gambling were forbidden, but from references to the beneficial 'herb' in Genesis, Revelations and the Psalms, ganja was venerated as a sacrament. This was an important aspect of the Rasta creed because it bound the movement closely to people at the bottom of Jamaican society, where Rastafari found most of its converts.

When Pinnacle broke up, the Rastas returned to the wasteland of urban Kingston, notorious ghetto areas like Trench Town and Back O' Wall, 'a desolate war-zone of zinc, cement and spit'.[4] They came back with nothing but their faith, found nothing except desperation and endless pressure, and consequently had nothing to lose. The ruling classes were terrified of the influx and sent the police in to crack heads at regular intervals. The notion that the Rastas were indeed a bunch of violent criminals seemed confirmed for business interests when a small group went beserk, burnt down a garage, killed the owner and a guest staying at a nearby motel. The Coral Gardens Incident of 1963 went into the legend of Rasta 'violence', but in truth it was a very isolated incident. Most Rastas have no interest in violent action – and with such a devotion to consuming vast quantities of the very finest sinsemilla ganja in chalices, chillums or spliffs the size of ice-cream cones, how could it be otherwise?

In fact, the Rastas were the spiritual alternative to the real lawmakers of the ghetto, the rude boys, and it was the revolution in their music that eventually gave Rastafari its public voice through reggae. The rudies were Jamaica's equivalent of Britain's teddy boys, mods and skinheads with a slice of small-time Chicago hoodlum thrown in. Dedicated to violence and getting drunk, they hung around the shebeens and clubs in shades and 'stingy brim' hats, earning a living through ganja dealing, pimping, gambling, riding shotgun for political heavies and large-scale ganja traffickers, and general hustling.

Music was a very important feature of ghetto life, not the passive strains of calypso, 'which couldn't carry the weight of the folk-urban rebellion taking place in Jamaica',[5] but American soul and r&b, the sounds of one dispossessed black population speaking to another. The music blared out of the island's dance halls from the massive speakers of the Sound Systems, run by youth cult heroes like Sir Coxsone, V Rocket and Duke Reid who would stop at virtually nothing to ensure that *their* systems had the best sounds. Jamaica had no recording plant of its own and there were simply not enough good records from America to go round, so in the late fifties two studios opened to record new Jamaican music, Federal Recording Studios and Coxsone's Studio One.

The new music was ska, the derivation of the word, like 'reggae', being ascribed to as many sources as those who cared to express an opinion. Essentially ska was a loose r&b calypso which emphasized the off-beat. As the sixties progressed and particularly after Independence, a distinctly more African sound emerged, whose pulse echoed the beat of burra drums which welcomed freed slaves and released prisoners back to their homes in the urban sprawl. As ska and bluebeat gave way to rock steady, the beat slowed and the lyrics began to reflect matters other than sex and romance. The key to these developments was Rastafari, as increasing numbers of musicians began to embrace its theology and express the concerns and visions of Rastafari in song. Rock steady can be likened to the erratic spit of an engine kickstarted into action, the strains of protest beginning to come through before giving way to the rhythmic purr and persistent throb of finely tuned reggae, Rastafari's most significant contribution to the culture of Jamaica.

Jamaican musicians were no strangers to ganja. Until well into this century, the principal entertainment for country people had been the Quadrille bands, a kind of Jamaican bluegrass. Using two guitars, fife, banjo and sometimes a fiddle or rhumba box, these bands would play waltzes and polkas, the music of their plantation bosses, at local dances and fairs. One of Bob Marley's relatives was a 'katreel' player around St Anne, where a particularly potent form of sinsemilla was grown. These musicians, like many in rural areas all over the world, had a special status in the community and their appetite for ganja and rum was legendary. But it was the Rasta musicians who first articulated what they regarded as the wonders of herb and the injustices of the ganja laws

195

which had plagued poor people for over half a century.

An early ganja hit was U Roy's 'Chalice in the Palace'. U Roy (Ewart Beckford) was one of the first DJs to rap over an instrumental dub version of somebody else's song; he took the Techniques' 'Queen Majesty' to tell how he shared a chalice with Queen Elizabeth at Buckingham Palace. The first hit for Sugar Minott was 'Oh Mr D.C.' in which he begs a policeman not to bust him because he needs to trade in ganja to feed his family. Both Black Uhuru and the albino DJ Yellowman have recorded songs about sinsemilla. Yellowman's version begins with a 'newscast' relating his court appearance on ganja charges followed by a shout of 'Cocaine will blow your brain, but sinsemilla is IR-IE!' The basic rhythm for the song was taken from the Mighty Diamonds' herb anthem 'Pass the Koutchie' (ganja pipe). This in turn inspired Musical Youth's UK hit 'Pass the Dutchie!' (The name was presumably changed so that the BBC censors would miss any reference to drugs, although in the light of their past record it is hard to imagine either song attracting their attention). The Itals, led by Keith Porter, and another reggae singer John Holt, have both recorded songs, 'Herb Pirate' and 'Police in Helicopter', which at the same time reflect the reasons for becoming involved in the ganja trade and the dangers of doing so.

In Bob Marley, reggae and Rastafari found an international voice; 'international reggae' was precisely the term used by poet Linton Kwezi Johnson to describe the Wailers' first Island Records album *Catch a Fire* in 1973. Once he began touring around the world as a superstar, Marley came under the usual pressures to try a variety of drugs like acid and cocaine. He always refused, but when it came to ganja Marley was the first ambassador. During his professional career he recorded several songs in praise of herb including 'Kaya', 'African Herbsman' and 'Redder Than Red'. From piecing together comments he made to various reporters about his ganja intake since he began serious smoking in 1966 until close to his death in 1980, it seems that he consumed over 300 kilos of the best ganja Jamaica had to offer. As a defiant gesture to those who claimed that ganja precipitated Marley's premature death, his widow Rita placed a stick of sinsemilla in his coffin and went on to score a hit single with 'One Draw', recorded with the same purpose in mind.

Public figures in Jamaica's tumultuous political arena are always likely to incur the wrath of somebody, and that somebody is always likely to try to settle the issue at the point of a gun. If Bob Marley was ever in any doubt that he was a potential target, they were dispelled in the most dramatic way when he narrowly missed assassination in

December 1976. Possibly for reasons of personal safety, he confined most of his public comments on ganja to the parameters of Rasta theology, although he was in any event drawn more to the mystical rather than the political aspects of ganja use. He told reporter Richard Cromelin: 'When you smoke herb, herb reveal yourself to you. All the wickedness you do, the herb reveal it to yourself, your conscience, show up yourself clear, because herb mek you meditate. Is only a natural t'ing and it grow like a tree.'[6] Occasionally, however, Marley did respond to questions about legalization, especially when Michael Manley's PLP were in power in the seventies and there was an influential groundswell in favour of legalizing the trade:

> Herb is the healin' of the nation. Manley can say whatever, but police still get their order from somebody. I mean ... there are people who live in evil and think it is right. For instance, now, a Rastaman sidding and smoke some herb, with good meditation, and a policeman come see him, stick him up, search him, beat him and put him in prison. Now, who is this guy doing these t'ings for? Herb just grow, like yam and cabbage. Policemen do it for evil. Dem don wan' know God and live, dem wan' ha'fe dead yunno![7]

Despite being photographed innumerable times spliff in hand, Bob Marley appears to have fallen foul of the law only once, sometime in the sixties, for what he later dismissed as a traffic offence. Peter Tosh took an altogether more militant stand. Possibly, once he had lost the protection of being part of 'Bob Marley and the Wailers' and went solo, he became more vulnerable. In 1975, he was beaten up by the police and the song written to record the event, 'Mark of the Beast', was banned in Jamaica, as was his personal herb statement 'Legalize It'. (This despite the fact that the government had the same action in mind.) He was on the receiving end of more harassment following the release of 'Equal Rights' in 1978, culminating in a police beating which almost killed him. He described what happened in an interview for *High Times*:

> TOSH: Well, I was standing at an office arranging a European tour. I was waiting for my musicians. I had a joint in my hand. Two guys came up behind me. One guy came behind me and just took it out of my hand. He was there looking at me. I took it back from him. He didn't tell me who he was. I just see him standing there smiling. I just took it from him and said, 'What happened?' And he was trying to get it back from me. When I see him trying to get my stick from me, my mind told me he was a beast, so I just tore it up and [*blows*] threw

it away. He didn't like *that*. So he started up his aggressiveness, and tried to do what he want, to take me to jail. But I realized he was a beast. He found out he couldn't manage me physically, so he went for his friend. His friend came with his gun and tried and failed, too. That didn't work so he went to find some more friends. And that still didn't work. Well, one of them closed his fist on his gun and punch at my face. I moved away and the one who was standing behind me, he got the lick in his face, and it cut him. It began to bleed.

Well, one policeman in his uniform came. I knew he was a police. He said, 'What happened?' I told him what happened. Well, he told me to walk with him to the station, and I walked with them to explain the situation. When I walked to explain what happened, they ganged me. Put me in a cell. About ten of them ganged my head. And that is when I realized that I was in like Daniel was put in the lion's den. But Peter was put in the dragon's den. And because I was protected from the elements of death, see, I recovered. When they beat and beat and beat and beat for over an hour and found out I would not dead, they was *beggin'* me to dead. When I realized that they were *determined* to kill, I just took one blow, another blow, and all those blows. I just lie down. They were convinced that I was dead because I didn't even wink an eye. I didn't shake a limb; so they was convinced that when I was lying there I was dead. Well, after they was convinced I was dead and left me, I got up like a lion. And they was marvelled. And they said, 'Take him to the dumb cell.'

Well, the dumb cell is a cell that when they put you in, there is not even a breeze come in. It is all concrete and a door. The only hole is a keyhole. And that is where they was taking me. When the guy went to the dumb cell and push his keys – he has about twelve keys together – none of them could fit the place, *yet* there was the right key there. But it was not spiritually designed for me to go into that cell. Because they wanted me to bleed to death because I was bleeding furiously. So the doctors came to the place when they heard of what took place. They said no, doctor cannot see me. Lawyers came, they said no, lawyers cannot see me. But when they realize that the news was getting spread all over Jamaica they got two lorries of soldiers to take me to the hospital. I went to the hospital. My hand was broken. This hand was broken here. And my head was properly bashed in.

Well, I went to the hospital and the doctor stitched it up, put my hand in plaster of Paris. They took me back to jail. Then I find that I could not go into the cell. They didn't want me among the prisoners. [The jailer] was asking me if I wanted to go among the prisoners. I said Yes. They are not criminals. You are the criminals. So I went among them and they used their hot coca tea and bathed my hand and bathed my head. One of the prisoners look inside and say he was seeing *inside* of my head and saw my nerve going up like this [*wiggles his finger back and forth*].[8]

In an interview with the Legalize Cannabis Campaign, Tosh came to this conclusion: 'So the system continue, my brethren, and until I and I can tear it down physically, mentally and spiritually and make it look as if it wasn't there, boy, it will still be there, but as long man live in fear ... the shitstem [system] will still be there. You see.'[9]*

Although the reggae–Rasta–ganja connection fed into youth cultures all over the world, England proved particularly receptive to the message. In the early eighties it was often easier to get hold of reggae records, even Jamaican pre-releases, in London than in Kingston. And of course, several top reggae solo artists and bands achieved international exposure through British record companies like Island and Virgin. Among black communities throughout the country, 'Reggae took hold and helped to inject a much-needed sense of ideological and cultural solidarity into the lifestyle and thinking of disaffected and anti-social young people, not only because it was an easy kind of dance music, but also because its messages and self-conscious critical and political commentaries on society were relevant to ... particular needs and desires.'[10] Not least of these desires was the establishment of ganja smoking, not so much to go high or deep, but as the defiant political gesture which has proved central to many of the country's racial explosions in recent years.

Less dramatically, and more closely tied to fashion and style, reggae won back the hearts of a section of Britain's white youth to black music. In the sixties, mods and skinheads demonstrated a close affinity with ska and bluebeat. However, the 'Africanization' of the music as it metamorphosed into reggae alienated these groups and they switched their allegiance to mainstream rock, particularly heavy metal and glamrock. But it was the very ethnicity of reggae that attracted punks in the late

*Around 8 p.m. on Friday 11 September 1987, three men on motorbikes rode up to Tosh's house. One of the men was a regular visitor to the house and so the trio were admitted without question. Once inside, the men shot six people, including Peter Tosh who died two days later. Of the remaining five, one died instantly and the other four survived. Although some jewellery and cash were stolen, there have been strong rumours that the murders were drug-related. In what turned out to be his last interview given to *Musician*, he said: 'If gunmen come tomorrow to get I, I'm not afraid. Jah will protect I ... Bullets can't come through I because I'm a wall.'

seventies. Although it never informed the sound of punk, '[reggae] carried the necessary conviction, the political bite, so obviously missing in most contemporary white music.'[11] And with the music came the marijuana, back in fashion among a new generation of style-conscious youth normally contemptuous of any artefact of the sixties.

Despite the new heroes who emerged from punk, New Wave and New Romanticism, reggae retained much of its popularity in England through the eighties, both in its purer form (Bob Marley, Sly and Robbie, Misty in Roots, Sugar Minott, Burning Spear, etc), and as a rhythmic pulse informing the sound of white pop, from the Police and Madness to Culture Club. Undoubtedly, however, reggae has lost its political edge and, although the essence of ganja still permeates the sound and the religion, public affirmation of this from reggae musicians has subsided during the anti-drugs backlash.

The example of Jamaica has always been the best answer to those who claim that smoking marijuana leads to heroin use; despite such large-scale use of marijuana on the island, Jamaica has never had a heroin problem. However, in line with many Caribbean islands, Jamaica has now become a stop-over point for cocaine passing from South America to Florida. Indeed, the island is something of a cocaine smugglers' paradise, because the ganja trade has supplied it with so many hidden airstrips. With cocaine on the island and reggae artists touring the world, the drug has inevitably permeated the music industry; Wayne Smith and Dillinger have recorded songs about it, while Gregory Isaacs has been busted for it. As expressed in reggae, Rastafari stands for everything that is harmonious, balanced and natural. Some musicians will wish to retain the fundamentals, others won't. How the music responds to the snap of a cocaine rush remains to be seen.

13

Copping ...

Dealers rip off bands left, right and centre. They're probably doing even better now, because it's cut much more than it was – especially in the UK.

Tour manager

Roughly speaking, one can say that the music business and the illicit market in drugs grew up together from their early beginnings as minority activities in the jazz jaunts of New Orleans. Popular music is now the property of multinational corporations with many subsidiaries, thousands of employees and profits running into millions. It is impossible to place illicit drug trafficking on any commercial league table because dealers tend not to submit audited accounts. However, through the intervention of organized crime (which also has a stake in the music industry), drug trafficking has a worldwide complexion involving the economic and political stability of whole countries, widespread corruption from the highest levels downwards and financial transactions on a breathtaking scale.

Music meets the drug scene at several points along the distribution network, providing those in the industry with limitless supplies of every type of drug. This ready access is the key to the problems which can accrue for musicians, technicians, DJs and company executives fighting for survival in a high-pressure business where longevity counts for little and you are only as good as your last product.

At the basic level, dealing in small quantities goes on between friends as in any drug-using circles. Some musicians become known as people with especially good contacts which have developed alongside their need to finance a spiralling drug habit – Papa John Phillips was one such example. Jazz too has thrown up some notorious 'Jesuit junkies' well-known within the community. Musicians can also become conduits between dealers anxious for free-spending star business and those in privileged positions who need to keep more than an arm's length from their source of supplies.

Small drug-using cliques exist in all areas of the business including the record companies. A former employee of EMI remembers, 'We had this thing going in our department, just a few of us, and I was the person who knew how to get stuff. Outsiders didn't really know about it, but one day this guy comes up to me right in the middle of the office party and says he wants some dope. I mean, how stupid can you get, right in the middle of the office!'[1] Musicians in particular can always rely on 'well wishers' who want to bask in reflected glory, to supply them with tasty titbits, a situation which can rapidly get of control. Jimi Hendrix spent far too much of his time in an acid haze because he could not say no to the legion of camp followers eager to claim that *they* turned him on. So desperate was Free manager John Glover to keep parasites away from guitarist Paul Kossoff that he actually had policemen posted outside the dressing-room door.

But sometimes it is the managers themselves who exploit a musician's dependency on drugs to keep them in line. Guitarist Steve Miller saw this happen to Barry Goldberg, keyboard player with Electric Flag: 'Barry really got into trouble. His manager tried to control him through drugs and he became a junkie for a while and he was down and out. His manager would go "That's great Barry, as long as you do what I tell you to do, here's a little smack, whatever you want." '[2] Miller also had this comment to make about Janis Joplin's manager Albert Grossman: 'I was astounded by what I saw. When I saw Albert Grossman letting Janis Joplin play concerts because she was off heroin and only drinking a fifth of booze a day, I thought he should have been arrested.'[3] Roadies, road- and tour-managers often figure as important intermediaries between dealers and customers. In fact their drug connections may be the main reason they get hired in the first place, like Scooter Herring. One tour manager who has been on the road for thirty years with several top bands recalled, 'I remember being in Germany at a gig, sitting in the backstage office. On the table in front of me was a huge pile of coke about six inches high. I had to divide this for the crew and the band. I wrote down who was getting what and it came out of the band's wages. The crew got theirs free, but the band had to pay. On some tours I seemed to be doing nothing but sorting out drugs – on others, well, they just turned up.'[4] Payment in kind to road crews is not uncommon. Particularly with cocaine, drugs represent more than just a perk of the job, they are a very bankable commodity. Cocaine can be resold as it is, or 'cut' to increase revenue. The entire crew of an American artist who toured recently in Britain was paid off in this way.

Record companies also play their part in the supply of drugs to their musicians. 'Hospitality' is normally taken care of by the Artists Relations Department (not to be confused with Artist and Repertoire or A&R). A band's special requirements are made known to AR and the rest is up to them. Promotion and publicity can also get involved. For example, when hijacking became a favoured means of attention-grabbing by political groups in the seventies, security was stepped up on internal flights in the States and a major record company was highly embarrased to have most of its promotions team busted for cocaine. An ex-AR man says he was most unhappy at having to score drugs for people:

> It was no good buying sub-standard stuff for the Americans, because they'd know straight away. You have to be very aware of connections. Ludicrous things happen and they are taken as normal. When I was working for the company, this big name flew in to promote his latest solo album. We had to go to this massive suite at his hotel to see if he was okay, and if he needed anything. We get there and he's whacked out of his head. His small child, about four years old, looks me straight in the eye and says, 'Mummy and Daddy said I mustn't call them joints. I must just call them cigarettes.'[5]

Drugs (along with women and cash) have always been part of the social grease of the industry. Journalists become accustomed to being offered drugs in the hope of eliciting favourable reviews. One British journalist who worked extensively for the music press in the seventies, was among this fêted group:

> It was all this 'let's be part of the hip drug circle' business. Early in the seventies, joints were being rolled the whole time; coke came in around 1974–5. This tended to appear more informally than in an office interview situation. You'd have a press do, a launch. Somebody from the record company would whip out some coke or you'd go back to the office at night or to the artist's home. It was no big deal.

The motivation of these executives was very transparent:

> Mainly they are trying to look, do and feel right in an industry that's all about being chic and up to date. The drugs would change, so did the booze. It would be Southern Comfort, then gin and tonic, as the

business got grimmer financially through the seventies. Same with the drugs. In '76 everyone had to be smoking thai* and nobody would be so gaffe as to bring out smack, although it was sniffed quite a lot then.

In turn, some of the journalists began to live the life they reported on:

It was a time of being elegantly wasted – all to do with snorting heroin, being fucked up, losing your teeth and being brainless. On the papers I worked for, cliques would evolve, a secret language developed and it would get quite complicated working out what level of consciousness different people were on. This code actually came out in the features – someone would write about 'traces of snow on the window' and so on. Then people started dying, friends of mine, the mood changed and those who were once elegantly wasted looked pathetic.[6]

Nor are the company men themselves immune from the dangers inherent in regular drug use and believing you can be someone you are not. One band manager remembers:

This guy who worked for Atlantic in the mid-seventies is now a very bad junkie. He's been to every clinic, but nobody can do anything. He started out as a young, dynamic, keen record guy. Then he started hanging round this one particular band on their tours – he wanted to be one of them and now he hasn't had a job for God knows how long. He's a real down and out, still on heroin.[7]

Disc jockeys, too, particularly in America, have long been a target for company favours. In the early days of rock 'n' roll, money, prostitutes and gifts were on offer in exchange for playing certain records. The scandal which broke in the early sixties over what became known as 'payola' has since been interpreted by rock historians as an orchestrated attempt to shove rock 'n' roll off the air. It certainly destroyed the career of pioneering rock DJ Alan Freed, who was indicted twice, in 1960 and 1964, and died shortly afterwards, a broken humiliated man – while other non-rock DJs cashed in with impunity. With the increasing popularity of cocaine in the entertainment world, 'payola' gave way to 'drugola'.

Washington journalist Jack Anderson was the first to break the initial 'drugola' scandal in March 1972. Record company employees came forward with tales of drug 'saloons' held by promotion staff, where

*Thai sticks – a form of marijuana.

cocaine, marijuana and assorted pills were handed out to DJs, station managers and performers. Unknown artists took it upon themselves to supply drugs to DJs hoping to secure airplay for records that otherwise would have sunk without trace. The promotions man of a well-known record company bought plays with $20 lots of marijuana and then apparently complained that he was having trouble 'losing it' in his expense account.

Stanley Gortikov, President of the Recording Industry Association of America (RIAA), issued a trenchant statement calling for companies to sort themselves out for the overall good of the industry. Any pay-for-play policy was 'unconscionable, immoral and commercially self-destructive'. He went on to urge companies to conduct investigations and surveillances to root out those dealing in payola/drugola among their own employees and those working for companies as independent promoters and distributors.

When questioned by Anderson and others over exactly how records were promoted, the record companies proved singularly reticent about supplying information. However, it would appear that as a result of all this adverse publicity, salaried promotional teams shrank in size, while more independent promoters were engaged to get airplay for records. In such a cut-throat business, no company was going to risk another stealing a march by making any genuine attempt to stop payola. Instead, they adopted an arm's-length policy, which in effect said, 'Here's the record, get it on the air, but we don't want to know how you do it.' In consequence, the independent promoters became a powerful and feared force in the American music business during the seventies. Paid anything up to $15,000 a week for their services, these 'indies' used every means at their disposal to get records played on Top Forty radio – cash, women, holidays, threats of violence, but most usually cocaine.

Inevitably the wheel turned full circle and another 'drugola' scandal broke in 1986. NBC's *Nightly News* reporter Brian Ross ran a TV exposé. Only one DJ was willing to be interviewed on camera, Don Cox from Miami, who said it was quite common to be offered cocaine in return for pushing a particular record. However, his information soon dried up after he claimed he was beaten up and his family threatened with violence unless he stopped talking.

Officially, the major companies knew nothing about payola. Yet as soon as the story broke, many of the main promoters suddenly found their contacts in the companies were 'in meetings' when they called. Many companies insist on 'no payola' clauses in their contracts with independent promoters. Warner Brothers actually stopped using 'indies' in 1981; sales started to fall, so the arrangements were reinstituted.

Early in 1986, the RIAA launched an investigation into corrupt practices in independent promotion, but at a special meeting, CBS and one other label apparently vetoed the idea and it was dropped. However, after the NBC revelations, RIAA records of that meeting were subpoenaed by a Federal grand jury to see if there was a case for instigating criminal proceedings.

Drug expenses money can be 'laundered' in a number of ways. If a slush fund is operated there are usually no receipts anyway; services like prostitution or goods like cocaine are bought and handed over. Supplies of drugs to musicians in recording studios can be lost on expense sheets under euphemisms like 'extra keyboards' or 'additional vocals'. On the road, it's the accountant's job to do some creative accounting. One road manager said, 'I would purchase what was needed, put it through the accounts, tell the accountant what it was and ask him to hide it. Anything up to 10% of the whole tour expenses could go on drugs and with some of the bands I've been with, that could run into thousands.'[8] Drug requirements can appear, again euphemistically, as riders to tour contracts with promoters. Where the promoter gets his supply is his business, but one rider allegedly stated quite simply 'no snow, no show'. Some people make no attempt at euphemisms whatsoever. I have seen a neatly typed receipt to a British record company from one of its artists recording in Los Angeles: $936 – Food, gifts, entertainment, liquor; $1,275 – Cocaine.

The NBC story focused on a group of about thirty top promoters dubbed 'the Network', the prominent members being Joe Isgro and Fred Disipio, men with alleged links to the Carlo Gambino Mafia family in New York. Speculation has been rife for many years about the involvement of the Mafia and other elements of organized crime in the music business. Senate hearings in 1973 established a link between the Mafia and Roulette Records and judging by the treatment meted out to some of its artists, the same may well have been true in the late sixties of the subsidiary of a major US company. Also in 1973, an internal audit at CBS resulted in the firing of David Wynshaw, head of Artist Relations. CBS claimed that Wynshaw and label chief Clive Davis had conspired together to siphon off company funds for personal use. It seemed strange to those in the industry that Davis, who was doing extremely well for CBS, should be fired for allegedly embezzling sums of money for expenses like his son's Barmitzvah, for which he could easily have afforded to pay out of his own huge salary.

Digging deeper, it seems that Davis (now head of Arista Records) may have gone because Wynshaw was linked to a mobster named Pat Falcone, indicted in February 1973 for heroin dealing. In turn, Falcone had been involved with a number of CBS acts like Sly Stone and O.C. Smith, offering protection for Smith under a death threat for non-payment of gambling debts. Falcone had a New York base in the office of Frank Camparia, an ex-promotions man for a CBS subsidiary label, Epic Records. From here he performed security services for Jeff Beck, an Epic artist. All this was happening at a time when the Nixon administration was under threat from Watergate. Woodward and Bernstein's paper the *Washington Post* owned a Florida TV station and the FCC challenged its licence. With the industry worried about the FCC guidelines on song lyric content, the Senate payola hearings and CBS's own extensive investment in broadcasting outlets, the company was anxious to present a squeaky-clean image. In such circumstances, Davis was sacrificed. Wynshaw was to testify to the Senate that between 1971–3 $500,000 had been charged to CBS's promotions budget for payola payments.

Organized crime has more tangential, but equally significant holds on the industry. These include stadium food and souvenir concessions, concert staging and lighting, work permit applications (through the Musicians Union), the passage of equipment through ports of entry (courtesy of the Teamsters and the Longshoremen) and trucking. It is said that nobody does a major US tour without various pay-offs being made. Failure to co-operate at the very least ensures that your equipment is mysteriously stranded in the Nevada Desert while you're in New York or perhaps the stage crew don't turn up. And of course, organized crime is a major supplier of drugs. About 70% of the heroin coming into America is Mafia-controlled and other non-Italian criminal families largely control the cocaine trade from South America through Florida, the main access point into the States.

Some of the world's top bands have, in the past, carried such large quantities of drugs with them that drug enforcement agents have become convinced that they were involved in transporting drugs for sale on the US mainland. FBI agents were quoted as saying:

> We were told by insiders, that Presley's group had the same connections that the Rolling Stones had ... We were told on numerous occasions that members of the Stones provided drugs to the scene in some of the biggest and fanciest disco clubs in New York. However after watching them for months and months, we decided that the opposite was true, that if the Stones were doing drugs, which our sources said was positive and which they did little to hide, connections within the clubs were providing them with narcotics and not the other way round.[9]

207

Notwithstanding, there is evidence to suggest that the high-powered, high-financed worlds of rock and drug-smuggling do support one another on occasion. In 1981, a convicted smuggler, Harold Oldham, testified to a Senate sub-committee on international narcotics trafficking. One of his main activities had been the importation of North African hashish:

> While I was in Morocco, I met a rock star with a major rock group. Through my contact with him I came into constant contact with many of the major rock and pop groups in the United States and Great Britain. My association with these groups led me to the formation of Startrans, a company I set up for the purpose of renting luxury buses to these groups while they were on tour. Startrans was a legitimate US company and business, though it had been capitalized by significant amounts of narcotics money which had been laundered through the Caymans.[10]

Payments in kind to DJs and road crews have established drugs as not only the social grease of the business, but also its currency. In recent years, however, as bands have ventured into new territories, this has taken on an altogether different dimension, evolving along the lines of the long-standing legitimate practice in international commerce of supplying goods for services rather than cash. The major precondition for 'sweeping', as it is generally known, is that the buying country is without an exchangeable currency in terms of international finance – such countries would include those in Eastern Europe and South America. Supposing a company supplies a power station to Romania or a fleet of trucks to Paraguay. The supplier does not want payment in Romanian lei or Paraguayan guarani. These countries and others like them might be able to pay in US dollars, but more likely they will offer a commodity of their own in exchange – in the case of Romania it could be oil. However, a tanker load of oil is no good to the supplier as it stands – he needs the money. Therefore he will go to a dealer who specializes in selling off 'swops' and receives the proceeds of the sale. Naturally, this dealer plus any other intermediaries will charge a commission, so the value of any swop has to exceed the price of the original goods to cover this 'creaming off'.

Pop artists touring in Eastern Europe have come to similar arrangements, receiving, for example, cut timber or even forests in lieu of currency for concerts or royalty payments. For the touring band in South America there is one local product which is actually worth more than money as it travels round the world – cocaine. The trade in cocaine represents South America's biggest dollar-earner abroad; however shaky the political and economic base of the main producer countries like Bolivia and Colombia, without cocaine both countries would be seriously destabilized.

Where bands have taken cocaine in payment for tours and royalties in South America, the principle is the same as in legitimate business, but the practical arrangements are very different. Obviously, if any rock manager is going to get involved with South American cocaine dealers he had better know what he's doing; the dealers negotiate with guns, not over brandies in smart restaurants. The band might opt for cocaine to be supplied to them over a period equivalent to the monies owed, or they might opt to take the whole lot with them, which could run into several kilos, in which case a smuggling operation would be set up to get the drugs home.

Alternatively, the drugs might be sold on behalf of the band and the proceeds laundered through off-shore banking accounts, to reappear a few months later in an account of the management's choice. Either way, elaborate and expensive precautions have to be taken every step of the way to ensure that the band doesn't get ripped off or busted. Such a payment system would be out of reach for all but the world's top bands.

At the other end of the drug-supply continuum is the medical profession. Doctors are not immune, particularly the younger ones, from the attractions of being associated with the rich and powerful world of rock music. Commenting on 'hangers-on' in the business, Little Richard's bass player, Eddie Fletcher, said it wasn't just female groupies who wanted to be around the legendary rock 'n' roller. 'I've heard doctors say "I don't think I'll go in this week. I'll just travel back east with y'all." And the management just couldn't get rid of them.'[11]

Primarily, however, it has been in pursuit of profit that doctors have been more than happy to supply the drug needs of musicians, whatever the health cost. Without wishing in any way to understate the potential harm done by those who traffic in illegal drugs, they at least make no pretence of acting in the best interests of their clients nor are they bound by a code of professional ethics. Doctors are, and it makes the activities of those who recklessly prescribe drugs for gain all the more reprehensible.

In American law, it has never been accepted that to prescribe opiates like morphine and heroin to help maintain somebody's habit is legitimate medical practice. British law takes a very different view: up to 1968 it was perfectly legal for a doctor to prescribe these opiates and cocaine to addicts, most of whom would have become dependent through original prescriptions for chronic pain. But as the sixties progressed, increasing numbers of younger people, including several jazz musicians, began using doctors as a ready source of pure heroin to feed habits derived from recreational rather than therapeutic drug use. Few doctors were willing to see such people, because of the problems they caused for the staff in the surgery. Those who were prepared to treat addicts often prescribed heroin in vast quantities. During the course of one year, one particular doctor wrote out prescriptions for heroin totalling six kilos. Some of these doctors genuinely believed that prescribing on demand kept their patients out of the black market and ensured a relatively stable lifestyle free from fears of police harassment, the degradations of street life and so on. Unfortunately, these doctors were unable to provide the kind of support needed to encourage their patients to become drug-free after a stable period. And in fact the black market in London was actually created by this over-prescribing on the grand scale. Invariably a user would ask for (and get) prescriptions in excess of his personal requirements and then sell the surplus. British jazz musicians who sold heroin around the clubs of Soho were usually selling their own surplus drugs in order to finance the purchase of their next doctor's prescription. And there were some doctors who could not even be credited with genuine if misguided beliefs; they saw no further than their bank balance.

After 1968 it became an offence for any doctor to prescribe heroin or cocaine to someone he knew would be using these drugs to support a habit. Only those with special licences could prescribe in the old way and these were granted only to doctors working the drug clinics set up at the same time. There was one loophole: doctors could still prescribe these drugs to relieve symptoms of organic illness such as pain, so a doctor could supply drugs pretending it was for pain, or having been conned into thinking it was. However the Home Office Drugs Inspectorate, who check pharmacists' records, would eventually become suspicious if one doctor was prescribing in this way on a regular basis. Of more significance is the range of powerful opiates still available to the doctor to prescribe to anyone, such as dihydrocodeine (DF-118) and dextromoramide (Palfium). Until recently dipipanone (Diconal) was readily available, but it has now been added to the restricted list along with heroin and cocaine. But whatever the rules and regulations applicable to opiate drugs, people with wallets to match their reputations and a pressing need for discretion have always found ostensibly reputable doctors willing to oblige. As well as secret trips to Harley Street, it is common practice for bands and solo artists to have a doctor travelling with them. In his Senate Testimony, smuggler Harold Oldham said that these doctors 'would liberally distribute pills – controlled substances to anyone in the troupe who wished them. It became a common sight on the chartered flights taken by these groups and elsewhere for the physician to set up shop. As soon as the plane took off, members of the troupe would literally line up at his shop for pills.'

John Lennon immortalized these Dr Feelgoods in 'Dr Robert' (on *Revolver*), the same guy who gave hot shots to Warhol and friends from the Factory. A notorious example of cash before care was the doctor who supplied jars full of tranquillizers, barbiturates and methaqualone (Mandrax and Quaaludes) to Paul Kossoff. It was these drugs, according to Free manager John Glover, that caused most of Kossoff's problems, but despite pleas by Kossoff's father directly to the doctor and to the profession's watchdog committee, the General Medical Council, the doctor continued to supply drugs to the ailing guitarist. Kossoff died in March 1976; the doctor is still in practice.

Perhaps the most famous rock doctor was Dr George 'Nick' Nichopoulos, personal physician to Elvis Presley and other members of the entourage. Opinions differed about Dr Nick. Some said he tried to keep Elvis away from even worse drugs than the ones he was taking and that he substituted placebos where he could get away with it. Others dismissed him as a disgrace to his profession, who profited handsomely from Presley's famed generosity and who was largely responsible for his death.

It is possible that Presley was the biggest drug hog in the history of rock. He used the large Merck prescribing manual for doctors like a mail-order catalogue and the list of drugs he consumed in cocktails of unknown quantities included Placidyl, Valmid, Dalmane, Valium, Mandrax and various barbiturates (all sedatives, hypnotics or tranquillizers); Hycomine, Codeine, Darvon, Dilaudid, Demerol and Meperidine (all painkillers); Dexadrine, Dexamill, Eskotrol, Ritalin and amphetamine (all stimulants). Ironically, he was virulently anti-heroin and even planned to have a local dealer 'eliminated' in *Death Wish* style. But because all his drugs were on prescription, he never made the connection between heroin and the drugs he consumed so voraciously.

Dr Nick was a classic rock 'n' roll doctor, on call day and night to tend the needs of his much-valued patient. On the day before he died, Presley took delivery of 150 Percodan and Dilaudid painkillers, 262 Amytals and Methaqualone and 278 Dexadrine and Biphetamine stimulants. How many of these he consumed is unknown, as is the exact cause of his death. Dr Nicks's prescribing habits came under close scrutiny when computer records revealed that during the last seven months of Presley's life, Nichopoulos had prescribed no less than 5,000 pills for him. A chemical soup had been swirling round Presley's system for years. Apart from an occasional yoghurt crash diet, Presley ate nothing but junk food and suffered from an alarming list of ailments, mainly of a respiratory and circulatory nature. Several drugs were prescribed for these, others (in combination with the mountains of ice cream and hot dogs) probably caused them. In the event, perhaps not surprisingly, the medical profession looked after its own: Nichopoulos was reprimanded, suspended for three months and put on probation for three years.

14

... And Coping

Rock 'n' roll is here to stay/Better to burn out/Than to fade away.

Neil Young

I've got a friend named Greenspan that says, 'I need a little cocaine to give me energy. I need a little liquor to give me courage. And I need a little pot to give me inspiration.' I believe this to be the case for many musicians ... I tend to stay slightly fucked up all the time.

Michael Bloomfield, 1944-81

It is clear that drugs of all descriptions, both legal and illegal, are available in any quantity to those working in the music business who want them and who have enough money and the right contacts. But why should they want them in the first place?

Most musicians don't get into problems with drugs; they are able to control their use in the same way as they (and people generally) control their drinking. Obviously some (and it may well be an increasing number) abstain altogether. Nevertheless, there is a high incidence of drug use throughout the industry and a correspondingly high occupational casualty rate. So what is it about musicians and the music business?

An attempt has been made earlier in the book (particularly in chapter six) to examine some of the attendant issues, like the adolescent aspects of musician psychology. However, such a complicated subject needs a lot of space and is more appropriately dealt with in a single chapter, both by way of a conclusion and in the light of the recent and more candidly documented era of pop and rock. In looking for patterns of behaviour, there is always the danger of forgetting that we are all individuals, that no two sets of motivating forces or personal circumstances are the same. The 'addictive personality' has yet to be identified. But the fact of individuality aside, what we are trying to make sense of here is a twisted skein of circumstance and psychology set against a background of easy access. And possibly the best way of getting a general feel for what goes on is to tease out some of the main threads of motivation for the use of drugs by musicians.* The fairly arbitrary labels I would attach to these threads would be practical and recreational, symbolic and emotional. It should be emphasized, however, that it is impossible to identify which factors are more significant than others, as they vary between individuals.

By any definition, being a professional musician can be a crazy way to make a living. Whether you are scuffling round Britain in a beat-up Transit van held together by string and God's munificence or criss-crossing the globe in a Lear jet on eighteen-month world tours, the principles are the same. It's just a question of degree.

In this world, you work while everyone else is at play and while the audience is at work, you're asleep. But that sleep may have to be taken when you are not tired, because of the travel itinerary, the show times, the press calls, the interviews, the sound check, the airport strike or whatever. The same goes with waking up. If you're lucky you might eat. And however awful you feel when the lights go up, you have to be some demonic superbeing for two hours *or* Joe Cool for as long as it takes to give that very important interview promoting the new album. Musicians cannot ring in sick, take days off (unless it is in the schedule), or turn up a week later with a sick note from the doctor. All sorts of horse dope has been pumped into people so that the show can go on. And in between these bursts of hyperactivity can be periods of cataclysmic boredom: hours spent in endless airport lounges, hotel rooms, dressing rooms, recording studios, trains, planes, buses and cars, each looking the same as the last.

In such a working environment, which cannot be fully appreciated by anyone who hasn't actually done it, it is very easy to jump on to a chemical carousel of drugs (including alcohol, of course) in order to go to sleep and wake up on demand, get you through the day, calm nerves, boost confidence and escape from boredom. It takes a special effort to avoid this potentially hazardous rollercoaster. One musician noted, 'My motto was to make sure I ate and slept because you get so caught up with the drugs and the frantic lifestyle that you actually forget to do

---

*I have deliberately excluded from the analysis others in the music business, like company executives, roadies, etc. They have their own pressures to face and many resort to drugs, but they don't have the pressure of being in the public eye.

those things and you can get very unhealthy and very sick on the road. So I always ate and slept properly, but I also took a lot of drugs. It was just normal.'[1] Guitarist Johnny Winter highlighted the tedium of touring as the starting point of his journey towards drug dependency: 'As the road got harder and I've got tired of playing the same songs over and over again, we took a little bit more. And then it was a little more until everybody in the band except Rick Derringer was in pretty bad shape.'[2]

Al Kooper captured some of the essential truths of the rock life on the road in his book *Backstage Passes*:

It's 1966 and we play in your college town gym ... You've arrived in the afternoon to your Holiday or Ramada Inn where the staff let you know you are most assuredly *not* welcome. You rush out to do a sound check where a skeleton crew is totally unprepared for you and the simplest matters wind up taking hours. You've maybe enough time to return to the hotel and shower (lunch, dinner – forget it – they wouldn't serve you in the restaurant even if you *had* time to eat), and then race back to the gym. Then it's wait around while the first act goes on late and plays twice as long as it's supposed to and the audience is real irritable just in time for you to go on.

Your big hour. Now that was *golden*. It was, for sure, the only enjoyment in the entire schedule. God forbid you played a lousy show; then suicide seemed like the only alternative to the boredom, frustration and futility. After a quick perusal of the premises for a smiling female (nope!), it's back to the hotel where the kitchen is (you've guessed it) closed ...

So practically all of us got high a lot. I'm surprised we weren't junkies ... Mostly we smoked hash, grass, opium and took some occasional mescalin. Imagine being revered on stage for that golden hour and then rushed back to your hotel cell. You felt like some talented animal in a zoo on temporary leave.[3]

And the next day, you do it all over again, and again and again and again. Drugs here were used to blot out the grind of being on the road, but Al Kooper also talked about 'the golden hour' on stage, and there is a great temptation after a gig to keep pumping the tremendous adrenalin surge that comes with a good performance. Musicians talk of an arrested orgasm when the show is over, and a few lines of cocaine in the dressing room keeps the whole experience on the boil, because whatever drugs you are using there is nothing like the high of playing a gig in front of a receptive audience when everything is cooking. And of course, if the concert is a disaster you may reach for something just as quickly. What musicians find particularly perplexing is the *unpredictability* of audiences. Al Kooper again:

> This was one of the major weirdnesses of being on the road. Sometimes you could play the best music you'd ever played and they'd just sit there on their hands, no encore, no nothin'. And then ... you shovel an hour's worth of dinosaur shit on 'em and get standing ovations and twenty encores. This usually helped to temper your respect for the people you played for.[4]

Eric Clapton has been quoted as saying with some bitterness that he could walk on with paper and comb and still get an ovation. Between themselves musicians are not happy to 'get away' with a bad gig, often contemptuous of an undiscerning, adoring audience. But then again, who wants to be booed off?

While on the road, a musician's leisure time is dramatically telescoped in comparison with that available to other working people. The working day is concentrated into, say, three hours instead of the normal seven or eight and these few hours are at the end of the day rather than at the beginning, after or during what for most people is leisure time. This means that a working musician's leisure or recreational time is quite limited both in the number of hours which can be devoted to it and by the advanced knowledge that another gig, which could be 500 miles away, has to be done tomorrow. Recreational time is thus robbed of reality to a certain extent and accrues an eerie, dislocated feel. Some musicians accept this and keep partying down to a minimum. Others chase the phantom and use drugs as a short cut to the party mood knowing that night will give way all too quickly to day and the sound of the tour manager hammering on the door. The physical constitution of musicians is legendary, as are the stories of after-hours excess – sex, drugs and rock 'n' roll in all its grim fascination. Few outsiders can stand this kind of pace – neither the lifestyle itself nor the chemicals needed to keep up with it – although many try. Some bands had a particularly fearsome reputation on the road – for drugs, damage and 'deviancy'. Led Zeppelin was one, the Stones another. Robert Greenfield in his account of the Stones' two-month tour of the States in 1972 relates the story of Bob Gibson, partner in a rock PR firm who had the Stones as one of their clients. Gibson decided to join the band for their whole tour. He lasted one week.

Paradoxically, despite all the aggravations of life on the road, many musicians start climbing the walls within a very short time of finishing a tour. This was graphically illustrated by Barbara Charone in her biography of Keith Richard. When he wasn't playing he did nothing but get wasted and watch TV. 'I can't live without being on the road ... every minute spent off the road, I either turn into an alcoholic or a junkie 'cause I've got nothing else to do.'[5] For Keith Richard heroin was itself a means to combat the withdrawal effects of not being on tour.

Many metaphors have been used to describe the music business – perhaps one of the more apposite is the feudal hierarchy. In this association, promoters, producers and company men are the lords of the manor, the musicians are knights, and the managers and public relations people are their retainers. Dancing attendance on the knights are the squires and peasants i.e. the roadies and 'go-fers'. The stage is the tournament arena where the band pleases the crowd or wins over the audience with a display of axe (or guitar) skills. But this imagery can be pushed beyond purely structural concerns to encompass the principles of heraldic protocol as a metaphor for the symbolic function that drugs can play in a musician's life. By virtue of their talent and the demands of their unconventional lifestyle, musicians of whatever genre often consider themselves as outsiders, running off at a tangent from the normal constraints put upon everyday behaviour. This outlaw status is very appealing to fans and from this derives adoration and hero worship. The musician becomes a blank slate on which the fans project their own desires, hopes, frustrations and unfulfilled pleasures. The knights of old who rode out to tackle the monsters on behalf of the people, were handsomely rewarded, should they survive, while their heroic deeds passed into legend and glory. A similar idea is abroad in the music business. The beast takes on many forms; in the sixties, it was often the music business itself, and musicians would tilt at the corporate windmill in the name of artistic freedom. But this many-headed hydra snapped back and few survived intact; some, like Hendrix, soared into rock immortality. Lessons have been learnt, the lambs lie down with the lions and the artists are nowadays just as anxious about their 'product' and turning up for accountants' meetings as the bosses who run the show. But still musicians do things that many wish *they* had the money and the nerve to do, and it has oft been expressed by musicians that they take the risks for ordinary people, they provide the vicarious thrills – in a very literal sense, they go out and 'chase the dragon'.

But the battles can be private as well as public: part of musician mythology is 'payin' your dues' and earning your spurs. Some musicians have regarded their drug experiences very much in this light, as a test, as a rite of passage like any Knight of the Round Table sent out on his quest. To quote Eric Clapton, 'There was definitely a heroic aspect to it.

I was trying to prove I could do it and come out alive.'

Soldiers on a crusade or musicians on the road develop a tight camaraderie and, within a band, drugs can be a very significant social cement which binds some or all of the members together. One sociologist has identified drug use and its associated rituals of preparation as one of any band's shared experiences. 'The sequential relationship of drugs before playing provides a sacrament which symbolizes the edge between onstage and offstage.'[6] This is fine, so long as all the members are involved in the same drugs with equal commitment, which is rarely the case. Where one or more persons are into heroin, the others will find it virtually impossible to communicate with them. Cocaine caused any amount of trouble in the Police because of the aggression it generated, while one member of the late Lynrd Skynrd was heavily into LSD, which tended to isolate him from the others. Eventually the social cement can crumble. One player described the demise of his band's bass player in a group of regular marijuana smokers: '... you'd start hearing these mistakes in the bass, it was really ragged ... just sorta falling apart. The thing is Mike was getting hung up on speed. First he was just popping and finally he was shooting up every morning. And he just looked like shit warmed over. Finally we just had to get rid of him, he was bringing the whole band down.'[7] The other side of the coin is peer pressure; one roadie remarked, 'A new member of a band I was with did come under a lot of pressure and ended up freebasing cocaine in a big way.'[8] Tony Sanchez, Keith Richard's supplier, said in his memoirs of life with the Stones: 'Working in the rock world and refusing to use cocaine is like joining a rugby club and preaching total abstinence. If you don't accept an occasional snort and proffer one in return, you are an instant outcast.'[9]

In tandem with camaraderie on the road comes a very deliberate policy of not only excluding outsiders, but making those who do try and get close feel very uncomfortable. Drugs are a prime instrument to achieve this, as illustrated by this tour manager:

A lot of musicians are quite nasty to people who are visiting them now and again, especially women. Suppose you wanted to pull somebody, say a girl out of the audience. If she visited the band or one of the crew and she didn't want to take the drugs, then they'd pressurize her, call her chicken, etc. When you are on a tour, you are like a family and you're totally enclosed with everybody else. Whoever visits is an outsider ... you all know what's going on because you're on the inside, so it's, 'Oh, let's try and shock them, do a lot of drugs in front of them,' especially journalists. You get them to do it as well. And it was very nice being part of the in-group.[10]

A group like the Stones, who drew people to them like a magnet, often used drugs to stay one jump ahead of the hangers-on to emphasize the value of elitism as a *chic* commodity. As described by Robert Greenfield, on tour with the band in 1972, it was the year of the 'lude' (Mandrax) – 'great for falling down, fucking people you might not otherwise speak to and forgetting your name'. This was for the audience; backstage, the rock parasites were trying to impress the Stones with the quality of the heroin they bore as gifts like the Magi to Bethlehem. However, the Stones don't impress easily; the in-chemicals on that tour were coke, Kahula and cream and tequila with grenadine, to which the Stones added amyl nitrite. This drug, chemically related to nitrous oxide (laughing gas), is used for the treatment of angina as it opens up the vessels carrying blood to the heart. On the street it comes in small glass capsules which pop when crushed (hence the slang name 'poppers') and the nitrite is then inhaled. The effect is a bit like being hit in the face with a brick, especially if you are caught unawares. Open season was declared on smack carriers and the sport was to sneak up on somebody and snap a popper under his nose.

Drugs are also 'a reward' in their own right: access to limitless quantities of illegal drugs is one of the rewards for being a rock hero – they symbolize success. If you can afford to be cavalier with expensive commodities, be it drugs or cars, you must be doing well. The same principle applies to smashing up hotel rooms; you can indulge your adolescent fantasies and then get the accountant to write a cheque afterwards. Money gives you the freedom to be contemptuous of what most people would cherish, like a valuable car. It reinforces the 'rebel' image and the notion that as a big star you can do what you like, whether it's line after line of cocaine, driving a Rolls-Royce into a swimming pool or copulating with anything that moves. This is the instant gratification demanded by children – 'gimme it all – I want it now.' Speaking as someone who has had to minister to these demands, one personal manager says most musicians are like 'overgrown children – every whim seen to'. The music industry is like Never-Never Land, nobody wants to grow up, even relatively level-headed stars like Mick Jagger. In 1965 he told Ian Whitcomb, then enjoying brief glory as a pop star. 'You don't think I want to be singing "Satisfaction" when I'm forty do you? Christ on a bicycle, I'd rather be dead!'[11] Mick Jagger was forty-four last birthday. Musicians in the public eye face many pressures and it seems painfully true that the desire to succeed in the music business burns brightest in those whose frailties that same business is particularly adept at exposing.

Unlike the writer, the painter or the sculptor, the musician (among other performing artists) cannot reach the pinnacles of artistic fulfilment in private. This can only be achieved in the recording studio surrounded by other musicians and technicians or standing on a concert stage in front of thousands. And for that to happen, musicians have to sail the shark-infested waters of the music business. Through long-term contracts, advances against royalties and the universal truth that 'he who pays the piper calls the tune', the record companies generally hold their musicians in thrall: 'No, sorry, the tour's off ... you'll have to wait another six weeks to record ... No, we don't think you should go to New York and play with --, we'd ask too much anyway ... No, we can't really let you record this - where's the hit single?' And it isn't only the companies; at every turn somebody is waiting to screw you - managers, agents, promoters and music publishers. This is a war the public never sees, surfacing by implication when label changes are announced or litigation erupts. Musicians (especially black musicians) have been systematically cheated out of millions of pounds in royalties, while bands and solo artists have been destroyed by law suits which have kept them off the road until the public have forgotten who they are. Not surprisingly, this causes much resentment and anguish in private, where some musicians give vent to their personal view that these games constitute a cynical process of manipulation. As we have seen, drugs can play a part in this process, while becoming a chemical crutch when life turns sour. As a performing artist, the musician can get trapped between an audience whom he often regards as lacking understanding and critical judgement, and the industry with which he has to work but which has entirely different goals. The fans never want an artist to 'sell out', but the company demands a more commercial approach. On the other hand, neither the company nor the fans want progression. The audiences wanted to see Hendrix smash his guitar and both the company and the management saw this as the way to sell records and put bums on seats. Hendrix backed himself into a room full of mirrors from which he couldn't get out.

For the international rock star there is plenty to run away from - the press, the fans, the conmen, the hustlers and the whole rock circus. Everyone wants a piece of the star, everyone thinks they have a right to something because they bought an album or a concert ticket, or just because the person is famous and therefore public property. There is a proto-audience that lurks on the edges desperate to be part of the scene, trying to gain acceptance by bringing in drugs and in turn believing that if a musician gets smashed on *your* drugs, then what he does subsequently has something to do with you. As Barbara Charone noted, 'characters would go to great lengths suffering personal humiliation just to please the Stones'.[12] But probably the most invidious elements are those closest to the star, the personal entourage, something which John Lennon for one became all too aware of:

> I was used to a situation where the newspaper was there for me to read and after I'd read it, somebody else could have it. ... I think that's what kills people like Presley and others of that ilk ... The King is always killed by his courtiers, not his enemies. The King is overfed, overdrugged, overindulged, anything to keep the King tied to his throne. Most people in that position never wake up. They either die mentally or physically or both ... and that's how. the Beatles ended. Not because Yoko split the Beatles, but because she showed me what it was like to be Elvis Beatle and be surrounded by sycophants and slaves who were only interested in keeping the situation as it was. And that's a kind of death.[13]

In the midst of all this vested self-interest, a star may find there is nobody he can really trust, and so retreats into drugs in order to feel secure. Mike Bloomfield, who died in 1981 of a drug overdose, had an illustrious career as a brilliant blues/rock guitarist with Bob Dylan, Paul Butterfield, Electric Flag, Muddy Waters, John Hammond and Sleepy John Estes, together with a string of solo albums: 'People may think this or that about me. People may want this or that of me. I may want this or that of me. But I know if I take a particular chemical, I'll attain a state that I can rely on. So in this way, I think drugs make a musicians's life a little more dealable.'[14]

Eric Clapton has likened heroin dependency to being wrapped up in a large ball of cotton wool, totally insulated from the world. Clapton appeared to take up heroin, both as his piece of artistic dues-paying and as his 'permission' to step out of the limelight after some personal loss and critical failures.

From the 'safety' of drugs, too, one can create an illusion of independence, of *not* being tied to the throne, in control, even though what seems like an act of rebellion is in fact very conservative and ritualistic. And again from this vantage point, another illusion – that drugs are actually necessary to play better. This was part of the mythology of Charlie Parker and infected many musicians well into the sixties and seventies, particularly those who crossed over from jazz to rock. The belief has some validity, but only in the initial stages when a loosening of inhibitions may well be a stimulus to experimentation and

221

progression. Saxophonist Dick Heckstall-Smith, who made the transition with Alexis Korner, Graham Bond, John Mayall and Jon Hiseman, puts it like this: 'My time with alcohol and speed, especially at the beginning, actually improved my playing. I thought of things I wouldn't otherwise have thought of.' How does this come about?

Well, in a sense, music is not made by the fully rational, fully conscious human being; part of a musician's training is to 'get out of the way' and let the music flow through. The perfect artist is one whose individual human characteristics are as good as wiped off – the nearer to not-there they are, the more music can take command. Alcohol and drugs are a short cut to removing many of the properties of consciousness. Alcohol enabled me to concentrate, but my tolerance soon went up and the amount I needed to get me to the right level was also enough to physically slow me down. There was more work, more pressure, so I decided I needed something to speed me up. I had warnings when my head knew what I wanted to do, but my fingers couldn't do it. After five years came the real diminishing returns...'[15]

Those who are successful or who are on the verge of success can be suddenly panicked by it all, craving stardom while being afraid of it and sometimes paranoid of being exposed as a talentless fraud. After leaving Television, guitarist Richard Lloyd looked set for a successful solo career with the launch of *Alchemy* in 1979: 'The big business aspect of chew-you-up-and-spit-you-out corporate behaviour terrified me and the "we're gonna make you a star" machinery had me running hard and scared. Frankly I showed up at some very important business meetings three sheets to the wind and the corporate people just threw me in the toilet.'[16] It took five years for Lloyd to sort out his drink and drug problem; he finally made it back with *Field of Fire*, a solo album released in 1986.

But fear of success is more than matched by fear of declining popularity. However hard it may be to claw your way to the top, it seems much harder to stay there. Brian Jones was desperate for stardom, but the harder he tried, the harder life became. Like so many before and since, he fell into the fatal trap of believing he had to be larger than life, off stage as well as on. He could never keep any perspective or distance about being a Rolling Stone – it consumed him constantly, plaguing him with insecurities and anxieties. For Brian, it was showtime all the time; he won the battles that were no use to him as a trendsetter and a drug-hog. He drowned in a swimming pool, dosed into oblivion by alcohol and sedatives, but his love affair with LSD was his real downfall. He slipped into a twilight world of unreality, unable to do the one thing that might have saved his life – play music.

Janis Joplin was a classic overdriven soul wanting to grab as many life experiences as possible and stuff them in her mouth all at once. Her physical constitution was frightening; she deliberately embarked on the toughest gig schedules, indulging in endless partying, consuming on the way vast quantities of drugs and alcohol in exotic combinations. She said to a reporter not long before she died: 'I wanted to smoke dope, take dope, lick dope, suck dope and fuck dope.' But her mental frailty could not match her physical appetites. She was very dependent on people, terrified of loneliness, yet sometimes impossibly demanding and over-bearing, She begged and pleaded for love and attention and fell into the depths of despair if she felt rejected or used. Any signs of fading popularity in rock polls she took especially hard. For her, the band she fronted was never enough – like Art Pepper, she was most at home with her drug-using friends who hung around the fringes of the business. They demanded the least of her, treated her like royalty and understood her relationship with drugs, a relationship nobody else could fathom.

Drugs have claimed the lives of many rock, pop and jazz musicians, black and white, spanning all the decades of post-war modern music, but although the actual circumstances of their deaths were very different, several of them happened during periods of transition, re-adjustment to a new situation or a career decline – all associated with great apprehension or despair.

Frankie Lymon was one of the more extreme examples of too much, too soon. Fronting a vocal group, the Teenagers, Frankie Lymon had a number one hit at the age of thirteen in 1956 with 'Why Do Fools Fall In Love?' It remained in the Hot Hundred for five months and sold two million copies worldwide. Earning $5,000 a week, Lymon was smoking eight-inch cigars, causing mayhem in hotel rooms and sleeping with a procession of much older women. Within three years, it was all over; no further recordings were anything like as successful, he split with the Teenagers and was eventually dropped by his label.

Lymon came from a harsh Puerto Rican environment in Washington Heights and stumbled back there as a chronic heroin user while still in his teens. In 1961 he was rescued by two managers who put him through a drug cure at Manhattan General Hospital and generally tried to revitalize his career. He released two singles, both ignored, and found himself tied to the small print of a Columbia recording contract for five years. In 1964 he was back in the news, but only because he was convicted on a heroin charge. In January 1967 the black magazine

Ebony ran an optimistic interview with Lymon as he struggled once more to find his feet: 'I have been born again,' Frankie proclaimed, '... I'm not ashamed to let the public know I took the cure. Maybe my story will keep some other kid from going wrong ... I was lucky, God must have been watching over me ... nobody ever sold me a bad fix.' A year later, his luck ran out. On 28 February 1968, aged twenty-six he was found dead on the bathroom floor in his grandmother's apartment. Tragically, like his brother, he had succumbed to an overdose of heroin.

Although something of a pill-popper as a teenager, Free guitarist Paul Kossoff had no real problems with drugs until the band broke up. Free were formed in 1969 and by 1970 had three albums under their belt. Their single 'All Right Now', taken from their third album, pushed them into the big league. It could have been a recipe for disaster: they were a young band (Andy Fraser, the bass player, was only fifteen when they started out) and they had found fame and fortune very quickly. However, according to manager John Glover, there were no destructive habits in the band and they formed a very tight self-contained unit which successfully absorbed all the pressures of the business. When the follow-up album and single failed to chart, however, the fortress crumbled, with singer Paul Rodgers and Andy Fraser, who together wrote all the songs, quarrelling bitterly. Yet so self-contained were Free, that when Andy anounced that the band was finished, it came as a great shock to everyone, including the management.

Drummer Simon Kirke was very upset, but managed to cope; Paul Kossoff was devastated. He was an exceptionally gifted guitarist with a unique feel and sound and also a very sensitive person. Free meant everything to him and without it he was lost. Fraser and Rodgers tried bands of their own which failed. Simon Kirke got Paul involved in a studio band which released one album, *Kossoff, Kirk, Tetsu and Rabbit*, and Kossoff also did some Island studio sessions for Robert Palmer and Jim Capaldi. But the collapse of Free had turned Kossoff to drugs: 'Pills were really his problem,' says John Glover. 'Valium, Librium, Mandrax, Tuinal – you name it, he'd take it. He had the most astounding resilience – he just took them by the handful.' Kossoff was spending much of his time in the company of other drug-using friends like Uriah Heep's bass player, Gary Thain. (In 1974, Thain survived electrocution on stage in Dallas, but quit Uriah Heep soon after saying they were insensitive to his injuries. A heroin user, he died of an overdose in February 1976. Paul Kossoff survived him by one month.)

With all the splinter bands failing, John Glover persuaded Free to reform for a farewell tour and then see what happened. Free II limped on from January to July 1972, when Andy Fraser quit again; their US tour had been badly hampered by Kossoff's non-appearance at several gigs. He was out of the band by October, replaced by Wendell Richardson from Osibisa who remained until Free broke up for the last time in July 1973. John Glover takes up the story:

Despite all the problems, I agreed to manage him [Kossoff] as a solo artist and Back Street Crawler was formed in 1975. We had to use three Americans because it was extremely difficult to get any British musicians who would work with Paul.

At that time, strenuous efforts were being made to persuade the doctor involved to stop handing out these drugs like sweets. But we couldn't get it stopped. He stayed with me and my wife for a while, so I know what he was like and he really wanted to get out of this drugs thing. But I'm convinced that all these drugs together severely affected his mind – part of him wanted to be straight, the other part staying wrecked.

I told Paul that I was going to hire somebody to be with him all the time, and everywhere they played I insisted the promoter provide police backstage to discourage people from giving him drugs. I just couldn't understand it – you'd tell people, his friends, 'Please don't give him any, they're killing him, you've seen him on stage, he can't play.' But it made no difference.

Whatever I did, he'd find a way. We were recording once at Olympic Studios. He went to the toilet, climbed out of the window, got in his car, drove off and we lost him. He went to a dealer, picked up a load of pills, took them all and then wrecked four cars in the Portobello Road, plus his own. He abandoned the car and went back to his flat where we found him eight hours later. The following day he was full of remorse. The smallest thing would send him off on a bender, like if somebody said anything about a solo he'd played. That day, as it happened, it wasn't so small: he'd just got back from a doctor who told him he was going deaf.

Paul couldn't do anything about it in the sense that all he wanted to do was to play music. So if you took him out of the environment where music was, he'd be very unhappy. Trouble was, that's where the drugs were as well. While Back Street Crawler was being established, he was reasonably straight, but once we started touring, he went completely over the top and that's when he was admitted to hospital. [This was in August 1975. The UK tour to promote the debut album was cancelled. Paul Kossoff was allegedly clinically dead for several minutes when his heart stopped.] In January 1976, we went to America to do the second album and a tour. Paul started on the pills again and the band were getting very angry. I went to his hotel room and had this furious row with him. He came at me with a bottle of Scotch; I pushed him and as he fell, he broke his little finger, his playing hand, would you believe, so he couldn't play anyway. After his finger healed, we did the tour, finishing with four dates in Los Angeles. There were a couple of girls around throughout that tour who obviously fancied Paul like mad. One of them was serious bad news and I had to keep throwing them out. We went to get the overnight plane to New York which left at 10 p.m. I was going to stay in New York to do the tour accounts while the band flew back to London. Before we left, Paul had been with this girl and she gave him a whole load of stuff – God knows what. We got the plane which was due in at 9 a.m. They called out to fasten safety belts, but Paul was not where he should have been – in the seat next to me. He was found dead in the toilet. His heart had stopped, but he must have been doing something.'[17]

This was on 19 March 1976. Six days earlier, the *Melody Maker* ran an article by Chris Welch called 'Save Our Stars', coming (as the headline pointed out) in the wake of Gary Thain's death and that of former Supremes star Florence Ballard, who was subsisting on welfare and whose death may also have been indirectly drug-related. Welch argued that the rock industry should act to try and prevent the waste of life and talent in the business:

> The singers, songwriters and musicians know the risks ... yet it is not always possible for people to be cold, calculating and rational ... [however] ... this is not to suggest that rock musicians are wholly innocents abroad. Talk to Jimmy McCulloch, the young lead guitarist with Wings, who has been playing professionally since he was fifteen, and he says firmly on the subject of pitfalls and exploitation: 'I'm no mug.'

On 28 September 1979 Jimmy McCulloch was found dead, apparently from the effects of drugs.

For fourteen years, bass player and lead vocalist Phil Lynott was the inspiration and driving force of Thin Lizzy, one of the finest bands ever to come out of Ireland. Throughout their career, they were an exciting, dynamic band, their image set by Lynott's cool, hard, machismo stance. Thin Lizzy had a stormy, unsettled history but enjoyed massive hits like the albums *Jailbreak, Johnny the Fox* and *Live and Dangerous* and chart singles 'The Boys are Back in Town' and 'Don't Believe a Word'. But despite pulling a large and loving crowd wherever they played, in 1983 it all went stale and sour and they called it a day. Lynott admitted to *Melody Maker* that he was the most reluctant of the band to split up; hardly surprising, as he had led Thin Lizzy for nearly all his professional life. He was never known for being exactly abstemious and had more than his share of drug convictions. But once Lizzy collapsed, his drug habit got worse, fuelled by the army of low-lifes that trailed after him. His solo career never took off and his marriage failed. An ex-girlfriend told a reporter; 'Sadly he could never face the fact that his days with Thin Lizzy were over. He had a jukebox in his house and every song was a Thin Lizzy record.' Drugs eventually destroyed his health and on 30 December 1985 he was admitted to Salisbury Infirmary with a serious kidney and liver infection. He died shortly afterwards.

Perhaps the one drug that has brought together all the rationales surrounding drug use in the music business is cocaine. It's a drug which can galvanize work rather than encourage sleep, it gives playtime a jet-propelled lift off, the world seems infinitely manageable and it crystallizes the industry's self-generated mythology. This drug for all seasons has also brought in its wake some serious problems for the industry over the past ten years.

Cocaine first became fashionable as an illegal drug among the Hollywood film aristocracy; 'joy powder' was readily available on the film sets – stars had bowls full of the stuff lying around at their parties. Aleister Crowley, whose book *Diary of a Drug Fiend* (1922) explored the effects of cocaine, wrote that Hollywood was populated by 'the cinema crowd of cocaine-crazed sexual lunatics'. By the end of the thirties, the fashion for cocaine had run its course to be replaced until the sixties by a whole clutch of synthetic stimulant amphetamines. Musicians, the new entertainment royalty, set the pace for cocaine's rediscovered popularity in the late sixties. Phil Spector is seen buying cocaine from Peter Fonda and Dennis Hopper in *Easy Rider* (1969). That same year, Phil Spector had a photo of himself sniffing cocaine printed on to his Christmas cards with the legend 'A Little Snow at Christmas Time Never Hurt Anybody'. *Esquire Magazine* put a golden coke spoon on its cover and cocaine-consciousness came of age in 1972 with the release of *Superfly,* a highly successful film about a black Manhattan coke dealer which spawned a classic soundtrack album and two hit singles. Since then, cocaine in all its forms – sniffed, smoked (i.e. 'freebase' or 'crack') and injected has become ubiquitous in the music and film industries and widely available throughout America. Statistics published in 1985 show that there are a purported five million regular cocaine-users in the States, while anything up to 10% of the population have tried the drug. In Britain the picture is unclear; certainly powdered cocaine circulates among media people and among those in higher income brackets, although there is evidence that cocaine is filtering down through the social strata. However, at the time of writing, Britain is nowhere near the 'cocaine epidemic' long forecast by police and politicians, although the amounts being seized are rising.

Cocaine has moved beyond high society; American documentaries on crack shown in Britain represent it as a stereotypical ghetto drug. Because of this, it has become commonplace to say that cocaine is no longer a 'champagne drug'. If this is meant to refer to its cost it is misleading. The effects of cocaine are very short-lived so that although a one-off purchase may be relatively inexpensive compared with ten years ago, to maintain a regular habit still costs a large amount of money. It is common to hear of people who are not celebrities (and thus not blatantly overcharged), spending tens of thousands of pounds in pursuit of cocaine.

Possibly one reason why cocaine is so popular in America is that it retains its jet-set image and is just as much a status symbol as any other material possession. So in this sense too, cocaine can still be regarded as a champagne drug. Its popularity can also be attributed to the fact that, unlike most other drugs, cocaine is a social chemical: 'Cocaine promotes a clubbiness among its followers. They will gravitate towards each other and form a sort of adenoidal freemasonry.'[18] And of course, with coke you don't need to go sticking needles in your arm.

Now that heroin use is levelling out in America, cocaine has given the drug-abuse industry a new lease of life. A number of doctors and academics are building careers on the platform, 'everybody thought cocaine was harmless, now we know it's not'. This, they argue, is because the symptoms which follow cessation of cocaine use were not previously regarded as true withdrawal symptoms on the heroin model, thus removing the bogey of physical addiction which, for many people, is the bench mark of a 'bad drug'.

The argument is somewhat disingenuous: the problems of cocaine have been documented since Sigmund Freud changed his mind about it last century. Over the last fifty years many blues and country artists like Victoria Spivey, Leadbelly, the Memphis Jug Band, Champion Jack Dupree, David Van Ronk and Hoyt Axton have recorded the ill-effects of the drug in their songs. A Los Angeles doctor who saw many musicians in his practice said back in 1974: 'Coke is an easy drug to abuse because it is so rapidly metabolized. But it also leaves the body rapidly, so the user, if he can afford it, does some more coke and when that detoxifies, he does some more. The next thing you know, he's in my office complaining of congestion, saying nasal sprays don't help.'[19]

The musicians who jumped on the cocaine bandwagon having been through speed, were among the first to find out the bad news: 'My nose got big enough to back a diesel truck in ... Everytime I blew my nose, there was flesh and blood on my handkerchief where it had eaten out my membranes.' (Little Richard). 'Cocaine is very insidious. I'm glad I've got it out of my system now. I can turn it down now, whereas before, I was always very tempted. It's a great feeling being able to say no.' (A Musician). 'The most deadly thing about cocaine is that it separates you from your soul.' (Quincy Jones). 'I couldn't stop, any more than I could stop breathing.' (Musician, after forty-eight-hour cocaine binge).

The trouble is that the 'edge' that comes with cocaine, the feelings of supreme self-confidence, are the very attributes necessary for success in high-pressure businesses like music. It gives you the illusion of clear-mindedness, a manipulative power over people, a control over yourself and a loathing of any kind of business etiquette. There is nothing emotionally sloppy about it: it offers a spurious sense of invulnerability that meshes with the business world's hard-headed materialism.

Eventually, however, with long-term use, this self-confidence can descend into aggression and paranoia. One manager says he can always tell if the person he is confronting face to face or even on the phone is doing cocaine: 'They get impossible to deal with, they're all over the place and you can't talk to them.'[20] *Rolling Stone* magazine asked Joni Mitchell what step in the music-making process was most likely to prove the undoing of a record. She answered, 'Cocaine! There are entire albums that would probably be very different if that drug didn't exist.'[21] According to Paul Kantner, the whole of Jefferson Airplane's album *Bark* was written under the influence of cocaine.[22]

Marvin Gaye, was totally besotted by it; he sniffed it, snorted it, ate it and rubbed it in his gums: 'No one will ever tell me it's not a great feeling. A clean, fresh high, specially early in the morning, will set you free – at least for a minute. There are times when blow [cocaine] got to me and sometimes I know it built up bad vibes inside my brain. I saw coke, though, as an elitist item, a gourmet drug and maybe that's one of its attractions.'[23]

Even when generally scarce, cocaine and heroin have always been easily available in the black ghettos of American cities. The social and economic climate of these areas tended to determine the nature of street drug use. Somehow, in the sixties, the white middle-class self-obsessed indulgences with LSD had no place in areas fighting for civil rights, gripped by urban squalor and torn apart by race riots. It has been said on a number of occasions that the police welcome or even encourage rampant drug use in black ghettos as an informal kind of social control, keeping the lid on potentially explosive situations.

Clarence Paul, a Motown producer, says there were a lot of drugs around the company in Detroit in the early sixties and that he and Marvin Gaye did their share of cocaine at that time. Gaye's biographer David Ritz said that in all the times he saw Marvin record, he was never straight; every major decision he took, he was high. On his 1983 summer tour, one of his musicians said, 'There was more coke on that tour than on any tour in the history of entertainment.'[24] Gaye obviously suffered from a whole battery of emotional problems and regarded cocaine as his trusted companion and possibly his final way out. 'Blow is what really let me fly. There were moments when I really thought I was gone. I'm talking about times – really down times – when I snorted up so much toot, I was convinced I'd be dead within minutes. I rather liked the idea of there being nothing left of me but my music.'[25]

Before his tragic death at the hands of his own father, Gaye's behaviour became increasingly bizzare. Oddly David Ritz doesn't seem to relate this directly to Gaye's long-term cocaine use, although a lay diagnosis of acute cocaine psychosis seems obvious. Gaye hired a top lawyer to investigate alleged conspiracies to shoot and poison him; he commanded his chauffeur to circle hotels several times before he would enter them and in the last ten months of his life he became totally obsessed with guns. Some of his friends tried to be light-hearted with him and dismiss his fears, but others had a vested interest in Gaye's paranoia and went along with all his demands in order to keep the gravy train rolling.

One form of cocaine which seems particularly captivating is smoked cocaine, or freebase. The technique is said to have been invented in South America for testing the purity of purchase, by separating the pure salt from any contaminants, using a strong solvent. After the process is complete, the theory is that only pure cocaine remains, leading to the stories that freebase and its ready-prepared form known as crack are super-addictive because they are so pure. In fact freebasing cannot remove all the impurities that can be found in a sample of cocaine. Nevertheless, it does act much faster than cocaine hydrochloride powder and wears off more quickly, so the potential for compulsive use is definitely there. Recently, health and law enforcement agencies in America have been expressing grave concern about the spread of cocaine in its smoked form.

As usual, the smart set got there first. Richard Pryor badly injured himself after a freebasing session back in 1980. He had been trying to filter the freebase in a pipe, using a burning cotton ball soaked in rum. The ball caught fire and Pryor suffered third-degree burns from the waist up.

Less explosive, but equally destructive, are the unfortunate circumstances in which Dave Crosby found himself as a result of compulsive freebasing. Crosby had been involved with drugs since the earliest days of his music career in the sixties and at times he got mighty annoyed at those who criticized his drug use, saying that he was stoned all the time when his name sold million of records and nobody moaned then – and if they thought they could do better, let them try.

However, once he got heavily into cocaine, he knew he was in serious trouble. In March 1982, he wrecked his car on the way to sing at an anti-nuclear rally and police found cocaine and a gun. From then on, he was a marked man. Three weeks later, he was caught freebasing in the dressing room of a Texas nightclub, where police found yet another gun. When the case came to trial in 1983, he was sentenced to five years. Normally for the small amount of cocaine Crosby had on him at that time, probation would be considered sufficient, but the judge regarded him as a public figure whose actions would always be held up for closer scrutiny.

While free, pending an appeal, Dave Crosby was arrested again on drugs and weapons charges. His luck turned when the judge allowed him to go to a drug rehabilitation unit in lieu of sentence. He stayed there seven weeks before absconding and eventually served four months in jail in 1985. At the time of writing, the appeal is still pending with Crosby looking at three years in a Texas penitentiary:

I know more about freebase than anybody! You think you plan to become an addict? It sneaks up on you. Oh, I'll just get a little high. I've kicked cigarettes, heroin, booze, everything, but this is the most horrible drug in the universe. It stays with you. I was in jail four months. Want to know how long I stayed clean when I got out? Two days. It never lets you alone. All I want to do is to be clean, man. But I'm scared I'm gonna crave it forever.[26]

As far as the physical effects of cocaine are concerned, the most famous (but actually quite rare) is septal necrosis, a perforation of the septum separating the nostrils. Plastic surgical repair is usually undertaken: nose jobs in the music business nowadays tend to mean internal scaffolding rather than cosmetic vanity.

Like amphetamine, deaths from the stimulant effects of cocaine are relatively rare. However, unlike amphetamine, cocaine has anaesthetic properties and in high doses these can depress the nervous system to the point where the heart starts skipping beats – known as the Casey Jones reaction, after the chugging locomotive of the Grateful Dead song. Death can follow through cardiac arrest or respiratory collapse, and the risk is greatly increased when cocaine is mixed with heroin to make speedballs. Most cocaine deaths recorded in America result from this concoction and also claimed the life of Meatloaf drummer Wells Kelly, when the band were in London. Cocaine was also implicated in the deaths of James Honeyman-Scott and Peter Farndon, both of the Pretenders.

When a musician (or anyone else for that matter) decides that the reasons for stopping drugs outweigh those for carrying on, how does he or she get help to achieve a drug-free life?

In America during the fifties, an era of regular incarceration for jazz musicians on drugs charges, several found their way to the prison treatment centres at Lexington and Fort Worth. For a brief time, too, there was a jazz musicians' clinic in New York. In the sixties, therapeutic communities like Phoenix House and Synanon provided a drug-free environment, while on the street outpatient methadone maintenance regimes were (and still are) widely favoured by the authorities. In Britain, too, there are methadone maintenance programmes, but since the mid-seventies, these programmes have been greatly reduced in duration as the wisdom of substituting one opiate drug for another, even in a controlled environment, has been questioned. However the advent of the AIDS epidemic has reopened the debate as it has become top priority to dissuade drug users from injecting their drugs by, for example, increasing the facilities for oral methadone maintenance programmes. Britain has therapeutic communities following the American example, including private clinics operating a style of psychotherapy known as the Minnesota Model, also imported from America.

Not surprisingly, well-heeled musicians seeking treatment normally book themselves into private clinics which offer detoxification and counselling programmes. Currently the much-publicized Betty Ford Addiction Clinic in the States seems to be the place to be seen, with the cachet of an exclusive nightclub. Others have sought out less conventional therapies.

There was a time when the keyboard skills of Nicky Hopkins graced the records of many a famous band, most notably the Rolling Stones. Then drugs took their toll and he disappeared from view, occasionally sighted in odd places – for example, slumped over a piano in a dude ranch owned by a mobster. The brainchild of L. Ron Hubbard, Scientology has attracted converts from the music business like Stanley Clarke and Chick Corea. The Scientologists also run a drug rehabilitation programme called Narconon. Hopkins went through the Narconon programme and is now quoted in a slightly chilling manner across the Scientologists' publicity:

L. Ron Hubbard is a pioneer in the truest sense of the word. He spent a lifetime researching and developing the only workable technology ever to enable man to become free.

It was this technology that literally saved my life a few years ago when I was totally caught up in the trap of drugs and had only a short time left to live. Not only was that problem terminatedly handled, but my awareness as a spiritual being and my artistic creativity have increased beyond measure.

I can never adequately express the love, admiration, respect and gratitude that I have for this superb being, who is surely the greatest friend Mankind ever had.

Thank you, Ron, for so very, very much.

Nicky Hopkins,
Musician, Composer

But probably the treatment most associated with rock stars is neuro-electric therapy, better known as the black box, developed by Dr Meg Patterson. The treatment was discovered by chance in 1972 when Dr Patterson was working with a Dr Wen in the Tung Wah Hospital, Hong Kong. Dr Wen was experimenting with electro-acupuncture, sending an electric current through acupuncture needles as a form of anaesthesia during surgery. On an island with a substantial addict population, many of his patients were addicts and in hospital they were obviously deprived of supplies. To their surprise, the doctors were getting reports from their addict patients that as well as being an effective anaesthetic, the electro-acupuncture was also relieving withdrawal symptoms on a scale which ruled out coincidence.

Back in England, the technique was adapted into a small box which generated an electric current through electrodes attached to the ears. Exactly why withdrawal symptoms are alleviated is still unclear; the most popular theory is associated with the discovery that the brain has its own natural opiates called endorphins. During a period of heroin dependency, the artificial painkiller replaces those found naturally in the brain. When heroin is stopped, the natural opiates do not rush back immediately to fill the space left by the heroin, and so the person suffers withdrawal symptoms. What the black box is supposed to do is to stimulate the natural opiates or endorphins quickly to occupy the space left by the heroin and so head off the misery of withdrawal.

In the very early days of her work, Dr Patterson had Paul Kossoff as one of her patients, but it was her treatment of Eric Clapton that earned her international publicity. The names of Clapton, Pete Townshend, Jack Bruce and George Harrison became associated with Dr Patterson as sponsors of a charity set up to fund a clinic at Broadhurst Manor in Sussex. Money came from the Robert Stigwood Organization – a rare example of the rock business becoming publicly involved in such a venture – and other commercial interests. The clinic opened in 1976 amid much ballyhoo and it was these other funders who began cynically to market 'the Black Box' as a 'cure for heroin addiction'. It isn't – and Dr Patterson never claimed that it was. In 1981, the funding ran out and, unable to attract government assistance, Dr Patterson and her husband moved to California where ironically they were sought out by Pete Townshend, whose own drink and drug habit had gone out of control. The Pattersons are now back in Britain, their most famous patient of recent times being Boy George.

So is it effective? Those who have undergone the treatment say it is, while critics in the medical profession claim that is has nothing more than a placebo effect. Research carried out in Britain has failed to demonstrate that neuro-electric therapy is any more effective in relieving withdrawal symptoms than methadone, let alone being any sort of cure, so it seems perhaps you pay your money and you take your chance. Some further points, however, are worth noting. When interviewed about their treatment, Dr Patterson's celebrity patients have gone on at some length about what a wonderful person she is, saying very little about the efficacy of the treatment itself. What may be more important than gadgets is the comfortable, non-challenging environment provided by Dr Patterson in contrast to the regimentation of the hospital clinic or the confrontational approach of the therapeutic community. Jerry Lee Lewis, admitted recently to the Betty Ford clinic, stormed out again, complaining that he wasn't getting the star treatment he thought he deserved. What the Pattersons are providing as much as anything is space and time out of the glare of publicity for rethinking and re-evaluation. At best the black box may aid detoxification, but whatever method is used, including cold turkey in a supportive environment, the coming-off is relatively easy compared with the staying-off. In the end, it is all down to the individual and to what life changes can be effected to render redundant the desire to use drugs on a regular basis.[27]

However effective the black box might be, it could not prevent Eric Clapton, for example, sliding into some very destructive drinking habits, causing more physical damage than his heroin use ever did. Clapton avoided the dangers of injecting by snorting the drug, and heroin, in any case, unlike alcohol, does not attack the body's vital organs. Since the mid-seventies he has been hospitalized more than once and warned very seriously about his alcohol intake.

Becoming an alcoholic after giving up other drugs is quite common among ex-users. Being a long-term, heavy drug user is an all-consuming occupation – all your physical and mental energies are channelled in one direction. When you stop, there is an enormous chasm to fill – and initially it has to be filled with something equally consuming of time and passion. For some it is religion and for others the bottle, but usually they survive. Some, like Jerry Lee Lewis, Dave Crosby and several others whose predicaments are not public knowledge, struggle on.

15

Just Say No?

You know it's the eighties when even Sly Stone is getting off drugs.
Rolling Stone

If most of those groups at Live Aid had donated their cocaine bills for the year, it would have saved as many lives.
Chris Maund, *Melody Maker,* 20 December 1986

I want to go straight / I want to go straight / I'm sick and tired of taking drugs / And staying up late.
Ian Dury 'I Want to Go Straight'

From about 1982 to 1986, the British government made several public statements which proclaimed that drug abuse was Britain's number one problem of social concern, 'the most serious threat to peacetime Britain,' as one politician put it. During that period, there was a steep rise in the number of heroin users and in the amount of drugs seized by police and customs. These figures continue to rise, even though government and media concerns have turned to AIDS. But the drugs issue won't lie down; drug users who share needles are one of the AIDS high-risk groups, forcing the government to support needle-exchange schemes in order to help prevent the spread of the disease.

Through that four-year period, drugs were given the highest priority by those government departments dealing with health, education and law enforcement. More money was made available for treatment and counselling services, special drugs workers were appointed to schools, new anti-trafficking legislation was passed and the police intelligence network was strengthened. And in an attempt to get the anti-heroin message across, the government ran a national TV and press advertisement campaign.

Beyond screening government warnings, the television companies

became heavily involved in the drugs issue with numerous documentaries, anti-drug themes built into dramas, such as the school serial
'Grange Hill', and specific campaigns organized by BBC's 'Drugwatch',
the Radio 1 'Drug Alert' initiative and TV's 'Action on Drugs', among
others. In America, there have been parallel developments both from
government (in the shape of Nancy Reagan's 'War against Drugs') and
within the entertainment industry. The music and film industries in the
States have come under heavy public scrutiny and government criticism
as alleged purveyors of pro-drug attitudes. Both industries have been
forced to respond with public declarations detailing what efforts they
have been making to de-glamorize drug use. So important has this issue
become in America that Senate hearings were held in 1985 at which
various media representatives were invited to provide depositions and
statements demonstrating how they were 'doing their bit' to warn of the
dangers of drugs. Michele Vonfeld of the rock video station MTV
submitted a written statement which began.

> At the outset, I wish to reiterate that MTV is keenly aware of its
> social responsibility to provide programing of the highest quality and
> to inform its viewers about social issues relevant to them. In this
> regard, our video channels have:
>> Voluntarily adopted program content guidelines relating to drug
>> and alcohol abuse.
>> Aired a significant number of Public Service Announcements
>> (PSAs) warning against drug and alcohol abuse in addition to
>> messages on behalf of a large number of community organizations.
>> Begun working with the New Jersey State Governor's 'Committee
>> on Children's Services Planning' to collaborate on the production
>> of a series of PSAs discouraging drug abuse by young people.

Probably because of rock's long-standing pro-drug image, those
musicians who went public in Britain with anti-drug sentiments received
a high profile in the media and started a trend of pop celebrities
becoming publicly involved in charitable works.

The impetus for rock's anti-drug face came from Pete Townshend. In
1984 he gave several interviews documenting his own problems with
drink and drugs and the help he received from Meg Patterson. He was
courted in government circles as a spokesman for young people and
invited to speak at the Conservative Party Conference in October that
year. But despite all the hype and the messianic feel to some of his
personal statements, Pete Townshend's 'Double O' charity has been
about the only music-based initiative that has put real money in the

coffers of drug services in Britain. Press releases and promises don't pay the bills.

The Double O was originally set up in 1976 by the Who (or the 'OO' hence Double O) to channel group funds into charitable works. Double O lay dormant when the band split up, but was revived by Pete Townshend after he had come through his own dependency problems. Approximately 90% of the charity's work is helping drug agencies to whom they have given in excess of £150,000 in the financial years 1985–7. Agencies who have benefited include Clouds House, Broadway Lodge and Phoenix House. Double O does not endorse any particular treatment method and has supplied funds to a range of modalities from neuro-electric therapy to behavioral therapies such as the Minnesota Model.

By no means does Double O confine its fundraising activities to music events, but some of its more notable evenings included the St James Square Balls held in 1985 and 1986 in conjunction with the Variety Club of Great Britain. These events were private, with 300 invited guests who came to listen to Elton John in 1985 and Courtney Pine in 1986 and donated several thousand pounds in the process. £25,000 was raised in 1985 when Pete Townshend's Deep End played the Brixton Academy with Simon Phillips, Dave Gilmour and Chucho Merchau of the Eurythmics.

There is a rather sad footnote to the Double O story. Once abstinent, some ex-users become heavily involved in crusading about the evils of drugs. But after a while, they want to push that part of their lives into the past. This has happened to Pete Townshend to the point where he has put a stop to Double O's work in the drugs field. It will remain a small private charity. Obviously good news for Pete Townshend because he is continuing to put distance between himself and dangerous times, but unfortunate for the agencies the charity was supporting. Sally Arnold ran Double O for the past two and a half years and is currently engaged in writing a guide to fundraising for other agencies which also incorporates information about the projects the charity has funded.

Dire Straits, and in particular bassist John Illsley, have become involved in sponsoring the Life Education Project, founded in Australia by the Reverend Ted Noffs. The project uses audio-visual aids to demonstrate the effects of drugs on the body and was launched in British schools in 1986.

Interspersed with these sustained efforts have been several 'one-offs' involving the music business. In Britain these have included GLC anti-heroin campaign gigs in London and the charity concert given by Lenny Henry and starring Elvis Costello which raised £15,000 for

Broadreach House in Plymouth. Feargal Sharkey has been photographed wearing a 'Heroin is a Life Sentence' T-shirt, a slogan also taken up by Madness, Big Country and Tom Robinson, while on 20 February 1986 the *Daily Mail* carried the headline, 'Steer Clear of Drugs or You'll Finish up Dead Says Ozzy', reporting that Ozzy Osbourne had recorded an anti-drugs message for Yorkshire Police. EMI released an album called 'Live in the World', organized by the anti-smack campaign and with proceeds going to Phoenix House, and the record covers of the Streetsounds and Streetwave Labels have carried the following announcement:

Hard drugs kill – and the people who sell them are MURDERERS. If you see someone dealing hard drugs, do something about it, put a stop to it. Merely wanting our environment to improve isn't enough – it's gotta start somewhere, we have got to take responsibility, we have got to take action against those murdering scum.

Just about all of us have got a younger brother or sister, cousin or nephew. Is it going to be the right time when we see them jacking up? Let's clean it up now. Step one: PUT THESE ANIMALS AWAY!

Predictably there have been some sour notes struck since rock rolled up its sleeves on the drugs issue. In his pre-Live Aid days, Bob Geldof tried to organize an anti-heroin gig at the Hippodrome in London. At that time (1984), musicians were possibly still wary of nailing their colours to the mast over drugs and several acts pulled out, much to Geldof's now famous chagrin. In the end, the organization by the sponsoring charity was so bad that the whole event was cancelled.

And so it has been with many other much-touted projects. Rock is no stranger to grandiose schemes which fail through a combination of poor organization, over-optimism, overblown egos and the machinations of self-seekers. The drugs bandwagon provided an ideal vehicle for aspiring Geldofs to make a name for themselves. Fortunately, most of these schemes fizzled out in the planning stage, partly because the same group of stars were getting tired of being asked to do charity gigs. More important, some of these crusading efforts miss the point entirely when trying to recruit the services of musicians. Many musicians use small amounts of illicit drugs from time to time, some marijuana or perhaps a line of cocaine, and they would feel uncomfortable being involved in strident, gung-ho exhortations not to touch anything because it's all so evil. They might be attracted to more realistic campaigns which recognized that kids will try drugs of all descriptions from alcohol and glue to heroin, but that valuable lessons can be taught about how not to come to undue harm and what to do if you notice a friend's drug use becoming a problem.

So what is one to make of all this activity? Certainly enterprises like Double O, which was sincere and well organized (despite having only two staff boxed up in a rabbit hutch off Covent Garden), are to be praised for generating much needed cash for services which are still very stretched, despite government initiatives. But as far as anti-drug messages are concerned, one gets a strong smell of razmatazz and a desire to clean up sullied images.

All the advice to the government prior to the advertising campaign was 'don't do it – it's a waste of money', and once the evaluations were made, the best that could be said for the campaign was that it hardened anti-heroin sentiments among those who were already negative in their attitudes towards drugs. Far from deterring youngsters, the wasted image portrayed in the adverts had a degree of romantic appeal and the accompanying poster accrued pin-up status. In that sense, pop stars who spout anti-drug messages are no more in touch with young people than Whitehall civil servants and government ministers. How can anyone seriously believe that a tax-exiled celebrity has anything to say to a kid living in rural Devon or the sprawling conurbation of Greater Manchester?

Because of this obvious distance between 'broadcaster' and 'receiver' one could interpret the message of some of music's drug survivors as 'I came through it because I'm a bit special but you're not, so don't do it.' And of course, it's easy to be anti-heroin when you spend much of your time nose down in a pile of cocaine.

And what of the music business itself? Behind the public pronouncements, how far does anti-drug feeling extend? Some musicians like Frank Zappa and Bruce Springsteen have always taken a hard line against drug use in their bands. But now even *Rolling Stone*, flagship of the sixties counterculture, has announced that it reserves the right to test employees for alcohol and drugs, thus falling into line with the big push among American employers towards compulsory urine testing. It is also true that among those musicians now in their forties who grew up with *Rolling Stone*, the use of drugs has significantly diminished.

But for the stars of the post-punk era it would seem that old music habits die hard, with drug revelations about Boy George, Modern Romance, Duran Duran, Julian Lennon, Topper Headon (Clash), Keith Levene (PIL), Nik Kershaw (pop's own supergrass, according to the *Daily Mail*) and the deaths of Sid Vicious, Malcolm Owen (the Ruts) and members of the Pretenders. And followers of the Mission, a much heralded band for the late eighties, cannot have failed to notice their commitment to putting the sex and drugs back into rock 'n' roll.

What seems to be happening in the entertainment business (particularly the American film industry) is the dawning of an age of denial. This can only be bad news. Irrespective of what reasons and whose fault, jazz, soul, country, pop, folk and rock, have lost too many of their brightest stars to drugs, usually through fear of their addiction being made public. Most of music's drug survivors have been the ones who got into treatment; but for the moment, with the AIDS panic in full cry, fear and denial is the name of the game.

Will there ever be a time when musicians don't take drugs? Realistically speaking, no. The music business does not exist in a vacuum; it operates within a society where drug use is universal. Moreover, inside the industry itself special conditions prevail. Temperamental artists try to co-exist with very hard-nosed businessmen; drugs are supplied in abundant quantity to soak up the huge amounts of money available to buy them; punishing schedules are worked for which the term 'unsocial hours' might have been invented. Extreme situations demand extreme 'remedies', most of which are illegal, often serving to exacerbate unhealthy circumstances.

What hope for change? The business is unlikely to be taken over by nice, kind people who wouldn't dream of ripping anybody off. Artists are unlikely to relinquish their egos and live in peace with themselves, their fellow artists and the men in suits. And some might argue that if this did come to pass, the fire of music that gets people buying records and tickets would be extinguished. Or to put it another way, as a doctor once told an alcoholic musician: 'I can cure your drinking, but I might also cure your talent.'

POSTSCRIPT

However prominent the anti-drugs stance of the music business, it seems musicians will be forever marked men. A musician friend of mine was arrested at Heathrow on his way back from the Caribbean on charges of being a suspected drugs smuggler. No drugs were found (in fact, he hasn't even drunk alcohol for twenty years) and the arrest was made solely on the evidence of his employment status, his choice of holiday resort, dental floss and condoms.

To eager customs officials, condoms and dental floss constitute the necessary equipment for bringing drugs into Britain 'internally' from tropical climes. The method is known as body packing and I leave the rest to the imagination.

So musicians beware – keeping your teeth clean and following government guidelines on safe sex can seriously damage your freedom.

Appendix: *A Touch Too Much*

The highway to pop immortality is littered with the wrecks of smashed cars and planes, while in the toilets and motel rooms lie the bodies of those who've had a touch too much.

A number of factors contribute to an acute toxic reaction or overdose. Where heroin is concerned, those who resume injecting after a period of abstinence are especially at risk; too often they make the mistake of picking up at the dosage level where they stopped. In the interim, the body's tolerance has fallen and cannot cope with what has now become too powerful a dose. Janis Joplin has been off for six months prior to her death, although her passing was a classic drug death where all was not as it seemed.

Certainly her period of abstinence played an important role, but she might have lived through it had she not been drinking. Alcohol is implicated in many so-called heroin deaths: both drugs depress the nervous system and in combination, one will exacerbate the action of the other to the point where the respiratory system may pack up.

Deaths are also caused by the impurities contained in street drugs; paying over the odds for your supplies, as most famous musicians do, is no guarantee of quality. To die from an overdose of relatively pure heroin can take anything from one to twelve hours, starting with lethargy and progressing to prolonged coma during which time effective treatment can be administered. However, users have been found dead with the needle still sticking in a vein and research in America has identified quinine as the contaminant capable of causing sudden death.

Then again, users have succumbed to the 'hot shot'. The story goes that being accustomed to a New York heroin purity of no more than 5%, Sid Vicious's metabolism was unprepared for the 30% plus powder thoughtfully brought over from England.

Should those who inject their drugs survive the hazards of a shot too pure or too impure, or the dangers of using drugs in combination, there are other perils to avoid. In 1939, an epidemic of malaria broke out among New York addicts caused by using contaminated needles. The same unwise practice of sharing 'works' has also been responsible for the spread of hepatitis and AIDS.

But even those who snort their drugs are not immune from the uncertainties inherent in using illegal drugs of unknown constituency. At least two musicians have died through mistaking heroin for cocaine. Folk artist Tim Buckley was one, but the most celebrated case involved Robbie McIntosh, drummer with the Average White Band. On 23 September 1974, the band were at a party hosted by record company executive Kenneth Moss. McIntosh collapsed after snorting what he thought was cocaine but in fact turned out to be heroin laced with strychnine. Panic stricken at what he had done, Moss persuaded McIntosh's wife that everything would be all right if she took the drummer back to his North Hollywood hotel room instead of going to hospital. She took the advice and McIntosh died. Guitarist Alan Gorrie was very nearly another victim of the same batch, but he was saved by singer Cher who kept him walking about packed with ice to prevent him losing consciousness. Moss pleaded guilty to involuntary manslaughter and served four months with four years probation.

Overdosing is a shorthand description for a very complicated clinical phenomenon, but in the face of research conducted in 1984 it becomes almost inexplicable. It was already known that ex-users often exhibit the symptoms of withdrawal without going near any drugs, just by walking in the vicinity of an old drug-using haunt. It now seems that these Pavlovian-type responses may also be a factor in who survives an overdose and who doesn't. Out of an admittedly small sample of ten survivors of drug overdoses interviewed, seven had overdosed in circumstances unusual for their own drug use. For example a regular heroin user who usually injected alone was the sole overdoser in the company of others using a common supply. If this theory is correct, drug-using musicians are particularly at risk, as they are often away from home in strange places and in the company of people they don't know.[1] According to the memoirs of Peggy Caserta, a lover of Janis Joplin, the singer invariably shot up with her friends, but when she took her last fix she was alone.[2]

A verdict of death from overdosing can be a handy let-out for a coroner when no other impelling evidence presents itself like suicide, violence or obvious natural causes. Did Elvis die from one last handful of uppers or downers or did his heart just give out after years of drugs and junk food, i.e. natural causes? For a family and a business anxious for reputations to remain unsullied, the latter is much preferred.

244

Thus for all these reasons, determining the cause of death where drugs are implicated, is hardly an exact science. What follows is a list of those whose deaths appear directly or indirectly to have been attributable to the misuse of drugs.

Those Who Reportedly Died from the Direct Toxic Effects of Drugs

Deaths due entirely to alcohol have been excluded

SONNY BERMAN   16 January 1947
Star trumpeter with Woody Herman who overdosed on heroin aged twenty-three

HANK WILLIAMS   1 January 1953
Combination of alcohol and amphetamines

CARL PERKINS   17 March 1958
Pianist with Art Pepper and other West Coast Jazz musicians

DINAH WASHINGTON   14 December 1963
Combination of alcohol and amphetamine – like diet pills, although some reports quoted barbiturates as the cause of death

RUDY LEWIS   1964
Replaced Ben E. King in the Drifters, but died of a drug overdose the morning they were due to record 'Under the Boardwalk'

BRIAN EPSTEIN   27 August 1967
Died from an overdose of a bromide-based sleeping pill called Carbitrol

FRANKIE LYMON   28 February 1968
Heroin overdose

AL WILSON   3 September 1970
Guitarist with Canned Heat who was nearly blind and suffered from depression, died of a barbiturate overdose

JIMI HENDRIX   18 September 1970
Barbiturate overdose

JANIS JOPLIN 4 October 1970
Overdose of heroin, alcohol and Valium in combination

JIM MORRISON 3 July 1971
Some reports say heart attack, others suggest a heroin overdose. His widow Pamela died of a heroin overdose on 24 April 1975.

BRIAN COLE 2 August 1972
The bass player and vocalist with the Association died of a heroin overdose

RORY STORM 27 September 1972
Leader of Rory Storm and the Hurricanes, a popular Mersey band who boasted Ringo Starr on drums before he joined the Beatles. Storm took an overdose of sleeping pills in a suicide pact with his mother

PHIL SEAMAN 13 October 1972
Long time heroin user and one of the greats of British jazz drumming. He died of a heroin overdose

BILLY MURCIA 6 November 1972
Drummer with the New York Dolls overdosed on alcohol and pills

DANNY WHITTEN 18 October 1972
Guitarist with Neil Young's Crazy Horse, died of a heroin overdose. A roadie in the band went the same way

MISS CHRISTINE 18 October 1972
One of Girls Together Outrageous (GTO), a groupie collective who recorded an album in 1969 on Frank Zappa's Straight label. She died of a heroin overdose

GRAM PARSONS 19 September 1973
A major pioneer of country rock. Actual cause of death inconclusive, but possibly due to a combination of heroin, cocaine, alcohol and amphetamine. His manager stole the coffin *en route* to the funeral and burned the body in the desert, apparently in accordance with Parsons' wishes

VINNIE TAYLOR 17 April 1974
Guitarist with Sha Na Na, died of a heroin overdose

ROBBIE McINTOSH   23 September 1974
Drummer with the Average White Band died of a heroin overdose
thinking it was cocaine

NICK DRAKE   23 October 1974
British folk artist who died of an overdose of Tryptizol, a trycyclic anti
depressant

TIM BUCKLEY   29 June 1975
Heroin overdose. A case of mistaken identity – for cocaine

GARY THAIN   February 1976
Formerly bass player with Uriah Heep, Thain was found floating in his
bath dead from a heroin overdose. He was a very good friend of Paul
Kossoff; the *Rolling Stone Encyclopædia of Rock & Roll* cites their
deaths as occurring on the same day, 19 March 1976. Eerie, if true, but
in fact Thain died about six weeks earlier.

PAUL KOSSOFF   19 March 1976
Died *en route* home from a US tour with Back Street Crawler. Had a
history of heart trouble, but was known to have been involved in heavy
sedative drug-taking prior to his death

TOMMY BOLIN   4 December 1976
Star guitarist with a later permutation of Deep Purple. Died of a heroin
overdose

ELVIS PRESLEY   16 August 1977
The great mystery (or one of them at any rate). Presley had so disturbed
his metabolism with horrendous quantities of drugs, anything could
have happened, but the deathly hush from official sources suggests an
overdose. Few people believed 'cardiac arrhythmia'

GREG HERBERT   31 January 1978
Saxophonist with Blood, Sweat and Tears. Died of a drug overdose on
tour with the band in Holland

PETER MEADEN   5 August 1978
First manager of the Who, who committed suicide with pills

KEITH MOON   7 September 1978
Just one month later and by the cruellest of ironies, Keith Moon

overdosed on Heminevrin, the drug he was taking to help control his drinking

SID VICIOUS   2 February 1979
Heroin overdose

JIMMY McCULLOCH   29 September 1979
Former Wings guitarist died of an unspecified drugs overdose

MALCOLM OWEN   14 July 1980
Lead singer with British New Wave band, the Ruts. Owen died of a heroin overdose

TIM HARDIN   29 December 1980
Many long-term heroin users 'mature out' of their dependency by their mid-thirties. Sadly, Hardin didn't and died of a heroin overdose aged thirty-nine

STEVE TOOK and DAVE BIDWELL
Took was formerly with Marc Bolan in Tyrannosaurus Rex; Dave Bidwell played drums with the British blues band Chicken Shack. Took was sacked by Bolan because of his drugs problem. He finally teamed up with Bidwell in a band called Shagrat, which played only one gig, the principals reportedly being stoned throughout. Both Took and Bidwell died through overdoses as did both Took's girlfriend and Bidwell's wife

MIKE BLOOMFIELD   15 February 1981
A stellar blues guitarist and committed drug user, found in his car having apparently overdosed on heroin

JOHN BELUSHI   5 March 1982
Not strictly a musician, despite the *Blues Brothers* movie, but a drug hog of the first order. Died of a drug overdose – a mixture of heroin and cocaine known as a speedball. Had the same 'minder' who tried to keep Eagles guitarist Joe Walsh away from dangerous substances, but it didn't save him

LESTER BANGS   30 April 1982
One of the great names of rock journalism found dead in his New York apartment of a heart attack precipitated by stimulants

JAMES HONEYMAN SCOTT   16 June 1982
Guitarist with the Pretenders who succumbed to a cocktail of alcohol
and cocaine

PETE FARNDON   16 April 1983
Former bass player with the Pretenders and another 'speedball' victim

WELLS KELLY   20 October 1984
Drummer with Meatloaf and another victim of the heroin/cocaine combo

GARY HOLTON   25 October 1985
Vocalist with the Heavy Metal Kids, a mid-seventies British band, and
later TV star who died of a heroin overdose

Those Whose Deaths were Drug-Related

NB Most of these people were also heavy smokers; but the role of
tobacco in musician mortality cannot be properly ascertained.

FATS NAVARRO   7 July 1950
His death was officially listed as tuberculosis complicated by narcotics
addiction. Other sources say a heroin overdose

CHARLIE PARKER   12 March 1955
Death was officially attributed to stomach ulcers and pneumonia with a
contributing condition of advanced cirrhosis and heart disease. Parker
was thirty-five when he died; to the doctor he looked twenty years older

BILLIE HOLIDAY   17 July 1959
On admittance to hospital the diagnosis changed from non lethal dose of
heroin to a liver complaint complicated by heart failure and then
changed again to a serious kidney condition. Alcohol was probably the
real culprit, although years of heroin use would have done nothing for
her digestive system

BRIAN JONES   3 July 1969
Drowning associated with alcohol, amphetamine and 'sleeping pills'

CLYDE McPHATTER   13 June 1972
Lead vocalist with the Drifters, he had a long history of drug and alcohol

problems and died from complications arising out of heart, liver and kidney disease

LOWELL GEORGE   29 June 1979
One of the finest slide guitar players of all time, George led the awesome Little Feat. His drug problems, however, pushed him to the sidelines towards the end and he died of a heart attack related both to drugs and obesity

CARL RADLE   30 May 1980
Eric Clapton's first-choice bass player for nearly a decade, Radle had serious heroin problems and died of a chronic liver complaint

ALEX HARVEY   3 February 1982
Harvey was forty-nine when he died, ostensibly of a heart attack, although it was said this was brought about by the large amount of speed being pushed at him to maintain a punishing schedule

ART PEPPER   25 May 1985
He was on methadone at the time of his death. It seems as if after years of drug and alcohol abuse, his body just said 'enough'

PHIL LYNOTT   30 December 1985
Died in hospital from severe kidney and liver infection

Those Who Had a Long History of Drug Misuse but Died of Unrelated Causes

WARDELL GRAY   25 May 1955
The tenor sax player was found with a broken neck in the Nevada Desert probably killed by gangsters because of gambling debts. An official report said he was a drug addict, but no autopsy was performed

GRAHAM BOND   8 May 1974
One of the unsung heroes of British jazz-rock and r & b and a legend in the music business. Bond had a serious drug habit for many years, mainly heroin and opiate-based cough medicine, but in practice any-thing would do. A couple of months after being discharged from mental hospital, he died under a London underground train

MAMA CASS ELLIOTT   29 July 1974
Allegedly she died after choking on a sandwich in a London flat. It may have been fate that she died so close to Graham Bond in time and location. Bond and Mama Cass had something of a fling when he was in the States in the late sixties, sharing intimacies and syringes

DENNIS WILSON   29 December 1983
Beach Boys' drummer who drowned in the sea while swimming: the autopsy revealed alcohol, cocaine and Valium in his system

AND FINALLY ...

OTIS REDDING and RICK NELSON   10 December 1967
                                            31 December 1985
The stuff that rock rumours are made of. Both came down in planes, but ... one story that circulated after Redding's death was that he was out of his head on cocaine on the evening of the flight and that rescuers pulled him from the *pilot's* seat when it ditched in a Wisconsin lake. First reports of Rick Nelson's death were that the plane caught fire after a cocaine freebasing session. However, further investigation suggests that as usual the press took 2 and 2 and made 137. The only basis for the story was that all the bodies had contained recently ingested cocaine or alcohol. From this, knowing a little of the freebasing process, some hack made the quantum leap and came up with the freebase fire story

Notes

(Where the full reference is cited in the bibliography, only the first named author is cited here)

INTRODUCTION

1. *Narcotics Control Digest*, 21 August 1985, p.5
2. Bakalar, p.68

CHAPTER ONE

1. Latimer, p.40
2. Berridge, p.66
3. McNamara *(Step Right Up)*, p.27
4. ibid., p.65
5. Epstein, p.35
6. McNeal, p.77
7. Cook, p.119
8. Toll, pp.221-2
9. White (Charles), p.31

CHAPTER TWO

1. Carroll, p.238
2. ibid., p.307
3. Toll, pp.65-6
4. ibid., p.97

CHAPTER THREE

1. Mezzrow, p.98
2. ibid., p.4
3. ibid., p.18
4. Ostransky, p.2

5. Sidran, p.44
6. Before he switched to clarinet, Mezzrow wanted to be a saxophonist
7. Mezzrow, p.55
8. ibid., p.59
9. Morris, p.22
10. ibid., p.25
11. Mezzrow, p.72
12. ibid., pp.79-80
13. Leonard, pp.60-1
14. Mezzrow, p.99
15. ibid., p.100
16. ibid., p.175
17. ibid., p.210
18. Palmer, Robert: *Deep Blues* (London: Macmillan, 1982), p.31
19. Mezzrow, p.216
20. ibid., pp.345-6
21. ibid., p.275

CHAPTER FIVE

1. Ehrenberg, p.83
2. ibid., p.84
3. Leonard, p.37
4. ibid., p.38
5. Bonnie, p.34
6. Jones, p.113
7. Sloman, p.42
8. Anslinger, p.8
9. Anslinger private papers
10. ibid.
11. ibid.
12. *Variety,* 26 November 1969
13. Anslinger private papers

CHAPTER SIX

1. Hawes, p.9
2. This is not to suggest that bebop was 'born' in Kansas City, but that its political set-up in the thirties made Kansas a particularly fertile breeding ground for the development of new music
3. Hentoff, p.87
4. Taylor, p.180
5. Mailer, pp.2-3
6. Hentoff, p.87
7. Hawes, p.96
8. ibid., p.86

9. Pepper, p.5
10. Charles, pp.110-11
11. Russell, p.232
12. Reisner, p.80
13. Hawes, p.13
14. ibid., p.45
15. Pepper, p.226
16. Taylor, p.156
17. Pepper, p.97

Two researchers, Zinberg and Lewis, quote the case of an American jazz musician (unnamed) who was admitted to hospital a second time with hepatitis. Since he used junkie slang in his speech, it was suspected he might be an addict. He admitted ashamedly that he had tried heroin twice and hadn't enjoyed it either time. He begged his doctors not to tell his wife or family since he would lose the status of being hooked. He was so psychologically dependent on the *experience* of being a heroin user (he obviously wasn't dependent on the drug), that the only way the hospital could get him to abide by the treatment regime for treating hepatitis was to play up the fact that having the disease was a sure sign of being an addict and so preserve his own self-image and esteem (Laurie, pp.52-3)

18. Hentoff, pp.84-5
19. Pepper, p.41
20. *Downbeat,* 20 February 1958
21. Hawes, p.32
22. Shaw, p.310
23. Reisner, p.19
24. ibid., p.52

CHAPTER SEVEN

1. O'Day, p.137
2. ibid., p.145
3. ibid., p.227
4. Holiday, p.132
5. Anslinger, p.199
6. O'Day, p.268

INTRODUCTION TO PART TWO

1. However, jazz was not entirely *passé* to young people; trad jazz remained part of the European dance scene to 1962
2. Hopkins (*Elvis*), p.119

CHAPTER EIGHT

1. Kerouac, p.114
2. Fong-Torres, p.450

3. Lyle, *British Journal of Addiction*, 1953, *50* p.52
4. Spear, *British Journal of Addiction*, 1969, *64* p.254
5. Brown, p.38
6. Burchill *(Damaged Gods),* p.34
7. Like the Krays and the Richardsons, the Nash gang was one of London's major criminal organizations of the sixties
8. Wilson, C.W.M. (ed): *The Pharmacological and Epidemiological Aspects of Adolescent Drug Dependence* (Oxford: Pergamon, 1968), p.266
9. Interview with author
10. Clarke (Steve), p.32
11. ibid., p.24
12. Marsh, p.122
13. ibid., p.140
14. Pidgeon, John: *Facing the Music. History of Rock,* 1982, *4*, p.808
15. Stein, p.295
16. ibid., p.266
17. Bockris, p.31
18. *Melody Maker,* 1 March 1986
19. Gay and Elsenbaumer, p.197
20. *High Times,* March 1984
21. *New Musical Express,* 11 December 1976
22. Speed was also an integral part of the Northern Soul dance circuit in the clubs of northern towns like Wigan

CHAPTER NINE

1. Hofmann, Albert: *LSD: My Problem Child* (New York: McGraw-Hill, 1980), p.15
2. Lee, p.57
3. ibid., p.71
4. Robinson, p.135
5. Chapple, p.305
6. ibid., p.20
7. Jackson, p.45
8. DMT is a synthetic hallucinogen similar to that found naturally in psilocybin mushrooms. The confusion of initials which represents the pharmacological shorthand of hallucinogens was captured in *The Alphabet Song* (1968), an unashamedly pro-drug anthem by David Peel and the Lower East Side.

A-B-C-D-E-F-G–LSD and DMT, P.O.T. and L-S-D
D-M-T & amphetamine
P-O-T and L-S-D, L-M-D and D-M-T S-T-P
D-M-T L-S-D got hold of me
Smoke pot, Smoke pot, everybody smoke pot.
Smoke pot, Smoke pot, everybody smoke pot.
Smoke pot, Smoke pot, everybody smoke pot.

ABCD P-O-T, L-S-D and amphetamine
D-M-T S-T-P heroin and C-O-P, L-S-D, P-O-T C-O-P
A-B-C L-S-D
Help! I'm stoned
Help! I'm stoned
Help! I'm stoned
L-S-D P-O-T, D-M-T S-T-P C-O-P & amphetamine
Here comes the cat with heroin

9. Metzner, p.304
10. Gray, p.119
11. ibid., p.192
12. 'Yellow Submarine' has often been thought of as referring to barbiturates or amphetamines. This suggests it was probably an oblique reference to LSD
13. Other acid-pop singles included 'San Francisco Nights' (Eric Burdon); 'I Can Hear the Grass Grow' (The Move); 'Whiter Shade of Pale' (Procol Harum) and 'Mellow Yellow' (Donovan). One of the earliest mentions of LSD on record was a single released by the Gamblers in 1962
14. Chapple, p.108
15. Radio Caroline survived by moving into international waters
16. The oft-touted 'psychedelic revival' in the UK has never really taken off. The only artists who have established themselves in commercial terms have been the Psychedelic Furs, Julian Cope and the Mission.

CHAPTER TEN

1. The FBI later claimed that they set McCartney up. His luggage was screened as he boarded the plane in America and the marijuana was detected. But instead of arresting him, the FBI informed Japanese customs. Quoted in: Greenshaw, Wayne: *Flying High: Inside Big-time Drug Smuggling* (New York: Dodd Mead, 1984), p.91
2. Comment to author
3. Wiener, p.81
4. ibid., p.225
5. Under the Misuse of Drugs Act 1971, this regulation only applies to opium and marijuana and has been a quirk of British drugs legislation since 1920
6. Brown, p.282
7. *Musician,* August 1985, p.110
8. *Macon Telegraph,* 20 August 1979
9. ibid.
10. *Macon Telegraph,* 29 May 1976
11. *Macon Telegraph,* 20 August 1979
12. Although Davison was caught with a pound of cocaine, he was only charged with half that amount. The rest 'disappeared'. Nowadays, with the high-profile crackdown on drug dealing, for possession of half a pound of cocaine with intent to supply the convicted person probably would be sentenced to

at least five years in jail.
13. Cornwell, p.27

CHAPTER ELEVEN

1. Epstein, p.41
2. ibid., p.43
3. The study was conducted jointly by the Association of the Bar of the City of New York and the Drug Abuse Council
4. CBS Records ran a slogan in the late sixties 'The Man Can't Bust Our Music'. More recently, Yves St Laurent came up with some seductive marketing images for a perfume called Opium
5. *Variety,* 23 September 1970
6. Epstein, p.170
7. ibid., p.171
8. *Billboard,* 24 October 1970
9. ibid., 21 November 1970
10. ibid., 14 November 1970
11. *Rolling Stone,* 15 April 1971
12. ibid.
13. *Billboard,* 27 October 1973
14. For example, Schwartz (1972); Douse (1973); Robinson (1976).
15. Stillman, Deane and Weiner, Rex: *The Woodstock Generation* (New York: Viking Press, 1979)
16. Schwartz 1972
17. Bearing in mind that most of the overtly drug-oriented songs tend to be anti-drug, an interesting variation on the theme of drug lyrics and youthful experimentation with drugs has been demonstrated by Arlene Marks in a study entitled 'Adolescents Discuss Themselves and Drugs through Drugs', *Journal of Substance Abuse Treatment,* 1986, *3*, pp.243-9. In this study, Marks used the lyrics of drug-related rock songs as a starting point for discussion about alcohol and drugs with a group of juvenile offenders. The aim was that through a medium young people could relate to, they could come to a better understanding of what drug dependency was all about.
18. The furore in America about the allegedly malevolent influence of rock on young people stimulated a discussion in Canada in June 1986 hosted by the Addiction Research Foundation of Ontario (ARF). The public debate was entitled 'Rock's Role in Drug Use: Myth or Reality?' The platform panel included female heavy-metal artist Lee Aaron and other members of the Canadian music business. Not surprisingly, the panel decision was in favour of 'myth'. This sparked off a lively debate with dissenting voices through the letters page of the *ARF Journal.*
19. When commentators wish to point to a recent example of how rock glorifies drug use, 'Cocaine', written by J. J. Cale, but popularized by Eric Clapton, is often quoted. It is alleged that Clapton sings: 'She's all right/she's all right/she's all right/cocaine'. After many careful listenings to J. J. Cale's

original version on the album *Troubadour* (1976), I must conclude that what he actually sings is, 'She don't lie/she don't lie/she don't lie/cocaine'. This is an altogether different sentiment, expressing the notion that cocaine will provide the effect the user is looking for, but being non-committal as to whether this is ultimately good or bad. To my ears, however, Clapton *does* sing the offending lyric on the album *Slowhand* (1977). For some reason it seems he changed the lyric. Interviewed in *Musician* (November 1986), Clapton was asked specifically about the association young people might make between a guitar hero and a very infectious, popular song about cocaine. 'Thank God,' said Eric, 'J. J. wrote a very ambivalent song there... I mean he's written a song that is so two-way... I can sing that song now and be anti-cocaine. And I actually think it's more anti- than pro-, but most people don't recognize that.'

CHAPTER TWELVE

1. Dr Lambos Comitas in an interview with *High Times,* 1978, *32*, p.33
2. Henman, p.45
3. ibid., p.85
4. Davis *(Reggae Bloodlines)*
5. Pryce, p.152
6. Davis *(Bob Marley)*, p.135
7. ibid., pp.145-6
8. *High Times,* September 1976, p.89
9. *Home Grown,* 1979, *1* (5) p.13
10. Pryce, p.156
11. Hebdige, p.63

CHAPTER THIRTEEN

1. Comment to author
2. *Dark Star,* 1978, *3*, (6), p.15
3. *High Times,* March 1982 p.99
4-8. Comment to author
9. Greenshaw, op. cit., pp.91-2
10. *See* Bibliography, Official sources, item 3
11. White (Charles), p.168

CHAPTER FOURTEEN

1. Comment to author
2. Cable, p.180
3. Kooper, p.103
4. ibid., p.99
5. Charone, Barbara: *Keith Richard* (London: Futura, 1979), p.10
6. Bennett, p.77
7. ibid., p.33

8. Comment to author
9. Sanchez, p.212
10. Comment to author
11. Whitcomb, p.195
12. Charone, op. cit., p.12
13. *Newsweek,* October 1980
14. *High Times,* June 1983, p.42
15. Interview with author
16. *Musician*, December 1986, p.25-6
17. Interview with author
18. Du Noyer, Paul: 'Cocaine', *Q* magazine, 1986, *1* (1) p.53
19. Hopkins, *Cocaine Consciousness,* p.313
20. Comment to author
21. *Rolling Stone,* 4 December 1982
22. *Dark Star,* 1978, *3* (6) p.15
23. *Ritz,* p.114
24. ibid., p.139
25. ibid., p.121
26. *Rolling Stone,* 1985
27. In fact, Boy George was eventually brought off heroin using the standard technique of a reducing dose of methadone to replace the heroin. In later comments to the press, e.g. *Observer*, 28 February 1987, he was none too complimentary about 'the black box'.

APPENDIX

1. Siegel, Shepard: 'Pavlovian Conditioning and Heroin Overdose: Reports by overdose victims', *Bulletin of the Psychonomic Society,* 1984, *22* (5), p.428-30
2. After Otis Redding's death in 1967, rock managers began taking out insurance policies on the lives of their valuable stars. Following Janis Joplin's death an unsavoury court case was heard because the insurance company refused to pay out. Suicide was not part of the policy and the company claimed that a self-inflicted overdose was tantamount to suicide. It took four years for Joplin's manager Albert Grossman to obtain a decision in his favour.

Bibliography

Official Sources

Harry J. Anslinger Collection, Pennsylvania State University

Hashish Smuggling and Passport Fraud: The Brotherhood of Eternal Love. US Senate Committee on the Judiciary, 3 October 1973 (Washington: USGPO, 1973)

International Narcotics Trafficking. Senate Committee on Governmental Affairs, 10-18 November 1981 (Washington: USPGO, 1981)

International Study Missions. Senate Select Committee on Narcotics Abuse and Control (Summary Report 1984)

The Role of the Entertainment Industry in Deglamorizing Drug Use. US Senate Committee on Governmental Affairs, 20 March 1985 (Washington: USGPO, 1985)

US Narcotics Control Programs Overseas: An Assessment. Congress Committee on Foreign Affairs, 22 February 1985 (Washington: USPGO, 1985)

Articles

Allsop, Kenneth: 'Jazz and Narcotics', *Encounter*, June 1961, pp.54-7

Ashley, Richard: 'Patent Medicines', *High Times*, November 1979, pp.59-63, 97

Bakalar, James and Grinspoon, Lester: 'Why Drug Policy is So Harsh', *Hastings Center Report*, August 1983, pp.34-9

Baumeister, Roy: 'Acid Rock: A Critical Reappraisal and Psychological Commentary', *Journal of Psychoactive Drugs*, 1984, *16* (4), pp.339-45

Beckley, Robert and Chalfant, H. Paul: 'Contrasting Images of Alcohol and Drug Use in Country and Rock Music', *Journal of Alcohol and Drug Education*, 1979, *25* (1), pp.44-51

Berger, Monroe: 'Jazz Resistance to the Diffusion of a Culture Pattern', *Journal of Negro History*, 1947, *23*, pp.461-94

Brecher, Edward: 'The "Heroin Overdose" Mystery and Other Occupational Hazards of Addiction'. Chapter in : Brecher, E (ed.), *Licit and Illicit Drugs:*

The Consumers' Union Report, Boston, Mass.: Little, Brown 1972

Catholic Commission for Racial Justice: 'Rastafarians in Jamaica and Britain', Notes and Reports No. 10, January 1982

Corzine, Jay and Sherwood, Janis: 'The Occupational Orientations of Jazz Musicians: Some Recent Findings and a Re-examination of the Evidence', *Sociological Spectrum,* 1983, *3,* pp.317-37

Curry, Andrew: 'Drugs in Jazz and Rock Music', *Clinical Toxicology,* 1968, *1* (2), pp.235-44

Dickson, Donald: 'Bureaucracy and Morality: an Organizational Perspective on a Moral Crusade', *Social Problems,* 1968, *16* (2), pp.143-56

Douse, Mike: 'Contemporary Music, Drug Attitudes and Drug Behaviour, *Australian Journal of Social Issues,* 1973, *8* (1), pp.74-80

Farren, Mick: 'Sex, Drugs and Rock 'n' Roll', *Home Grown,* Summer 1979, *1* (5), pp.16-18, 39

Federal Communications Committee: 'Licensee Responsiblity to Review Records Before Their Broadcast'. In: Coombs, Robert H., Fry, Lincoln J. *et al* (eds) *Socialization in Drug Abuse* (Cambridge Mass.: Schenkman, 1976)

Gannon, Frank: 'Pot, Pop and Acid', *New Society,* 21 September 1967

Garon, Paul: 'If Blues was Reefers', *Living Blues,* Autumn 1970, *3,* pp.13-18

Gay, George, Elsenbaumer, Robbie *et al*: 'A Dash of M*A*S*H – the Zep and the Dead: Head to Head', *Journal of Psychedelic Drugs,* 1972, *5* (2), pp.193-203

Gay, George: 'You've Come a Long Way, Baby! Coke Time for the New American Lady of the Eighties', *Journal of Psychoactive Drugs,* 1981, *13* (4), pp.297-313

Hall, Stuart: 'The Hippies: an American Moment', Sub and Popular Culture Series Occasional Paper No. 16, Birmingham University, 1968

Hebdige, Dick: 'The Style of the Mods', Sub and Popular Culture Series Occasional Paper No. 20, Birmingham University, 1974

Hopkins, Jerry: 'Cocaine: a Flash in the Pan, a Pain in the Nose', *Rolling Stone,* 29 April 1971, pp.1-6

Hopkins, Jerry: 'Cocaine Consciousness: the Gourmet Trip', *Journal of Popular Culture,* 1975, *9* (2), pp.305-14

Kane, Joe: 'Dope Lyrics – the Secret Language of Rock', *High Times*

Lauderdale, Pat and Inverarity, James: 'Regulation of Opiates', *Journal of Drug Issues,* Summer 1984, pp.567-77

Leech, Kenneth: 'Amphetamine Abuse', Evidence to the Advisory Committee on Drug Dependence, 1969 (unpublished)

Lyle, George: 'Dangerous Drug Traffic in London', *British Journal of Addiction,* 1953, *50,* pp.47-55

McNamara, Brooks: 'The Medicine Show Log: Reconstructing a Traditional American Entertainment', *Drama Review,* Fall 1984, *28* (3)

Malyon, Tim: 'Just Another Cash Crop? The Cannabis Market Present and Future', *Ecologist,* 1980, *10* (8/9), pp.293-9

Margolis, Norman: 'A Theory on the Psychology of Jazz', *American Imago,* 1954, *11,* pp.264-91

Melly, George: 'A Jazzman's View of Dope', *Home Grown*, 1979, *1* (5), pp.20-2

Merriam, A.P. and Mack, R.W: 'The Jazz Community', *Social Forces*, 1960, *25*, pp.211-22

Pharchem Newsletter: 'The Nation's Toughest Drug Law: Evaluating the New York Experience', *Pharchem Newsletter*, 1978, *7* (10) pp.1-3, 7-9

Post, William and McGrath, James: 'Potents and Potions – Precursors to Modern Drug Use and Abuse', *Journal of Drug Issues*, 1972, *2*, pp.50-6

Preble, Edward and Casey, John: 'Taking Care of Business – the Heroin User's Life on the Street', *International Journal of the Addictions*, 1969, *4* (1), pp.1-24

Robinson, John and Pilskaln, Robert *et al*: 'Protest Rock and Drugs', *Journal of Communications*, 1976, *26* (4), pp.125-36

Schwartz, Elaine and Feinglass, S.J. *et al*: 'Popular Music and Drug Lyrics: Analysis of a Scapegoat'. In: *US National Commission on Marijuana and Drug Abuse*, Vol. II (Washington: USGPO, 1973), pp.718-46

Seymour, Richard: 'The Chemical Muse', *Street Pharmacologist*, 1982, *5* (6) pp.5-7, 14-17

Shapiro, Harry: 'Singin' the Blues on Reds', *Home Grown*, 1980, *1* (8) pp.29-33

Siegel, Shepard: 'Pavlovian conditioning and Heroin Overdose: Reports by Overdose Victims', *Bulletin of the Psychonomic Society*, 1984, *22* (5), pp.428-30

Sloman, Larry: 'Copping – Stories from a Lifetime of Getting High on the Road by Michael Bloomfield as Told to Larry Sloman', *High Times*, June 1983, pp.42-5, 66-7, 93

Smith, David and Luce, John *et al*: 'The Health of Haight Ashbury', *TransAction*, 1970, *7* (6), pp.35-45

Smith, Roger: 'Status Politics and the Image of the Addict', *Issues in Criminology*, 1966, *2* (2), pp.157-75

Spear, H.B.: 'The Growth of Heroin Addiction in the United Kingdom', *British Journal of Addiction*, 1969, *64*, pp.245-55

Spencer, Neil: 'The Ja Connection', *New Musical Expresss*, 16 October 1976

Sutter, Alan: 'The World of the Righteous Dope Fiend', *Issues in Criminology*, 1966, *2* (2) pp.77-222

Swenson, John: 'Peter Tosh Captured: Dread or Alive', *High Times*, November 1981, p.9

Taqi, S.: 'Approbation of Drug Usage in Rock and Roll Music', *Bulletin on Narcotics*, 1969, *21* (4) pp.29-35

Tosh, Peter: 'Rasta, Reggae and Ganja', *Home Grown*, Summer 1979, *1* (5)

Winick, Charles: 'How High the Moon – Jazz and Drugs', *Antioch Review*, Spring 1961, pp.53-68

Winick, Charles and Nyswander, Marie: 'Psychotherapy of Successful Musicians Who are Drug Addicts', *American Journal of Orthopsychiatry*, 1961, *31*, pp.622-36

Winick, Charles: 'The Use of Drugs by Jazz Musicians', *Social Problems*, 1959, *7*, pp.240-53

Books

Abel, Ernest L.: *Marihuana – the First Twelve Thousand Years* (New York: Plenum Press, 1980)

Albertson, Chris: *Bessie* (London: Barrie & Jenkins, 1972)

Algren, Nelson: *The Man with the Golden Arm* (New York: Doubleday, 1949)

Allsop, Kenneth: *The Bootleggers: The Story of Chicago's Prohibition Era* (London: Hutchinson, 1961)

Anslinger, Harry J. and Ousler, Will: *The Murderers: The Story of the Narcotics Gangs* (New York: Farrar, Strauss and Cudady, 1961)

Ashley, Richard: *Cocaine: Its History, Use and Effects* (New York: St. Martin's Press, 1975)

Auld, John: *Marihuana and Social Control* (London: Academic Press, 1981)

Austin, Gregory (ed.): *Perspectives on the History of Psychoactive Drug Use* (Rockville, Md: National Institute on Drug Abuse, 1978)

Bakalar, James and Grinspoon, Lester: *Drug Control in a Free Society*, (Cambridge: Cambridge University Press, 1984)

Becker, Howard: *The Outsiders: Studies in the Sociology of Deviance* (New York: Free Press, 1963)

Bennett, H. Stith: *On Becoming a Rock Musician* (Amherst, Mass.: University of Massachusetts Press, 1980)

Berridge, Virginia and Edwards, G: *Opium and the People: Opiate Use in 19th-century England* (London: Allen Lane, 1981)

Block, A.A. and Chambliss, W.J.: *Organizing Crime* (New York: Elsevier, 1981)

Blum, Richard: *Society and Drugs* (San Francisco: Josey Bass, 1969)

Bockris, Victor and Malanga Gerard: *Up-tight – The Velvet Underground Story* (London: Omnibus, 1983)

Bonnie, Richard J. and Whitehead, Charles H. *The Marihuana Conviction: A History of Marihuana Prohibition in the United States* (Charlottesville, Va.: University Press of Virginia, 1974)

Boot, Adrian and Thomas, Michel: *Jamaica: Babylon on a Thin Wire* (London: Thames & Hudson, 1976)

Boot, Adrian and Goldman, Vivian: *Bob Marley: Soul Rebel – Natural Mystic* (London: Eel Pie, 1981)

Brake, Michael: *Comparative Youth Culture* (London: Routledge & Kegan Paul, 1985)

Brown, Peter and Gaines, Steven: *The Love You Make: An Insider's Story of the Beatles* (London: Pan, 1984)

Buerkle, Jack V. and Barker, Danny: *Bourbon Street Black: The New Orleans Black Jazz Man* (Oxford: Oxford University Press, 1973)

Burchill, Julie and Parsons, Tony: *The Boy Looked at Johnny: The Obituary of Rock and Roll* (London: Pluto Press, 1978)

Burchill, Julie: *Damaged Gods* (London: Century, 1986)

Cable, Michael: *The Pop Industry Inside Out* (London: W.H. Allen, 1977)

Campbell, Horace: *Rasta and Resistance: from Marcus Garvey to Walter Rodney* (London: Hansrib, 1985)

Carr, Ian: *Miles Davis: A Critical Biography* (London: Quartet, 1982)

Carroll, Peter and Noble, David: *The Free and the Unfree: A New History of the United States* (Harmondsworth: Penguin, 1977)

Caserta, Peggy and Knapp, Dan: *Going Down with Janis* (New Jersey: Lyle Stuart, 1973)

Cash, Johnny: *The Man in Black* (London: Hodder and Stoughton, 1975)

Cashmore, Ernest: *Rastaman: The Rastafarian Movement in England* (London: Unwin, 1983)

Chambers, Ian: *Urban Rhythms: Pop Music and Popular Culture* (London: Macmillan, 1985)

Chapple, Steve and Garofalo, Reebee: *Rock 'n' Roll is Here to Pay.* (Chicago: Nelson-Hall, 1977)

Charles, Ray and Ritz, David: *Brother Ray: Ray Charles' Own Story* (London: Macdonald & Jane, 1978)

Charters, Sam: *The Legacy of the Blues* (London: Calder & Boyars, 1975)

Chilton, John: *Billie's Blues: The True Story of the Immortal Billie Holiday* (London: Quartet, 1975)

Clarke, Sebastian: *Jah Music: The Evolution of the Popular Jamaican Song* (London: Heinemann, 1980)

Clarke, Steve (Comp.): *The Who in Their Own Words* (London: Omnibus, 1979)

Cohn, Nik: *Pop from the Beginning* (London: Weidenfeld & Nicolson, 1969)

Coleman, Ray: *Survivor: The Authorized Biography of Eric Clapton* (London: Sidgwick & Jackson, 1985)

Cook, Bruce: *Listen to the Blues* (London: Robson Books, 1975)

Cornwell, Hugh: *Inside Information* (London: Stranglers Information Service, 1980)

Courtwright, David: *Dark Paradise: Opiate Addiction in America Before 1940* (Cambridge, Mass.: Harvard University Press, 1982)

Cox, Barry and Shirley, John *et al: The Fall of Scotland Yard* (Harmondsworth: Penguin, 1977)

Davis, Clive and Willwerth, J. Clive: *Inside the Record Business* (New York: William Morrow, 1975)

Davis, Stephen: *Bob Marley* (London: Arthur Barker, 1983)

Davis, Stephen and Simon, Peter: *Reggae Bloodlines: In Search of the Music and Culture of Jamaica* (London: Heinemann, 1979)

Dowley, Tim and Dunnage, Barry: *Bob Dylan: from a Hard Rain to a Slow Train* (Midas, 1982)

Epstein, Edward Jay: *Agency of Fear: Opiates and Political Power in America* (New York: Putnam, 1977)

Erenberg, Lewis A: *Steppin' Out: New York Nightlife and the Transformation of American Culture 1890-1930* (Chicago: University of Chicago Press, 1981)

Fong-Torres, Ben (ed.): *The Rolling Stone Rock 'n' Roll Reader* (New York: Bantam, 1974)

Freemantle, Brian: *The Fix* (London: Michael Joseph, 1985)

Friedman, Myra: *Buried Alive: The Biography of Janis Joplin* (New York: Bantam, 1974)

Gillespie, Dizzy and Fraser, Al: *Dizzy: To Be or Not to Bop* (London: W.H. Allen, 1980)

Gleason, Ralph: *The Jefferson Airplane and the San Francisco Sound* (New York: Ballantine, 1969)

Goldman, Albert: *Elvis* (Harmondsworth: Penguin, 1982)

Goldman, Albert: *Grass Roots: Marijuana in America Today* (New York: Harper & Row, 1979)

Gorman, Clem: *Backstage Rock* (London: Pan, 1978)

Gray, Michael: *The Art of Bob Dylan* (London: Hamlyn, 1981)

Green, Shirley: *Rachman* (London: Michael Joseph, 1969)

Greenfield, Robert: *A Journey Through America with the Rolling Stones* (London: Panther, 1975)

Grime, Kitty: *Jazz Voices* (London: Quartet, 1983)

Harrison, Hank: *The Grateful Dead* (Star Books, 1973)

Hawes, Hampton and Asher, Don: *Raise Up Off Me: A Portrait of Hampton Hawes* (New York: Da Capo, 1979)

Hebdidge, Dick: *Subculture: The Meaning of Style* (London: Methuen, 1979)

Helmer, John: *Drugs and Minority Oppression* (New York: Seabury Press, 1975)

Henman, Anthony *et al*: *Big Deal: The Politics of the Illicit Drugs Business* (London: Pluto Press, 1985)

Hentoff, Nat: *The Jazz Life* (London: Peter Davies, 1962)

Herman, Gary: *Rock 'n' Roll Babylon* (London: Plexus 1982)

Himmelstein, Jerome L. *The Strange Career of Marihuana: Politics and Ideology of Drug Control in America* (London: Greenwood Press, 1983)

Holiday, Billie and Dufty, William: *Lady Sings the Blues* (New York: Doubleday, 1956)

Hollingshead, Michael: *The Man who Turned on the World* (London: Blond & Briggs, 1973)

Hopkins, Jerry: *Elvis: The Final Years* (London: Omnibus, 1981)

Hunter, Ian: *Diary of a Rock 'n' Roll Star* (London: Panther, 1975)

Inglis, Brian: *The Forbidden Game: A Social History of Drugs* (London: Hodder & Stoughton, 1975)

Jackson, Blair: *Grateful Dead: The Music Never Stopped* (London: Plexus, 1983)

Jones, Max and Chilton, John: *Louis: The Louis Armstrong Story 1900-1971* (London: Studio Vista 1971)

Joynson, Vernon: *The Acid Trip: A Complete Guide to Psychedelic Music* (Todmorden, Lancs: Babylon Books, 1984)

Kaplan, John: *Marijuana: The New Prohibition* (New York: The World Publishing Company, 1970)

Kelleher, Maureen *et al*: *Drugs and Society: A Critical Reader* (Dubuque, Iowa: Kendall/Hunt, 1983)

Kennedy, Joseph: *Coca Exotica: The Illustrated History of Cocaine* (New York: Cornwall, 1985)

Kerouac, Jack: *On the Road* (Harmondsworth: Penguin, 1976)

King, Rufus: *The Drug Hang-up: America's Fifty-year Folly* (New York: W.W.Norton, 1972)

Kooper, Al and Edmonds, Ben: *Backstage Passes: Rock 'n' Roll Life in the Sixties* (New York: Stein & Day, 1977)

Lacker, Marty *et al*: *Elvis: Portrait of a Friend* (New York: Bantam, 1980)

Latimer, Dean and Goldberg, Jeff: *Flowers in the Blood: The Story of Opium* (New York: Franklin Watts, 1981)

Laurie, Peter: *Drugs: Medical, Psychological and Social Facts* (Harmondsworh: Penguin, 1974)

Lee, Martin, and Schlain, Bruce: *Acid Dreams* (New York: Grove Press, 1985)

Leech, Kenneth: *Keep the Faith Baby* (London: SPCK, 1973)

Leonard, Neil: *Jazz and the White Americans: The Acceptance of a New Art Form* (Chicago: University of Chicago Press, 1962)

Levine, L.W: *Black Culture and Black Consciousness* (Oxford: Oxford University Press, 1977)

Lomax, Alan: *Mister Jelly Roll*, 2nd ed. (Berkeley: University of California Press, 1973)

McKnight, Cathy and Tobler, John: *Bob Marley: The Roots of Reggae* (London: Star, 1977)

McNamara, Brooks: *Step Right Up* (New York: Doubleday, 1976)

McNeal, Violet: *Four White Horses and a Brass Band* (New York: Doubleday, 1947)

McNicoll, André: *Drug Trafficking: A North-South Perspective* (Ottawa: North-South Institute, 1983)

Mailer, Norman: *The White Negro* (San Francisco: City Lights Books, 1970)

Marsh, Dave: *Before I Get Old: The Story of the Who* (London: Plexus, 1983)

Mezzrow, Milton and Wolfe, Bernard: *Really the Blues* (New York: Random House, 1946)

Mingus, Charles: *Beneath the Underdog* (Harmondsworth: Penguin, 1975)

Morris, Ronald L.: *Wait Until Dark: Jazz and the Underworld 1880-1940)* (Bowling Green, Ohio: Bowling Green University Popular Press, 1980)

Musto, David: *The American Disease: The Origins of Narcotic Control* (New Jersey: Yale University Press, 1973)

Napier-Bell, Simon: *You Don't Have to Say You Love Me* (London: New English Library, 1982)

Nelli, Humbert, S.: *The Business of Crime: Italian and Syndicate Crime in the United States* (Oxford: Oxford University Press, 1976)

Neville, Richard: *Playpower* (London: Paladin, 1971)

Norman, Philip: *The Stones* (London: Elm Tree, 1984)

Nuttall, Jeff: *Bomb Culture* (MacGibbon & Kee, 1968)

O'Day, Anita and Eells, George: *High Times, Hard Times* (London: Corgi, 1983)

Oliver, Paul: *Songsters and Saints* (Cambridge: Cambridge University Press, 1984)

Ostransky, Leroy: *Jazz City: The Impact of Our Cities on the Development of Jazz* (New Jersey: Prentice-Hall, 1978)

Palmer, Tony: *All You Need is Love* (London: Futura, 1977)

Parssinen, Terry: *Secret Passion, Secret Remedies: Narcotic Drugs in British Society 1820-1930* (Manchester: Manchester University Press, 1933)

Peebles, Andy: *The Lennon Tapes* (London: BBC, 1981)

Peele, Stanton and Brodsky, Archie: *Love and Addiction* (New York: Taplinger, 1975)

Peele, Stanton: *The Meaning of Addiction: Compulsive Experience and Its Interpretation* (Lexington, Mass.: Lexington Books, 1985)

Pepper, Art and Pepper, Laurie: *Straight Life* (London: Collier Macmillan, 1979)

Phillips, Joel and Wynne, Ronald: *Cocaine: The Mystique and the Reality* (New York: Avon Books, 1980)

Pichaske, David: *A Generation in Motion: Popular Music and Culture in the Sixties* (London: Macmillan, 1979)

Pryce, Ken: *Endless Pressure: A Study of West Indian Life-styles in Bristol* (Harmondsworth: Penguin, 1979)

Reisner, Robert: *Bird: The Legend of Charlie Parker* (London: Quartet, 1974)

Ritz, David: *Divided Soul: The Life of Marvin Gaye* (London: Michael Joseph, 1985)

Rolling Stone: *Rock Almanac: The Chronicles of Rock Music* (London: Macmillan, 1983)

Rosenbaum, Marsha: *Women on Heroin* (New Brunswick, NJ: Rutgers University Press, 1981)

Rubin, Vera and Comitas, Lambros: *Ganja in Jamaica* (Amsterdam: Mouton, 1975)

Russell, Ross: *Bird Lives!* (London: Quartet, 1973)

Sanchez, Tony: *Up and Down with the Rolling Stones* (New York: William Morrow, 1979)

Sander, Ellen: *Trips: Rock Life in the Sixties* (New York: Scribner, 1973)

Scaduto, Anthony: *Bob Dylan* (London: Abacus, 1972)

Scullatti, Gene and Seay, Davin: *San Francisco Nights: The Psychedelic Music Trip* (London: Sidgwick and Jackson, 1985)

Shapiro, Harry: *Just a Crazy Dream: The Life of Graham Bond* (unpublished manuscript)

Shapiro, Harry: *Slowhand: The Story of Eric Clapton* (London: Proteus, 1984)

Shaw, Arnold: *52nd Street: The Street of Jazz* (New York: Da Capo, 1971)

Sidran, Ben: *Black Talk* (New York: Da Capo, 1971)

Silver, Gary (ed.): *The Dope Chronicles 1850-1950* (San Francisco: Harper & Row, 1979)

Slowman,Larry: *Reefer Madness: The History of Marihuana in America* (New York: Bobbs-Merrill, 1979)

Stallings, Penny: *Rock 'n' Roll Confidential* (London: Vermillion, 1984)

Starks, Michael: *Cocaine Fiends and Reefer Madness: An Illustrated History of Drugs in the Movies* (New York: Cornwall Books, 1982)

Stein, Jean: *Edie: The Life and Times of Andy Warhol's Superstar* (London: Panther, 1984)

BIBLIOGRAPHY

Taylor, Arthur: *Notes and Tones: Musician-to-Musician Interviews* (London: Quartet, 1983)

Tendler, Steward and May, David: *The Brotherhood of Eternal Love* (London: Panther, 1984)

Titon, Jeff: *Early Downhome Blues* (University of Illinois Press, 1977)

Toll, Robert C.: *Blacking up: The Minstrel Show in Nineteenth-century America* (New York: Oxford University Press, 1974)

Tosches, Nick: *Hellfire: The Jerry Lee Lewis Story* (London: Plexus, 1982)

Trebach, Arnold: *The Heroin Solution* (New Haven: Yale University Press, 1982)

Turner, Steve: *Conversations with Eric Clapton* (London: Abacus, 1976)

Tyler, Andrew: *Street Drugs* (London: New English Library, 1986)

Waller, Maurice and Calabrese, Anthony: *Fats Waller* (London: Cassell, 1977)

Whitcomb, Ian: *After the Ball* (London: Allen Lane, 1972)

White, Charles: *The Life and Times of Little Richard* (London: Pan, 1984)

White, Timothy: *Catch a Fire: The Life of Bob Marley* (London: Elm Tree, 1983)

Whitney, Malika and Hussey, Dermott: *Bob Marley – Reggae King of the Word* (London: Plexus, 1984)

Wolfe, Tom: *The Electric Kool-aid Acid Test* (London: Weidenfeld & Nicolson, 1969)

Young, James: *The Toadstool Millionaires: A Social History of Patent Medicines in America before Federal Regulation* (Princeton, NJ: Princeton University Press, 1961)

Index